My Exquisite Purple Life

Insights from a Woman Who Never
Should Have Made It but Did.

by
Aideen T. Finnola

BALBOA
PRESS
A DIVISION OF HAY HOUSE

Balboa Press books may be ordered through booksellers or by contacting:

Balboa Press
A Division of Hay House
1663 Liberty Drive
Bloomington, IN 47403
www.balboapress.com
1 (877) 407-4847

Because of the dynamic nature of the Internet, any web addresses or links contained in this book may have changed since publication and may no longer be valid. The views expressed in this work are solely those of the author and do not necessarily reflect the views of the publisher, and the publisher hereby disclaims any responsibility for them.

The author of this book does not dispense medical advice or prescribe the use of any technique as a form of treatment for physical, emotional, or medical problems without the advice of a physician, either directly or indirectly. The intent of the author is only to offer information of a general nature to help you in your quest for emotional and spiritual well-being. In the event you use any of the information in this book for yourself, which is your constitutional right, the author and the publisher assume no responsibility for your actions.

Any people depicted in stock imagery provided by Thinkstock are models, and such images are being used for illustrative purposes only.
Certain stock imagery © Thinkstock.

Print information available on the last page.

ISBN: 978-1-5043-9655-4 (sc)
ISBN: 978-1-5043-9656-1 (hc)
ISBN: 978-1-5043-9672-1 (e)

Library of Congress Control Number: 2018901048

Balboa Press rev. date: 02/14/2018

Contents

Acknowledgments vii

Introduction ix

Author's Note xiii

Chapter 1   How It Began 1

Chapter 2   For the Adventure of It 19

Chapter 3   I Was Up For It.. 31

Chapter 4   Oh Yeah? Watch Me! 43

Chapter 5   So What? 59

Chapter 6   The After-Market Add-On................................. 75

Chapter 7   It Wasn't My Fault, But It Was My Responsibility 89

Chapter 8   I May Have Been a Slow Learner, But At Least I Wasn't a "No Learner" 107

Chapter 9   I Am Hurt 125

Chapter 10 The A-Man 141

Chapter 11 Following Felix 155

Chapter 12 My Exquisite Purple Life 175

Epilogue..193

Work With Me...205

Acknowledgments

To every character who has played a part in my life adventure, good, bad, or ugly, I thank you for showing up! To my many dear and precious friends who believed in me, believed in this book, and helped make it what it is, your encouragement, support, and contribution have meant the world to me. Although, for legal reasons, I cannot name you here, just know that I love you all more than words can say! Eternal gratitude to May, my muse on the other side, who poured out inspiration like molasses, so thick, so sweet, so rich, and so beautiful; she made the writing process such an effortless joy!

Introduction

In my late twenties, whenever I shared stories from my childhood, during which I was raised in a Christian cult, I was told by friends and strangers alike that I should write my autobiography. These comments only became more frequent and more adamant in my early forties after I discovered that my husband of eighteen years was a closeted gay man. Although I knew that much of my life experience was unique (to say the least!), I never thought of it as extraordinary in any way, and certainly not worthy of an autobiography. In addition, I had never had even the slightest bit of interest in writing an autobiography! The thought of writing a chronological "I was born on blah, blah, blah, and I grew up blah, blah, blah, etc., etc., etc. . . ." account of my life totally turned me off; as my teenage self from the eighties would have said, "Gag me with a spoon!"

In my early twenties, when I was getting my degree in secondary education, people would often tell me how much they disliked teenagers, because teenagers don't know anything but they think they know everything; these same people would marvel at why I was choosing to teach teenagers because they didn't know how I could tolerate teenagers. The funny thing is that the blissful ignorance of teenagers was one of the things that I liked most about working with them! Teenagers are so blissfully unaware of how little they know, and they are so gloriously confident and passionate about what they think they know. I have fond memories of being a teenager and feeling so sure of what I thought I knew; I hated my twenties because that was when it hit me that I didn't know *anything*! By the beginning of my thirties, I felt like I might know one or two things . . . maybe. By the time I turned forty, for the first time in my life, I really felt like I might actually know something!

Having amassed a decent collection of insights gained from my unique life experiences, I wanted to share my thoughts with the world. I wanted to share because I had been so richly blessed and helped on my life journey by others who did not keep to themselves the life insights they had gained. As the late Maya Angelou said many times, "When you get, give; when you learn, teach."

I started this book as a "here's what I know" dialogue about what I had learned from my life experiences, but everything I wrote came out way too "know it all," and if there's one thing I have learned on my life journey it is that I don't, and never will, know it all! Everything I wrote was, once again, provoking the feeling of "Gag me with a spoon!" I wrestled with this book for months until I just gave up and put it on the back burner. Wanting to keep myself writing, I decided just to let myself write about any random thing that was on my mind. As I continued to write, individual stories from my life came to the forefront of my mind, and I wrote out detailed accounts of them not knowing that they would go anywhere. After nearly a year of this meandering writing, I stepped back, took inventory of all the electronic scraps scattered about the desktop of my computer, and realized that they all fit into the original chapter outline of the book that I had put on hold. As I began to work my life stories, which I had written out, back into the outline of the insights I had originally wanted to share, I found it to be so much more palatable; I was so much happier with what I was writing, and I was thrilled to have discovered a more relatable way to share what I felt so compelled to share!

I think of the human experience as if we are a group of children sitting together around a table all coloring our own pictures—the masterpieces that are ourselves and our lives. Each of us has our own pile of crayons (our own experiences) from which we select the colors that we create our lives with. In our pursuit of the most exquisite and colorful life experience, we can and should draw from each other's piles of crayons (each other's experiences) to enhance our own masterpieces. I share my life experiences and insights to offer you my pile of crayons; if I have any colors that can enhance your masterpiece, help yourself!

I have watched *Master Class* on the OWN network since the very first episode. The first time I heard Oprah say, during the opening, "treat your life like a classroom," I nearly injured myself jumping off the couch shouting, "I do; I have; I did; I do!" For as far back as I can remember, I have paid attention to and taken mental notes on all of my life experiences, good, bad, and ugly; I have compulsively studied this thing we call life and been gripped by a relentless desire to puzzle it out. In this book, I offer you my notes; if you find anything useful, feel free to copy!

I do not presume to know everything, or even to know anything, definitively or objectively. I do not present my insights to you as truth to influence or convert you to the perspective on life that I currently hold; I only offer my insights in the hopes that they may be a help and a blessing to you, as so many others' shared insights have been to me. This quote, by an unknown author, perfectly captures my feelings on this matter:

> I would not interfere with any creed of yours, nor want to appear that I have all the cures. There is so much to know, so many things are true. The way my feet must go may not be best for you. I give this spark, of what is light to me, to guide you through the dark but not tell you what to see.

Namaste, shalom, God bless, Goddess bless, blessed be, and so on 'til we meet again...

"I show my scars so that others know that they can heal."
~Rhachelle Nichol'

Author's Note

Author's Note: All the stories in this book are completely true, but to protect the identity of the individuals, all names, places, dates, and physical descriptions have been changed.

CHAPTER ONE

How It Began

I was supposed to be in bed, fast asleep. My parents had told me that they were having a meeting that night. As I lay in bed, unable to fall asleep, I could hear people with unfamiliar voices arriving, one after another, to the little two-bedroom apartment with bars on the windows in the rough part of Chicago where we—my parents, my younger sister, and I—lived. I knew that I was strictly forbidden to get out of bed, but after a while, curiosity got the better of my little seven-year-old self. I snuck out of my room and crept silently (probably not . . . I was seven) down the hallway that led to the living room.

Even before I got far enough to see anything, I heard whiney, mournful singing; I don't remember recognizing the song, but my adult reference for it would be something along the lines of "Kumbaya, My Lord." When the song ended, I heard quiet and strange speech that didn't sound anything like the adult conversation that I was used to hearing. Everyone seemed to be talking at once, but not to each other and not with the construct of normal conversation; I also heard words that were unintelligible. Fascinated, I inched my way toward the opening of the living room until I could see as well as hear.

What I saw was even stranger than what I had been hearing! All of the adults were sitting with their eyes closed, their heads lolled back, and their palms upraised. Sure enough, they were all talking, but no one was talking to each other; no one was even looking at each other! The tone of their voices was just as whiney and mournful as the song they had finished singing, and some of them even sounded like they were moaning! All cues indicated to my little seven-year-old mind that something was wrong with these adults, but none of them seemed concerned. Unbeknownst to me, I had just stumbled across the

1

very beginnings of the weirdness (to state it benignly) that was to become the hallmark of my life from my childhood through my early twenties.

———————

I was born a redheaded stepchild. Well, okay, so I was never a stepchild, but I was born a redhead and may as well have been a stepchild—that's how little I felt I belonged in my family of origin. My mother and I were different in every way possible. She had straight, black hair and I had curly, flaming-red hair; she was a petite five foot two and I grew to be five foot six. She had brown eyes and I had my father's bright blue eyes. Although we rarely clashed, in addition to looking nothing like each other, we were like night and day in our temperaments. Try as I might, I never could make any sense of her, and I never had a feeling of home with her. I had a greater affinity for and a stronger feeling of home with my father, from whom I got my curly red hair and my height (he was six foot two). In many ways, both in our physical appearance and in our temperaments, he and I were like two peas in a pod. This did cause us to clash at times, and we quickly parted ways philosophically and religiously as I entered adulthood. My sister and I were as different in our temperaments as we were in our physical appearance; she was a brunette, had skin that could tan, and grew to be a petite five feet tall. Despite our differences, my sister and I could have been friends, but with parents who neither guided nor protected us, it became impossible.

I was raised by hippies turned Jesus freaks—no joke. These two seemingly-opposite movements, hippie and Jesus freak, had fanaticism and extremism in common, which were things that my parents excelled in. My parents relished being perceived as weird, and proudly thumbed their noses at conventional living. The couch in our living room had been pulled out of someone else's trash; if you sat on it in the wrong spot, you crashed to the floor. There were no labels on any of the food items in our refrigerator because my health-fanatic, hippie mother made *everything* from scratch (for a while she even churned her own butter). I never had new clothes, the kind that come with price tags, because we did all our clothes shopping at thrift stores (the grungier the better). I have seen photos of myself at preschool age looking like the quintessential wild child of hippies, my curly red hair an uncut and uncombed mess, wearing only my father's old under-shirt as a dress.

Both of my parents came from excruciatingly dysfunctional and abusive families, and in their childhoods, endured experiences that are the stuff of *Law and Order SVU* episodes; in a later generation, the things my grandparents did to their children would have landed them in prison. When my parents met each other, just out of college, they were already carrying a crippling weight of pain that rendered them incapable of not doing harm to each other, and subsequently, to their children; they never really stood a chance. Despite their efforts, they failed miserably in their attempts to heal their own pain or prevent the pain that they caused each other, and my sister and me.

In my life, I have never known two people to hate each other more vehemently or put more effort into inflicting pain on each other (emotional pain, psychological pain, and, on occasion, physical pain). It was like being raised by dogs who were bred to fight; they attacked each other every chance they got, and unfortunately, my sister and I had ringside seats for all their fights. Despite their passionate profession and fanatical practice of the Christian faith, screaming, swearing, name-calling, and my mother in tears, face down at the kitchen table, were daily occurrences in my childhood. Throughout their more than half a century of marriage and parenthood, they did a monumental amount of harm to each other and to their two daughters.

When my sister and I were still in early single digits, my parents got caught up in the Catholic Charismatic Renewal movement. Several years later, they left our extended family behind in Chicago and moved to San Francisco to join an ecumenical, fundamentalist, charismatic, evangelical Christian cult. Being ecumenical meant that the membership was comprised of both Catholics and Protestants, who maintained their individual denominational practices and doctrinal beliefs in addition to their participation in the cult. Being fundamentalist meant that the belief system and world view that was preached by the leaders and practiced by the members was extremely conservative (literal interpretation of the Bible) and apocalyptic (I grew up believing that the world was going to end at any moment, with the bodily rapture of the true believers who had accepted Jesus Christ as their personal Lord and Savior, followed by seven years of tribulation ending with the second coming of Christ, who would pass final judgment on all nonbelievers and throw them into the "Lake of Fire" to burn for all eternity). Being charismatic meant that everyone in the cult believed in and practiced the "gifts of the Spirit," among which were speaking in tongues, interpretation of tongues, prophecy, healing by the laying on of hands, and performing miracles. Being evangelical meant that everyone zealously and regularly tried to proselytize anyone they crossed paths with to bring new members into the cult.

I feel compelled to say here that this is just entirely too much religion, doctrine, and dogma to shove into one group, let alone to expect a single person to believe and practice! It was as if the cult leaders took everything out of their refrigerators and kitchen pantries, mixed all of it together, and baked it for far too long at way too high of a temperature; in the end, no matter how they served it up, the result was neither attractive nor easy to swallow! It brings to mind what my father used to call the "curry principle." The curry principle states that "if one tablespoon of curry seasoning is good, then two must be better." It was just another in a long line of ironies that my father, who was the author of the curry principle, could not apply the logic of it to his own life and religious practice. (Just in case the logic of the curry principle went sailing past you . . . two tablespoons of curry seasoning is *not* better! One tablespoon of curry seasoning will make a dish beautiful; two tablespoons will ruin it!)

I was eight years old when I attended my first cult prayer meeting. At that time, the membership was just over a thousand; it later grew to over three thousand members. The large numbers in attendance necessitated a large venue for the prayer meetings; the first prayer meeting I attended was held in a local high school gymnasium. In later years, when the membership was at its peak, we met in university auditoriums. The memory of my first cult prayer meeting is hazy because I was so young, but several moments of the whole experience stand out vividly. If my parents offered me any explanation about or warning of what was to come, I don't remember it; what is burned into my memory is when, immediately following the upbeat opening song, the crowd erupted with thunderous clapping, deafening shouts of "Praise Jesus! Glory be to God! Hallelujah!" along with incoherent babbling (speaking in tongues), erratic jumping, and wild hand waving, all of which completely bewildered and terrified me! We were sitting in the bleachers, which only intensified the experience because hundreds of adults jumping on the flimsy wooden bleachers made them shake horribly; I really did think that the world was going to end!

By the time I was a teenager, every inch of our house was plastered with religious propaganda. My father regularly accosted random strangers on the street to share "the good news of Jesus Christ." My birthday parties always included getting prayed over by the "laying on of hands;" this stressed me out for many reasons, not the least of which being that my father always placed his hand heavily on the top front of my head, completely squashing my bangs, which I had spent so much time and hairspray perfecting (it was the eighties). My mother had stockpiled enough nonperishable food—fifty-pound sacks of flour, dried beans and rice, five-gallon drums of peanut butter, innumerous gallons of water, etc.—to survive the imminent apocalyptic biblical "end times" preached about by the cult leaders. My whole life had become consumed by my parents' membership in and devotion to the cult; I can't remember a time in my childhood or adolescence when I felt normal or accepted—outside of or within my family.

Of all the wrongs I suffered at the hands of my parents, the most painful and damaging was being told every day and in every way that who I am was wrong and bad. I was told that God loved me unconditionally, but I was taught that my sins made me vile in his sight. It was my perceived sinfulness that was the constant focus of my parents' anxiety and disapproval. They believed that I was defective on a very core level and in need of constant correction. Their fear for the fate of my immortal soul gripped them so fiercely that they took severe measures to force me into who they felt I needed to be, according to the teachings of the cult leadership and their own dysfunctional needs.

In accordance with cult teachings, my parents took the discipline of their children very seriously. My father had fashioned a paddle out of a wooden two-by-four plank which he also used as a doorstop for their bedroom door; I heard him joke once, with a friend, that he liked to keep it in plain sight to inspire fear. When I was deemed to be disobedient, which often was daily, I was made to lie face down on my parents' bed while my father raised the two-by-four paddle up over his head with both hands and came down, with the full force of his might, repeatedly on my backside. Before it began, I was allowed to ask "how many" I was going to get; I don't remember a number smaller than six, and more often than not, the answer was in the double digits. I remember seething with hatred toward my father after every time he spanked me, and feeling powerless to do anything more than think, "I hate you! I hate you! I hate you!" over and over again in my head; once, I made the mistake of yelling it out loud, which only landed me face down again for another spanking. I was seventeen years old, physically a woman and practically an adult, when I got my last spanking. Apparently, I had sassed my mother, and my father, in an attempt to justify his actions, said, "If you are going to act like a child, I am going to discipline you like a child." It was such a humiliating violation! When I described my childhood experience of spanking in a therapy session in my early twenties, my therapist emphatically exclaimed, "Aidy, you were beaten!" I gave her my conditioned response and said, "No, my father was just spanking me." She said, "No, that was not spanking; that was beating! He beat you!"

The cult that my parents raised me in had all the classic characteristics of a cult, and my parents aspired to be model members. As such, they followed the extreme teachings without question, surrendered their own judgment (what little they had) in favor of the judgment of the cult leaders in all matters big and small, ranging from which house they bought to how they dressed, and socialized and associated only with cult members, even to the exclusion of extended family members with whom we spent very limited time.

Several years after moving cross country to join the cult, my parents built a new house in a developing neighborhood and moved into the cult's very first "cluster." A cluster was a neighborhood comprised mostly or completely of cult members. By the time our house was built, there was only one house in our neighborhood that wasn't owned by cult members, but the owners of that house moved soon after our cluster took over the neighborhood; I can't imagine what our cluster did to those poor people's property value!

By the age of twelve, I had become completely isolated and knew nothing of the world outside of the cult. I remember a time once during my high school years when my maternal grandmother visited us; she took me aside when my parents weren't looking and anxiously urged me, "Aidy, don't drink anything they give you *ever*, especially if it is Kool-Aid!" This made absolutely no sense to me at the time. Years later, when I was in my thirties, I watched a documentary on Jonestown, and it broke my heart to think that my grandmother was that worried for my life!

In their pursuit of status within the cult, my parents enforced extreme rules and placed impossible expectations on my sister and me, so that we could present as the perfect Christian family (according to the extreme teachings of the cult). I was not allowed to have any friends who were not in the cult. Dating was declared to be for the purpose of entering into marriage only, and therefore was restricted to adults who were deemed to be ready to move toward marriage. Although I spent much of my junior high, high school, and college years dreaming about having a boyfriend, I did not go on my first date, hold hands with, or kiss a guy until I was twenty-two.

All elements of secular culture were deemed to be sinful and were forbidden. I was not allowed to wear fashionable clothes because they were considered to be materialistic and worldly. I remember begging my parents for a coveted pair of Gloria Vanderbilt jeans (the '80s equivalent of Citizens, Sevens, or AGs) for Christmas when I was in eighth grade. They gave in after I presented a particularly persuasive argument, but bought them two sizes too big for me to make sure I didn't look sexy; my mother watched me like a hawk to keep me from trying to shrink them in the dryer.

I wasn't allowed to listen to any music other than Christian music; to this day, when my peers reminisce about '80s music, I am lost because it wasn't the soundtrack of my adolescence the way it was for everyone else my age. The television of my generation was another thing I completely missed out on; I was a college junior when my parents bought their first television set. Throughout my childhood, I remember my father eagerly pontificating about the evils of the boob tube to anyone who would listen. To this day, I do not know who killed JR or why Joanie loved Chachi. Once a week, I was allowed to go next door to my best friend Mallory's house (whose family was also in the cult but mysteriously had a TV) to watch *Little House on the Prairie*, because my parents deemed it to be safe and wholesome enough.

Rarely were we allowed to go to the movies, and never to anything more than "G" rated. My father took us to see the original *Rocky* movie when it came out in the late seventies, which was rated "PG," but made us walk out in the middle of it because it was so violent. He made a huge scene as we exited, loudly exclaiming about the evils of gratuitous violence, while my sister and I followed behind him with our heads hung in shame and embarrassment.

Like most fanatical religious groups, there was a strict gender hierarchy in the cult; men were to lead and women were to follow. My father was supposed to be the head of the household with total and final decision-making power in all areas; my mother was supposed to follow the biblical admonition to submit to her husband in all things. She struggled with the practice of submitting, which caused a lot of fights between her and my father, but, in retrospect, was a precious example of assertiveness and independence that became a tiny flickering beacon of inspiration for me. My father struggled just as much with the biblical admonition to love my mother the way that Christ loved the church. Love, respect, kindness . . . these were not practiced or modeled in my childhood home.

It was a very depressing existence for two main reasons. One, I was cut off from the majority of the human experience that was available to be had, and two, I was constantly beaten down—physically, psychologically, emotionally, and spiritually—by my parents and the only community I knew, the cult, because I was sinful. Of course I didn't know it at the time, but by early adolescence I was clinically depressed. I had little to compare my feelings to; any fleeting joy I might have experienced in early childhood, before my parents "found the Lord," was a distant and foggy memory. I didn't realize that it was not normal to feel so sad that you wanted to die. Perhaps feeling like I wanted to die somehow made sense to me because I had been taught that my sinfulness made me deserving of being damned to Hell. I remember sitting at the kitchen table when I was thirteen and flatly remarking to my mother that I didn't think I would make it to the end of my life, because life was just too hard.

When I was in eighth grade, my parents pulled me out of school to homeschool me, because the public junior high school was too worldly and they feared the wicked influence of my secular classmates on me. Since I spent every day that year doing my lessons at the kitchen table, my mother actually noticed how lethargic and spiritless I had become. Concerned that I was depressed, she took me to our family doctor. There was no help to be had for me there since our family doctor was, of course, a cult member. The doctor immediately dismissed the idea that removing a teenager from her peer group and confining her to the house to be homeschooled would have any negative effect; on the contrary, the doctor praised my parents' bravery for sequestering me from the evils of the world.

Even in the midst of my sadness and lethargy, I tried to assert myself, albeit not very gracefully or effectively because I was only thirteen. I screamed and yelled a lot at my parents, who remained unmoved and only increased my spankings. I plotted to run away but never succeeded. I wrote scathing daily accounts in my diary. I tried my first cigarette; I got caught and punished. I tried to sneak out to go to a rock concert; I got caught and punished. Along with the spankings, I also got grounded, which, looking back, is pretty funny because there was so little that my parents allowed me that there was therefore very little for them to deprive me of as a punishment; my whole life had become one unending punishment.

Like all children, on a primal level, I equated the lack of my parents' love and approval with death, and it created that level of anxiety in me. After my one brave year of attempting to assert my independence and individuality, I caved and "gave my heart to Jesus." I remember sitting in a prayer meeting looking up at my mother as she swayed with her hands raised in charismatic prayer and thinking, "I can't go on like this." I was so weary and felt more alone than any thirteen-year-old ever should. I asked my mother to step outside with me, and I said to her, "I give up." She was thrilled! She thought that I meant that I was ready to give my life to Christ. What I actually meant was, "I give up; you win. I can't make it on my own without your love and approval. I will do whatever it takes to win your love and approval even if it isn't genuine!"

Thus began the next decade of my life, during which I exerted a monumental effort to reject who I was and become who they wanted me to be. I became a model member of the cult; I wholeheartedly embraced and practiced all the teachings and championed the extreme way of life that had been forced on me. I cut off all ties with anyone who wasn't in the cult. I faithfully attended all the meetings three to five times a week. I enthusiastically joined in the efforts to proselytize the rest of the world for Christ and bring more members into the cult. I voluntarily opted out of every standard adolescent activity and experience—dating, popular music, most movies, rock concerts, dances, parties, etc. When I look back on those years, I marvel at what I was able and willing to cooperate with and subject myself to; quite frankly, I can't believe I did it, but when I remember how much I felt as if I had no choice and how much I felt as if my very life depended on it, I understand.

After my eighth grade year of homeschooling, my parents found a very small, very conservative Baptist high school to send me to. Although the school wasn't part of the cult, it was very similar in ideology and practice. The primary purpose of the school was to get kids "saved," which took priority over academics; I remember having to write out my salvation testimony on the entrance application. My parents were more than happy with the school's focus on and mission of salvation over academics. Looking back, it seems so incongruous, because both of my parents were Montessori educators with degrees from Princeton and Yale; it just goes to show how much of the Kool-Aid they had already drunk by that time. By the time I was a senior in high school, I had become so completely indoctrinated into the cult ideology and way of life that, although I was the valedictorian of my senior class, my greatest ambition was to get married, subjugate my will and my life to my husband's authority, and start having babies as soon as possible.

The bitter irony was that although I met and exceeded every one of my parents' extreme demands, I never won their love and approval. It remained the elusive proverbial carrot that was always dangling just out of reach, and I remained the proverbial gerbil on the wheel running after it, thinking that surely someday I would get it. For decades and well into my adulthood, even after they had left the cult, my parents continued to find fault with me and make it clear that I, on the whole, fell short of who they needed me to be. I was never able to win their hearts on my own merits. I was always "too much this and not enough that." I was too rebellious and not submissive enough; I was too gregarious and not demure enough; I was too much of an independent thinker and not enough of a believer/follower/conformist . . . etc., etc., etc.

As fate would have it, I did not end up getting married and having babies right out of high school as I had hoped. Instead, on the complete opposite end of the spectrum, I ended up pursuing an undergraduate degree in history and secondary education at UCLA. In truth, my parents would have preferred that I go to a strictly Christian college, but they had no money for my college tuition; as a Montessori teacher, my father made very little money, my mother, per the mandates of the cult teachings, was a housewife, and they faithfully tithed at least ten percent of their gross income to the cult, which made our modest family budget even tighter. My maternal grandfather, who was a self-made millionaire in the 1950s, offered to pay for my college tuition, but he was clear that his offer was only for a quality education which was not to be had, in his opinion, at a Christian college; he was a staunch atheist. My parents would never have allowed me to go to such a secular and liberal institution as UCLA, but the cult had a satellite ministry on the campus so I could stay within the cult bubble; in fact, my cult experience was the most intense during my college years.

All my college roommates were cult members, so I remained insulated from anyone outside of the cult. In addition to the Saturday night Lord's Day ceremonies (a Christianized version of the Jewish Sabbath ceremony), Sunday morning church services, and Sunday afternoon three-hour-long prayer meetings, which were already a part of my weekly schedule growing up in the cult, we had Wednesday night courses, weekly men's or women's group meetings, and daily morning and evening prayer time. Everyone involved in the campus branch of the cult went through a set of courses (on Wednesday nights) designed to intensely indoctrinate new members. During the summers, we were separated into men's and women's "summer households." In summer household, we lived together in sorority and/or fraternity houses on the college campus, which we rented for the summer. The goal of summer household was to create a very intense, monastic-like religious life of early morning prayers (five in the morning or earlier), evening prayers, communal living (no one had a bedroom to themselves), and all meals together as well as mandatory household chores. It was a very demanding and isolating experience; the first time I ever felt seriously suicidal was when I was living in summer household after my freshman year of college.

In college, I had my very first "pastoral leader"; a pastoral leader was a member of the cult who was deemed to be more advanced in their "walk with the Lord" and therefore qualified to pastor a less advanced member. All adult members of the cult had pastoral leaders; all husbands were the pastoral leaders for their wives and underage sons, mothers were the pastoral leaders for their underage daughters, single women had female pastoral leaders, and all men (single or married) had male pastoral leaders. The only two cult members who didn't have a pastoral leader were the founding leaders, who supposedly pastored each other, and in the end, had a huge falling out which split the cult.

We were taught to respect and follow the direction of our pastoral leaders without question, and pastoral leaders were given free rein to probe into any and every area of our lives. Nothing was off limits. For example, my first pastoral leader in college asked me if I masturbated. It wasn't an option to respond with anything resembling boundaries (which I wasn't raised to have anyway) and say something like, "I don't feel comfortable with that question," and certainly not, "None of your damn business!" My feeble attempt to defend myself against this gross boundary violation was to lie and say, with as much innocence as I could muster, "No, of course I don't masturbate; that's a sin!" Needless to say, the pastoral leader system was fraught with voyeurism and abuse; ultimately, it was the blind and dysfunctional leading the blind and dysfunctional.

Even though the majority of my time at UCLA was spent going to prayer meetings, it was instrumental in the expansion of my mind beyond the distorted and fringe world view I had been raised with. It was the beginning of a slow, growing awareness that did not fully surface until after I was finished with college, and unfortunately, not until after I had spent four more years of my life living the way I had been raised. As a result, I made it to age twenty-two having completely avoided all the major experiences and developmental stages that most people in Western cultures usually experience and go through from adolescence to adulthood. What proved to be the most tragic and detrimental was that I had zero relationship experience with men.

In my final year of college, I was deemed by my parents and the cult leadership to be ready to move toward marriage. Only a decade later than my peers, I was finally allowed to date! Whoo-hoo! I was overjoyed and completely oblivious to the dangers that awaited me. I was chronologically twenty-two, but emotionally, psychologically, and developmentally, I was still a pre-teen, since my parents had surgically removed my adolescence, and with it, the crucial and necessary developmental stages contained therein. I was not equipped to enter into a marriage relationship; I was equipped to handle, at most, "going with" a guy and breaking up after a few weeks, as is typical for a beginner in relationships. Letting me get married at that point in my life was about as responsible as giving a child a loaded gun to play with; I had no more concept of the seriousness or consequences of my actions. To compound the problem, not once did my mother teach me anything useful or practical about men, relationships with men, or marriage, and what she and my father had modeled for me was disastrous.

On New Year's Eve of that year, I met and fell deeply and tragically in love with a man who deliberately concealed from me the fact that he was gay; eighteen months later, we were married. At this point in my life, I had not encountered any gay men or lesbian women, *or so I thought*. In keeping with the bigoted and exaggerated stereotypes I had been taught, I thought they all wore sparkly outfits or combat boots (or both?) while waving rainbow flags and marching jauntily in fabulous parades. Looking back, I realize that I knew plenty of gay men and lesbian women in the cult, but they were all closeted; they escaped my notice at the time because, as is almost always the case, they did not fit my given stereotypes. Basically, I was so clueless about gay men that I wouldn't have known a gay man if he stood at the altar with me!

I was primed by my family of origin to be comfortably familiar with dysfunction and abuse, and I was completely unequipped to accurately assess my future husband's character or my relationship with him before I committed to him. I evaluated him with the oh-so-discriminating criteria of a thirteen-year-old; the top two things that most impressed me about him were that he was "so cute," with his aquiline features, wavy black hair, and bright green eyes, and was "such a sharp dresser," although he expertly avoided wearing anything sparkly. Although he was, in reality, a weak and unscrupulous man, I believed him to be my Prince Charming and blindly devoted myself to him accordingly. In classic Machiavellian fashion, he took advantage of my devotion to him and asked me to marry him in order to pass himself off as heterosexual. Years later, he told me, "I only married you because I was expected to get married and you were willing." I'm telling you, Hallmark should grab that quote for one of their cards, because that's about the most romantic sentiment I've ever heard! "Happy anniversary, Honey; thanks for 'being willing!'"

For the next twenty years, he effortlessly continued the relentless disapproval of me begun by my parents with seamless continuity, but added his own twist to take it to the next devastating level. Not only did he also constantly tell me that everything about *who* I am was wrong (always too much this and not enough that), in addition, he told me that *what* I am—a woman—was wrong. He didn't have the honesty or decency to tell me directly that the reason he wanted nothing to do with me was because I was a woman and he wasn't attracted to women; nonetheless, he made it clear, loud and clear, that he thought there was something wrong with me. He was so blunt and harsh about his loathing for my female body that he even went so far as to tell me that when he looked at my vagina, all he saw was an undeveloped phallus. During my eventual divorce decades later, I joked that my marriage totally would have worked if it hadn't been for my pesky vagina problem!

The strictest rules of sexual purity had been imposed on me by my parents and the cult teachings. I was raised with the classic virgin-whore dichotomy perspective on female sexuality. I was taught that truly godly women did not have sexual desire or even really enjoy sex; they only participated in sex to meet their husbands' needs. Men were prone to the sin of lust, but only ungodly women lusted. All through high school and college, I regularly heard talks (sermons) on sexual purity where it was plainly stated that women were responsible for helping men to avoid the sin of lust by dressing modestly and making sure that our behavior was always non-sexual in nature.

Everyone in the cult called each other Brother and Sister, which was part of the whole de-sexualization programming; after all, how can you lust after your brother or your sister? We all greeted each other with hugs, but *only side hugs*, because as we were instructed, a full-frontal hug between a Brother and a Sister could cause the Brother to lust. Besides the fact that side hugs are awkward any day of the week, especially when everyone knows that their expressed purpose is to be lust-free, they are also downright disgusting in the summer heat; I suffered many a damp shirt shoulder after being released from the sweaty pit side hug of a Brother who was awkwardly trying to remain lust-free! I remember expressing my frustration to a Brother once, saying, "I feel like I am responsible for the lust of all men just because I have breasts!" and knowing, as soon as I had said it, that my comment alone was grounds for rebuke.

I grew up surrounded by "saintly" women who gave all appearances of complete asexuality. By the time I was in college, I was sure there was something wrong with me because I did have sexual desire and I was interested in sex even though I knew nothing about it beyond the basic biology lesson. I felt so sinful for the thoughts and feelings I had; I consoled myself with thinking, "Well, at least whoever I marry is going to be a happy man!" It was not until I was in my mid-twenties, when I got out into the real world and crossed paths with real, sexually self-possessed women, that I began to feel normal.

I was taught that sex and all sexual activity outside of marriage, beyond chaste kissing and hand holding, was sinful. I was also taught that sex was first and foremost for the godly mandate of procreation, and that the pleasure of it was a secondary and unnecessary byproduct (especially for the woman). Needless to say, I was also taught that masturbation was a perversion and a sin. Since I was raised Catholic, in addition to what I was taught about sex by the cult, I was also taught that the use of birth control, the practice of abortion, and the use of in vitro fertilization (or any other medical aid for fertility) were all sinful because they were considered to be a usurpation of God's supreme and exclusive role in creation. The only acceptable birth control was the use of the rhythm method, which is also known as Natural Family Planning (we jokingly called it "natural family pregnancy" because it was so ineffective). Natural Family Planning is a method of birth control where the woman tracks her ovulation and abstains from sex when she is fertile (never mind the fact that this is when the woman will most enjoy sex). Prior to meeting my husband, I had remained "pure" with the exception of self-exploration (which I repented for nightly!), but I eagerly looked forward to and regularly fantasized about the time when I could get married and have as much sex as I wanted without it being sin.

Although we did more than just kiss and hold hands before we got married, my fiancé and I made it to our wedding night with both of our virginities intact. This happened primarily because of my fiancé's insistence that we not have sex until we were married; I was more than ready to "go all the way," eternal damnation be damned! At the time, I thought it was because he was so noble and respectful; I now know that it was because he was trying to put off for as long as possible that which he was deeply dreading—having sex with a woman. Only ten days after losing his virginity with me, he asked me, with an exasperated sigh, in response to the lingerie I had put on, "Do we *have* to have sex *every* night?" He was only twenty-six. I was crushed and completely confused!

He had had a little dating experience prior to us meeting, whereas I had had none. He hadn't joined the cult until he was in medical school at UCLA; he was brought in by his older sister who had been previously evangelized by some cult members. As was the practice in the cult, when we were dating, I asked him to confess to me the extent of his prior sexual activity so I could judge his purity. He told me that he had messed around with his first college girlfriend and gone so far as to fondle her vagina; when I asked him how he felt about it, thinking he would say that it had excited him but that he knew it was a sin, he said "touching a vagina frightened me." Although his answer makes perfect sense now, I had absolutely no categories at that time for what he said; I was completely confused, so I just dismissed his response.

After we were married, he divulged to me that in high school when his buddies had gotten ahold of a porno to watch and he saw a man having sex with a woman for the first time, he ran to the bathroom and vomited; he also told me that he vomited on our wedding day right before I walked down the aisle. For the entirety of our marriage, he used sex as a weapon, withholding it as punishment and initiating it only to appease me when I was angry with him. I once tried to refrain from initiating sex to see how long it would take him to initiate; I gave up after two months. He told me at the end of our marriage that, in all the years we were sexually active together, he had not once actually *wanted* to have sex with me; he said he only ever felt *ambivalent*, at best. For so many years after my wedding night, I often found myself thinking bitterly, "This is what I saved myself for?"

He not only wanted nothing to do with me romantically and sexually, he wanted nothing to do with me at all; he didn't want to talk with me; he didn't want to go anywhere with me; he didn't even want to sit on the couch next to me to watch TV. He knew all along why our marriage wasn't working, but he never had the decency at least to say, "I don't know what is wrong but it's not you." Instead, he capitalized on any and every one of my alleged shortcomings to blame me for the problems in our relationship and to keep me in a weakened state, distracted by my own pain, so that I would not figure out the truth. He told me that he would want to be with me if I lost the twenty pounds of residual pregnancy weight, or kept the house cleaner, or had dinner ready on time, or toned down my colorful personality. So, because I was starved for affection and just as desperate for his love and approval as I had been for my parents' love and approval, I jumped through every hoop he held up for me, just as I had for my parents, only to be blamed in a new way for his lack of love and desire for me. For twenty years, he sustained a relentless, all-pervasive attitude of arrogant disdain and loathing toward me; just as it had been with my parents, his love remained the elusive proverbial carrot that was always dangling just out of reach.

Miraculously, I had survived my parents' rejection without a total loss of my self-esteem, but barely; on the heels of my parents' rejection, rejection from the man I was deeply in love with was crushing and just short of completely devastating. The heartache I shouldered for decades splintered me into a million painful shards; it almost broke me. Many times, I cried rivers of tears and wailed heartache from the depth of my broken being. I felt so alone, so sad, and so frightened for so long.

The pain was so confusing because it was so nebulous. Unlike the overt and identifiable abuse that I had suffered from my parents, the abuse from my husband had no handle. From the outside, he appeared to be an enviable husband; he was a good provider, helped around the house, and shared parenting responsibilities. My family and friends often just looked at me in confusion when I would confide that I was unhappy and in pain. The ceaseless subtle verbal criticisms, relentless attitude of disdain and loathing, and sexual manipulation, withholding, and rejection didn't register as important with anyone; in particular, I got little sympathy from my girlfriends, who were weary of being chased around for sex by their husbands (which I viewed with awe and envy). If he had hit me, it would have made sense to those around me. Instead, I was perceived as being the problem; I was labeled as being emotionally needy and unstable. The sad irony was that I *had* become emotionally needy and unstable as a result of the culmination of a lifetime of neglect, condemnation, and rejection. I had been living with a severe love deficit from before I was born, and it was rapidly catching up with me.

It is no wonder to me that by my mid-thirties, I was a pack-a-day smoker, daily drinker, chronically overweight, had had two extra-marital affairs, and was on a high dose of anti-depressants because I had seriously contemplated suicide more than once. What is a wonder to me is that it wasn't worse. What is a wonder to me is that I am still here. What is a wonder to me is that today, I am healthy, happy, and whole.

CHAPTER TWO

For the Adventure of It

All the EPT commercials I had ever seen were nothing like the scene that played out in the little bathroom of the 500-square foot, one-bedroom apartment I had moved into two years earlier as a glowing virginal bride. There were no tears of joy, there was no exuberant loving embrace, neither of us excitedly reached for the phone to share the news. There was only shock, there was only disbelief, there was only cold paralysis. We were sure there must be a mistake; this just could not actually have happened! We had been using condoms, carefully and faithfully, since the previous summer when a bad reaction had prompted me to discontinue taking the Pill. Not once had we had sex without using a condom, not once had a single condom broken, and we knew enough, at least, not to use the never-trusty "pull out" method!

I stood there limply holding the EPT with its devastating two blue lines, glowing as if penned in neon ink, muttering "How did this happen? How did this happen? How did this happen?" while my husband frantically searched through his medical text books for an explanation. After what felt like forever, he came across a handy bit of information which I would never have known on account of how I was raised, and on account of not having a penis: he discovered that pre-cum is ten times more concentrated with sperm than regular cum! Oh . . . My . . . God . . . ignorantly, we had not been careful enough before putting on the condom! Once I recovered from my shock and regained my voice, I practically screamed at my husband: "You're a medical

19

doctor, for chrissake! How did you not know this? We're not high school kids on prom night; how the hell did this happen to us?"

I was in my early twenties when I was first exposed to the ideas of modern spirituality (which is actually ancient spirituality, but we in the West like to think that we have discovered everything) through the audio programs and books of Deepak Chopra, Wayne Dyer, Ram Dass, Thich Nhat Hanh, and the like. Their thoughts and ideas were the fresh air I had been gasping for during the asphyxiation of my religious cult upbringing. With all the hunger of a famine survivor, I devoured these new ideas and embraced them with enthusiasm. All except one . . .

The one idea I really choked on was the idea that we choose all of our life circumstances and experiences before we are born. The idea is that, contrary to millennia of common understanding, life is not random; we are in control of our life circumstances and we chose and direct everything about our lives. Therefore, we are responsible for what has happened to us and for what will happen to us. The flip side of this idea is that since we choose and direct everything in our lives, we also have the power to create the lives we want going forward. That part I really liked; I liked the idea that I could create the life of my dreams, since, thus far, my life had been anything but that of my dreams, but I really balked at the idea that I had picked or was responsible for everything about my life thus far. I didn't mind taking credit for my positive qualities and the successes I felt I had created—my degree, my teaching career, my sparkling personality, my witty charm, etc.—but I didn't like the idea that I was responsible for the things in my life that I felt were beyond my control—the dreadful parents I was born to, the religious cult I was raised in, or the marriage I ended up in with an abusive man who intentionally deceived me. You can't tell me I willingly and knowingly picked those circumstances! Seriously? Because if it really were up to me, you better believe I would have made better choices! Really, if you could meet my parents, you would know that no one would ever willingly pick them to be raised by! What bride, in her right mind, would willingly choose to be lied to by her groom about his sexual orientation?

But I am an intelligent person capable of grasping logic. I understood that it cannot be that I have the power to create the future life that I want but my past was random and beyond my control. Thanks to Einstein, we know that time and space are relative and our concept of time as linear is an illusion—so, if I can create my future, I must have created my past. If my whole life is of my creation, then of course I am responsible for all of what makes, has made, and will make it up. Grrrrrrrrrrrrrrrrrrr . . . wailing and gnashing of teeth! Even though I grasped the cold and sound logic of the idea, I still rejected it on emotional grounds. You just could not get me to believe that I deliberately chose to be raised by my incompetent, abusive parents, or willingly chose an abusive marriage that turned out to be a complete fraud!

Then, a very interesting series of events happened to me, which removed any doubt in my mind that we, at the very least, pick our parents and the families we are born into. I was in my mid-twenties and I had just recently left the religious cult I was raised in. I was newly married with a plan—we were going to wait at least five years before starting a family. I was smart enough to know that I had issues from my own childhood and I wanted to address them before I became a parent, so I began to see a therapist on a weekly basis, and it was very productive.

Around this time, I developed pretty severe chronic PMS. At this time (the early '90s), Prozac was the darling drug of the psychiatric profession, and my therapist suggested that I might want to try going on Prozac for my PMS. Having been raised by a hippie mother, I had been taught to prefer a natural solution over a chemical drug solution, and a lot of this had stuck with me. I have always operated from the premise that the body is self-healing and driven to maintain health; I need only to support my body's healing mechanisms and refrain from behaviors that are destructive or hinder the body from healing itself. So, when my therapist suggested I start taking Prozac, I said, "Thank you, but *no* thank you!"

I wanted to find a way to relieve my PMS on my own, and this was long before Whole Foods was everywhere and natural remedies were as prevalent as their chemical counterparts. About a year prior, a friend had introduced me to meditation, and I was meditating here and there mostly out of curiosity and for the novelty of it. I decided that I was going to use meditation to try and resolve my PMS. I realized that I had been socialized to be at odds with my body and how it worked. I had been taught that the workings of my female body were, at the very least, a messy inconvenience, and, ultimately, they were the result of God's curse on Eve for her sin of eating the forbidden fruit in the Garden of Eden. In short, I was taught to reject and abhor the workings of my female organs as yucky and punishment for my sin (an attitude that my closeted gay husband was more than happy to reinforce). It seemed logical to me that my female organs might take umbrage with this attitude and treatment and react in a negative way, i.e. severe chronic PMS.

Having discarded the religious teachings I was raised with, I began to consider a different perspective on my body and its workings. I realized how silly it was to reject the natural workings of my female organs! For example, if I hadn't been having regular periods, I would have been worried and run to the doctor to find out what was wrong. If I hadn't been having regular periods, I would have feared that I would be unable to have children. I shifted my attitude to one of gratitude, and I began regular meditations focused on my uterus. I began by apologizing for the attitude of rejection and abhorrence I had held toward my uterus. I acknowledged that my uterus had always and only been doing its job, and that I shouldn't have been negative about it for just doing what it was supposed to do. I thanked my uterus for being so healthy and functioning so flawlessly. I expressed gratitude and appreciation that, someday, when I wanted to have children, my uterus would be there to do that for me.

As I shifted my attitude, my PMS significantly lessened. I became more and more peaceful and in harmony with my body. I continued with my meditations, following the same pattern of gratitude and appreciation, and the most interesting thing began to happen. When I was expressing gratitude toward my uterus for the future children it would create for me, a little girl, of about age six, began to appear in my mind's eye during my meditation. I was so intrigued! I was so curious about who this little girl was, so I began to interact with her. She was delightful! When she came, often she was holding hands with a little brother. I remember thinking to myself, "How curious! I am not planning on getting pregnant for another four to five years. I wonder why this little girl and her brother are here." Then this little girl began to come to me even when I wasn't in meditation. She would visit me when I was in the kitchen making dinner, at the table grading papers, sitting on the couch watching TV, etc. Still, I just thought the whole experience was very curious because I was twenty-dumb and I was certain that I wasn't going to get pregnant for quite a few more years. Are you laughing? I am now! Ah, how dim we can be when we think we know so much!

This went on for about three months until the beginning of the summer. I was scheduled to go on a weeklong workshop for my teaching job at the end of the school year. Several days before I was due to leave, I got a call from a dear friend who lived in another state—a five-hour drive. The man she had been dating for several years had died suddenly, and she was distraught. I decided to make the drive to be with her for the funeral; I would be able to make it back home before I had to leave for my workshop. On the five-hour return drive home, the little girl sat in the front passenger's seat of my car, as palpable as if she were flesh and blood! We laughed together with tangible joy the entire drive home—all five hours! I got home late Saturday night with just enough time to pack for my workshop the next day and spend the night with my husband.

. . . and by now, you know where this story is going . . .

Sure enough, three weeks later I was a week late for my period, which was always on time. I wish I could tell you that I was thrilled; I wish I could tell you that knowing my daughter before I got pregnant with her made the unplanned pregnancy with her a pleasant surprise, but I can't. Being firmly attached to my plan for my life, as I was at that age, I was anything but thrilled! I had just escaped a severely restrictive and repressive childhood, I was *not* ready to relinquish my freedom in exchange for the serious responsibilities of motherhood. It wasn't until I was about four or five months along that I could smile graciously and not feel the urge to slap someone who beamed "Congratulations!" when I told them I was pregnant. In hindsight, I am sure that this was why my daughter decided to make herself known so strongly before she entered time and space. She knew that I wouldn't be expecting her, and she knew that I felt I wasn't ready to become a mother. Had I not known who she was already, I very likely would have chosen not to go through with the pregnancy; in fact, her father and I discussed that option.

I had not told my husband anything about what had been occurring in my meditations. He was a medical doctor, a psychiatrist, and a very left-brained, scientific kind of guy with nary a spiritual bone in his body; in addition, he had a mean and spiteful habit of mocking me for my interest in New Age spirituality. During our discussion about what course of action to take with our unplanned pregnancy, I told him about everything that had happened in my meditations over the previous three months. I concluded by saying that I knew that we had the choice to decline this girl, and that if we did, she would not judge us, but she would not come to us again. I intuitively knew that she wanted/needed to come to Earth then, and that if we declined her, she would pick someone else to come through. I knew that we would/could have other children, but if we said no to her at that time, she would not come to us again. That was something I could not live with! I knew her already, I felt bonded with her, and as much as I didn't want to become a mother at that time in my life, I knew I had to have her. So, she became my exquisite first born redheaded daughter, and I have had no regrets, only gratitude to her for picking me to be her mother!

After being so clearly chosen by my daughter, I could not doubt or question the idea that, at the very least, we choose our families. In my mind, it stood to reason that if we choose something as significant as our families, we likely choose everything else in our lives. It just didn't make sense to me that we would have a choice in something as big as the family we are born into, but not have a choice in the rest of the details. From this point on, I accepted, on academic grounds, that I chose all the details and circumstances of my life, but I still did not like the idea and I still did not understand why I would have chosen the specific, seemingly-unfortunate details of the life I found myself in.

Most of my thirties and into my early forties was the darkest time in my life; it was a time of just plain survival. Although I still pondered life's big questions, I did not make any visible strides in personal or spiritual growth; my energy was spent on making it safely through the day and living to see the next morning. It wasn't until my early forties that I began again to absorb what the contemporary spiritual teachers were sharing, and attempted to incorporate their thoughts into my personal growth.

To be honest, even into my early forties, I was still firmly attached to my victim identity, and it served me to wallow in self-pity and to indulge in the pity of others for the difficult childhood, marriage, and life I had had. I believed myself to be as helpless and tragic as Cinderella after midnight, sitting on the ground, dressed in rags, surrounded by broken pieces of smashed pumpkin, with silly little mice running around her feet. I did not want to be responsible for any of these perceived misfortunes that had occurred in my life, because I enjoyed using them as an excuse for why I was where I was in life and why I couldn't be expected to do any better. I felt that I was doing better than most would do in my circumstances, and in fact, I was. Looking back on this time in my life, I think this was fair; I had suffered, and was still suffering, quite a lot of abuse, heartache, and disappointment, and I was entitled to my fair share of time to lick my wounds and feeling sorry for myself. The problem was that, in the long run, operating from the place of my victim identity did not serve me. As much as I enjoyed playing the victim, I really wanted more; I wanted a better life than the one I was having as a victim.

So, I began again to ponder this idea that I had chosen the circumstances of my life. It really did make sense to my intellect, even if it offended my sensibilities. I decided, for the sake of argument, to accept that I chose all the circumstances of my life. From that premise, I began to ask "Why? Why would I pick these painful abusive experiences? Why wouldn't I pick loving, balanced parents who would nurture me with unconditional love and celebrate who I am? Why, if I were going to suffer at the hands of my parents, wouldn't I then pick a loving, supportive man to marry and help heal the wounds inflicted by my parents? Why would I add insult to injury, literally, and pick a man who was going to lie to me, emotionally and psychologically abuse me, and when I was in the deepest pit of suicidal despair, disregard me?"

Every time I pondered these questions, indignation rose inside of me screaming, "You are *crazy*! I *did not* pick these circumstances! *How dare* you blame me!" Each time, I pushed past the emotions and returned to the academic query, "Why? Why would I pick such seemingly unfortunate circumstances?" It took years for the answer to come to me; it emerged slowly in several phases, like Goldilocks' quest to find what was "just right."

At first, I mulled over the explanation I had heard so many others offer, which was that I chose these experiences to be taught lessons I needed to learn. This fit, but only somewhat. Like Goldilocks in Papa Bear's chair, I found this explanation to be "too hard"—it seemed to presume that I was ignorant, lacking, and in need of schooling. It could be argued that I was, and still am, most definitely ignorant, lacking, and in need of schooling (I am a human, after all), but having already dismissed the self-perception of defectiveness and inadequacy that I had been given in my youth, this explanation didn't sit well with me, so I pressed on with my query.

What came to me next was the acceptance that, for better or worse, I would not be the person I am today without the experiences I have had. By this time in my life, I believed myself to be essentially good. If I was good, then the experiences that produced me were, by default, good—or at least, served a good purpose. Like Goldilocks in Mama Bear's chair, I found this explanation to be "too soft"; it was just too nebulous and weak. This idea seemed to give meaning to my experiences, rather than having my experiences be random, pitiable events, but it didn't fully answer why I would have chosen these specific, arguably difficult, experiences. Couldn't I have become who I was with nicer experiences? Perhaps, I could have become an even better person with easier, nicer experiences. Again, why would I pick such miserable, painful, and, oftentimes, frightening experiences? Like Winnie the Pooh, I continued to "think, think, think . . ." and, eventually, like Goldilocks settling into Baby Bear's chair, I came to an understanding that, for me, was "just right."

In my early forties, I came across a new spiritual teacher named Mike Dooley; he also taught that we choose all the details of our lives and have the ability to create the future life we want. My response was the same: "You are crazy if you think I picked all this pain, confusion, and misery! But I do want to create a new life for myself, one that exceeds my wildest dreams . . . okay, fine, you win, I picked all this! But . . . why? *Why? Why?*" The phrase that Mike Dooley kept repeating in answer to this question was: "For the adventure of it!" Like a record needle stuck on a scratch in a record, this phrase stuck in my head and kept repeating, over and over and over again, "For the adventure of it . . . for the adventure of it . . . for the adventure of it . . . for the adventure of it . . ."

I kept thinking, "Adventure? I would *not* call my life an adventure! Thus far, I would call it an ordeal (*according to Random House unabridged dictionary an ordeal is: an extremely severe or trying test, experience, or trial*). Actually, I would call it a *harrowing* ordeal, and one which I had, at that point, barely made it through alive!

26

When I hear "adventure," I think of a tour of multiple European countries whose languages I don't speak, or a cruise to the Orient where I would be lost culturally, or, *maybe*, an African safari, *if* we traveled in a large, air-conditioned bus and stayed in a hotel. This is what adventure means to me. Risking my life climbing Mount Everest does *not* sound like an adventure; it sounds like complete lunacy and something that I would never, in a million years, willing subject myself to! I was born a land animal and I am very comfortable being a land animal! I enjoy and take great comfort in walking on the earth and breathing in the air every day. I have never felt even the slightest urge to try being an animal of flight and jump out of an airplane with nothing but a parachute to keep me alive, or to try being a water animal and scuba dive miles under the ocean with only a tiny tank of air to keep me alive.

When I thought more about it, I realized that not everyone feels the way I do about adventure. Not everyone defines adventure the same way I do. There are people who would be bored to tears on a cruise. There are people who would think that an African safari wouldn't be worth taking if they couldn't sleep out under the stars within earshot of the roaring lions. In fact, one of my girlfriends feels her life won't be complete until she gets to sky dive. I think she and the rest of them are crazy, but then again, I don't even ride roller coasters—nope, not even the kiddy ones! As I am able to admit that my point of view is subjective and not a universal standard (and not even necessarily normal), I can accept, in theory, that jumping out of an airplane or sleeping within earshot of lions could be, for some, an exciting adventure, and not the harrowing ordeal it would be for me.

I turned this logic toward the idea that I had picked my life experiences for the adventure of it. Would a different person experience my life as an adventure? What if, instead of being a different person, all that was necessary was a different perspective; could I then see it as an exciting adventure and not the harrowing ordeal that I had, up to this point, experienced it to be? From what perspective could I view my experiences positively, or even neutrally enough to call them an adventure? What if it wasn't a different person that was needed, but rather just for me to access a different part of myself? What if the perspective and the part of me necessary to make sense of all this were not bound by time and space? After all, time and space are illusions; it would stand to reason that all of what had happened to me within time and space was also an illusion. If all of what had happened to me within time and space was an illusion, then was it really a harrowing ordeal, after all?

As I thought more along these lines, it seemed that I might be getting closer to something that made sense. The problem I got stuck on was that all of my life experiences sure felt real; the physical abuse, the psychological abuse, the religious abuse, the emotional pain, the abandonment, the neglect, the rejection, the depression, the fear, *it all hurt so very much!* It all seemed so very tangible; I had a hard time dismissing it all as an illusion when it seemed and felt so real!

In his audio programs "Infinite Possibilities, The Art of Living Your Dreams" and "Leveraging the Universe and Engaging Life's Magic," (©Mike Dooley, www.tut.com) Dooley talks about all the many experiences we can have in life that "feel so real," but are not. He gives the example of the terror that we momentarily experience in the middle of a roller coaster ride. We experience definite physical peril, and yet we are completely safe. This experience is completely "real" in the moment, but once we are removed from the situation, we can see that it was only a simulated experience, an illusion. A horror movie, although terrifying while you are immersed in it, is not real. Although, in the dark of the theatre, you fully identify and sympathize with the characters to the point of physical response—your heart races, your palms sweat, you may even gasp, scream, or cry—there is a part of you, however momentarily suppressed, which knows that none of it is real. Could all the pain that I had experienced in my life also be only a simulated experience, an illusion? Could it be that I have actually been completely safe the whole time? Could I have actually voluntarily participated in all of these experiences truly for the adventure of it? Is that not, after all, why people voluntarily participate in the simulated terror of a roller coaster or the illusionary horror of a scary movie, for the adventure of it and because they know it's not real?

Dooley suggests that people embrace these experiences of simulated terror or illusionary horror not just for the adventure, but also for the challenge of "surviving" the experience. He gives the examples of the standard conversation between people waiting in line for the newest, most terrifying roller coaster—the excited and anticipatory conversation revolves around how scary it will potentially be and whether they can "survive" it—and the typical conversation between people who have just gotten off the newest, most terrifying roller coaster—the jubilant and relieved conversation revolves around how they "thought that they almost weren't going to make it" but in the end, it "was awesome and they can't wait to go again!" The fun of it is because none of it is real; the adventure of it is in embracing the challenge of remembering that it is not real, even in the midst of the experience.

It seemed logical to me that, as Dooley suggests, the same dynamics could very well be operating in my life here in the illusion of time and space. All the terror and horror that I thought I had experienced really could be simulated and illusionary. The part of me that is outside of time and space—my infinite, divine, perfect, omniscient, non-local self—could actually have chosen my entire life, each and every experience, and every last detail . . . for the adventure of it! If this really was the case, then none of it could be a mistake! How could my infinite, divine, perfect, omniscient, non-local self make a mistake? Knowing, as my non-local self would have known, that none of it would be real, *did I really think it would be fun?* Perhaps I did choose my life adventure, with all of its seeming perils, to see if I could rise to the challenge of remembering, in the midst of it, that it is not real. If I could remember that it is not real, then surely I could survive it; if I could survive it, then, wow, I would be so very proud of myself! Maybe this was why I had picked such seemingly-challenging experiences when I could have picked a life of ease—not only for the adventure of it but also for the bragging rights at the end. After all, how proud can you really be of yourself for "surviving" a cruise to the Orient? I'd be much more proud of myself for surviving a treacherous trip down the Amazon River in a leaky canoe!

CHAPTER THREE

I Was Up For It

Just like most mornings, my husband was brushing his teeth at the sink while I was toweling myself off after stepping out of the shower. My naked body was nothing new to me, but being naked in front of a man was still very new to me. Having never even so much as held hands with a man, much less been naked in front of a man, prior to being with my husband, my husband's opinion of my body was, at that point in my life, my only point of reference for its attractiveness. As I turned to hang up my wet towel, I caught my naked reflection in the bathroom mirror. I twisted around to appraise my backside, and with a momentary flash of self-approval, I said to my husband, "I have a nice ass, don't I?"

After straightening up from where he was leaning over the sink, he grabbed a hand towel, wiped his mouth dry, and impatiently asked, "What did you say?" With my naked backside turned toward him, I wiggled my hips side to side and tentatively repeated, "I have a nice ass, don't I?" Without hesitation, he hooked each of his index fingers under the outer edges of the curve of each of my butt cheeks, lifted my butt cheeks a few inches higher, and ungraciously said, "Well, it could be a bit more like this." He dropped my butt cheeks and walked out of the bathroom, leaving me in shock. Tears stung my eyes as I repeated his motion with my own fingers, watching my butt cheeks rise to where he said they should be, and wondering how I could get them there so that he would want me.

I began my life dying—literally. I was born a healthy eight pounds and some odd ounces on December 19, 1967. One month later, I weighed less than six pounds and was passing starvation stools. For some reason, which she "never can recall," my mother neglected to take me to my two-week doctor's appointment, so her failure to feed me adequately went unnoticed and uncorrected for my first month of life. At my one-month check-up, the pediatrician was alarmed by my weight loss, and when he discovered starvation stools in my diaper, he exploded at my mother, yelling, *"What are you doing to this baby?"* He sent her home with feeding supplements and a medical-grade scale; he demanded that she weigh me daily and call my weight into his office each morning. I'm certain the doctor was very close to taking me away from my mother—in a later generation, he would have. Knowing what I do now about human physiology in relation to starvation and dehydration, I know that I was very close to death. Had the doctor not intervened, it is very likely that within the next week or two, my organs would have begun to shut down and I probably would have died.

My mother, being an all-natural hippie, was breast feeding me, or at least she was attempting to. This was before the "Breast is Best" campaign of my generation of mothers. My mother was part of the "breast feeding makes everyone uncomfortable" generation of mothers, and as it was, there was little or no education, support, or community for mothers who wanted to breast feed. To make matters worse, I was my mother's first baby. Still, even the least experienced mother knows that a newborn baby is supposed to grow, not wither! I don't know how she failed to notice that level of weight loss, or, more to the point, failed to be moved to do something about it! I lost more than 25 percent of my body weight in one month—in the one month of my life that I should have been gaining and growing the most! To put it in perspective, my weight loss as a newborn is comparable to an adult weighing 160 pounds losing more than 40 pounds in one month—which can really only be achieved through starvation and would most definitely be noticeable!

My mother claims that she was unaware that there was a problem because, as she tells it, I never cried; my father remembers a very different story. In his account, I screamed and screamed until I passed out from exhaustion, then slept fitfully until I woke up screaming and started the cycle again. He remembers giving me a little bit of honey on the tip of his finger, and me attacking it as if my life depended on it—which, in reality, it did. I was a preteen when I first remember my mother telling the story of how she almost starved me to death from birth; why she ever told me is beyond me! This was not the only story of neglect from my early years that she later casually recounted to me with no shame, embarrassment, or even any awareness of how exceptionally lacking her parenting was.

When I was newly married, my husband and I were planning a camping trip. I called my mother to see if she and my father had any camping gear that we could borrow. In the conversation, she began to reminisce about the camping that she and my father did when they were young and newly married. She proceeded to tell me of a time that they went camping when I was just six months old. She said that she and my father didn't have a tent, so all three of us were sleeping out under the stars (wait, with a six-month-old baby . . . what?) and when it began to rain, she scooted me under a picnic table (again . . . what?). I was shocked enough that they had me sleeping out under the stars as an infant, and when she said it started raining, I thought for sure her next statement was going to be, "so we packed up and went to a hotel" or, at the very least, "so we slept in the car"—but, no, she scooted me under a picnic table! She recounted it as if she was proud of herself for taking measures to protect me from the rain, as if she thought this was evidence of her being a good and responsible mother. If I stretch my brain, I can concede that it was a different time, theoretically a safer time, and perhaps the threat of kidnapping wasn't as imminent as it would be today, but what about the threat of nature? I could have actually ended up being raised by wolves instead of only figuratively raised by wolves! In all fairness, wolves do a damn good job raising their young, and to my knowledge, have never been known to join cults; who knows, I might have actually been better off!

Unfortunately, these occurrences were not isolated. They were only a few in an entire childhood full of incidents where my mother and father catastrophically failed to protect me (and my sister) and deliberately turned a blind eye to my (our) gross and blatant suffering. My mother, and to a lesser degree, my father, were undoubtedly missing the parenting gene. My mother clearly lacked the animal instinct to protect and nurture her young. I remember my father having more of a nurturing and protective instinct. He was a Taurus and had all the bull-like qualities of his sign—stubborn, angry, and capable of doing a fair bit of damage when provoked—but he also possessed the comforting solidness that is the hallmark of an Earth sign. I have precious memories from my childhood of him holding me tightly while an emotional fire storm (a frequent experience for me as a Sagittarius) ravaged me, and saying over and over again, "You're okay; I've gotcha." Unfortunately, because of the traditional gender roles enforced by the cult, he abdicated much of the parenting responsibility, beyond corporal punishment, to my mother. Being raised primarily by a mother who lacked or circumvented her basic primal instinct to protect and nurture has had far-reaching and long-lasting negative effects.

Manipulation of food in my life did not end with the doctor-mandated formula that corrected my nearly-deadly newborn weight loss. My mother controlled food in my life with an iron fist. She was obsessed with keeping the 24-inch waist she had when she got married, and she extended her obsession to the rest of the household. My father was chronically overweight (oftentimes even morbidly obese), and his weight management was her personal crusade—a crusade at which she rarely succeeded. As a health food fanatic, she allowed no white flour or white sugar in the house, which meant an existence devoid of any and all treats. The only time we ever got treats was at Halloween, or if we were at someone else's house. For my eleventh birthday party, my mother baked a carob cake with carob frosting; I was humiliated and mortified as my friends, one after the other, gagged, spit it out, and refused to finish it! Even if you have never tasted carob, I cannot in good conscience recommend that you try it just to gain the experience—it is actually that dreadful!

Not only was my mother a health food fanatic, she was also tragically lacking in any cooking talent. As a result, what she served us was never palatable and rarely even edible. One of her signature dishes was chicken-a-la-king, which was so disgusting that my sister and I nicknamed it "chicken-a-la-throw-up-sauce." She did not consider it to be necessary, and certainly not her responsibility, to make good-tasting food, just to make good-for-you food (I have learned in my adulthood that the two are not mutually exclusive). I was to eat what she prepared, without complaint or protest, regardless of how bad it tasted. She employed the *Mommy Dearest* method of making me sit at the table until I ate what was served to me. If I did not finish my dinner, it was served to me, cold, for breakfast; if I did not eat it for breakfast, it was served to me for lunch, and so on. Having intense, even if only subconscious, memories of the excruciating sensation of starvation from the start of my life, I learned to choke down just about anything. The upside of this was that it seriously expanded my palate, and to this day, there is very little that I won't eat or at least try. I've even eaten haggis without flinching!

My parents were Montessori teachers and were very passionate about the Montessori teaching method. Their passion was not left at the classroom door; it pervaded every aspect of our family life in my childhood. Unfortunately, certain nuances of the "respect the child" principle, which is at the heart of the Montessori philosophy, escaped my parents! They implemented the Montessori philosophy in my childhood with their trademark fanaticism and rigidity.

When I was in first grade, they decided that they were going to use my school lunches as an opportunity to teach me how to make a sandwich and pack a lunch, and to give me a sense of ownership and responsibility in my little six-year-old world. It is a stretch to make a six-year-old responsible for packing her own school lunches, but it might have worked out okay if it hadn't been for the extreme fanaticism they, of course, layered on top. In a stroke of what my mother mistook for brilliance, she decided that we would all make our lunches for the whole week on Sunday night, and get it done in one fell swoop. This meant that by Friday afternoon, I was eating a five-day-old peanut butter and jelly sandwich (which didn't even taste good on Monday because it was made with all natural, no sugar, no salt peanut butter) and a five-day-old, very stale bag of unbuttered, unsalted popcorn for "dessert." Efficient, maybe; gross, definitely!!

Now, I know there are starving children in Africa, and in the grand scheme of things, I was lucky to have food, even five-day-old food, but compared to what my classmates brought in for lunch, my lunches were abysmal! I remember, every day, gawking in envy at what my classmates unpacked from their lunch boxes—white bread sandwiches, cookies, potato chips, Tastykake cupcakes and butterscotch krimpets, etc. Trading was out of the question because there wasn't a chance that anyone wanted what I had in my lunch! By the time I was in second grade, I had developed the delinquent behavior of raiding the other students' lunch boxes in the coat closet, where they were kept until lunchtime, and gobbling up as many cupcakes and cookies as I could find, as fast as I could, like a starving orphan. I remember sitting in a parent-teacher conference with my mother, my father, and my teacher because my treat-stealing had reached epic proportions, understandably upsetting the other students and their parents. All three adults stared me down with stern fury, and my father demanded to know *"Why?"* I sat there in terrified silence, and eventually managed to squeak out a tiny, meek, "I don't know . . ." Looking back on that scene, I want to scream, *"Really?* You are asking me 'why?' *Really?* It's *obvious*, you morons!"

As a child, it seemed such a mystery to me that everyone around me had access to foods that I did not. It wasn't just what my friends at school brought in their lunches; it was also what I was served whenever I was over at a friend's house. The world was full of glorious food, all of which, for me, was behind glass—and I was the little girl with her face pressed up against the glass wishing with all my might that I could have it. Once, during my elementary school years, I was at the grocery store with my mother and saw what I thought was the same thing I had envied in one of my classmate's lunches—a jar of candied dates. I begged and begged and begged my mother to get them for me; finally, she relented. I remember sitting in the grocery cart holding this glorious jar of coveted food and basking in the glow of having been atypically successful in persuading my mother to give me something. I couldn't wait to eat them when we got home! Unfortunately, I found them to be dreadful; they were entirely too sticky and too sweet! True to form, my mother made me eat every single one. I had begged for them; I had to eat them.

Like most American women, I have had a complex about my body over the course of my lifetime, and have struggled to keep a "perfect" figure (what is that, by the way?). I'm pretty sure that experiencing starvation at such a young age left a deep impression on my primitive brain, and has had continuing effects which are deeply rooted in my subconscious. I think I am more sensitive to the sensations of hunger (hunger makes me panic) and I enjoy being full, even overly full, more than normal (and more than I believe I would if I had not been nearly starved to death). I have almost never been heard to say, "I better stop eating now or else I am going to get too full and have a stomachache." My thoughts have always been more along the lines of, "Keep the food coming! I'll suffer the stomachache later!" I also have never been one of those tragic women who *"just can't eat"* when she is stressed; oh, please, stress just makes me eat more! I can count on one hand the number of times in my life when I was so stressed that I couldn't eat! When I look at the big picture of food over the course my life, it's a marvel that I'm not the star of *My 600 Pound Life*. In fact, I have never been any more than fifty pounds overweight; my times at that size have been few and far between, and twice because of pregnancy. For most of the overweight years in my life, which have been the minority of my total life years, I have only been twenty to thirty pounds over my medically recommended "ideal" weight.

I was thirteen years old and a freshman in high school when I went on my first diet. From as far back as I can remember, my mother had told me that I needed to be careful about what I ate because I was "prone to being overweight"; a declaration for which she had no supporting evidence or proof, but a declaration which has haunted me for much of my life. As a result, by age thirteen I was five foot six, weighed 118 pounds, and thought I was fat (the medically recommended weight for that height is 117 to 143 pounds). My mother and father were starting the fad diet of the day, which was the Mayo Clinic Diet, also known as the Grapefruit Diet. I asked my mother if I could go on the diet with her and my father; she said that she thought it would be a good idea, since I could "stand to lose a few pounds."

The Mayo Clinic Diet includes a meal plan with a daily caloric intake of only 800 calories, which was less than half the recommended caloric intake for a teenage girl of my height. This would be the second time in my life when I was at a healthy weight and my mother starved me (are you *sure* I picked this woman to be my mother?). I only lasted three days on the diet; after nearly passing out in the hallway in between classes at school, I gave up and abandoned the diet. My mother acted just as confused about why there was a problem as she had when she starved me as a baby, and furthermore, acted as if the failure was in my lack of will power.

The summer after my sophomore year in high school, I joined my best friend Mallory (from next door) and her family on a six-week road trip across the country to visit her grandparents in Florida. I knew that Mallory's family's eating habits were more "normal," and as such, the food they ate was more fattening (mac-n-cheese, hotdogs, sugary cereal, etc.); in my mother's house there was *no* temptation for someone who was trying to watch their weight. Prior to leaving, I expressed concern to my mother that I would not have control over the food I would be eating for six weeks; I was worried, per her conditioning, that I would get fat (I was still only 118 pounds). In an attempt to reassure myself, I said to her, "Really, how bad can it be, right? How much weight can I really gain in six weeks?" My mother casually responded, "Well, you could gain twenty pounds." This struck terror into my heart! I was so gripped by the fear she had so callously and recklessly planted in me that I practically starved myself the whole trip, and militantly swam 100 laps each night in Mallory's grandmother's pool. By the end of the trip, *I had actually lost weight!* I had also ruined my vacation and almost ruined my friendship; I was such a neurotic kill-joy that, to this day, Mallory still bitterly remembers how I behaved on that trip! Unfortunately, having been firmly convinced by my mother that I was fat, or about to become fat any minute, I continued to go on and off diets (most of them very extreme), with mixed results, for the next three decades of my life.

Over the years, the more I thought about having been starved at birth and all the rest of the controlling food craziness I had suffered under from my mother, the more I began to think that there were probably some pretty deep-seated issues which were behind my struggle with food. In my early forties, I went to see a hypnotherapist to see if I could gain any insight into these issues, or make a breakthrough on a subconscious level.

After sharing a brief synopsis of my life and my history with food with the hypnotherapist, she guided me through the basic relaxation visualization (walking through the woods, birds singing, etc.), and then began to tailor the scene to me specifically. She brought me mentally into an open field, and then told me to visualize my different "selves" walking up to greet me. First, she guided me to see myself as a newborn. I saw myself as a brand new baby and cradled my infant self in my arms—I saw the wild hunger in my eyes and how helpless and defenseless I was. Then, the therapist guided me to visualize myself at thirteen walking up to join me in the field—I saw the eagerness to express and assert myself as an individual for the first time. Then, the therapist guided me to visualize myself in my early twenties walking up to me—I saw the engagement ring on my finger and the love for a heartless man shining in my eyes. Then, the therapist instructed me to talk to each one of my selves and tell them anything I wanted to tell them, anything I thought that they needed to hear, and to give them what they weren't given that they needed.

First, I spoke to my infant self and expressed pity, empathy, and fear for the neglect she was about to suffer. I said,

> You poor, precious, helpless baby! I'm so sorry for what you are about to go through. I wish I could take your pain away! You don't deserve to be neglected nearly to the point of death! If I could, I would keep you safe; I would protect you!

Next, I spoke to my thirteen-year old self and expressed sympathy, support, and indignation for the oppression and nullification she was about to suffer. I said,

> You poor, fierce girl! I'm so sorry for what you are about to go through. I wish I could whisk you away and prevent you from sacrificing yourself the way you are about to do! You deserve respect and honor for who you are, not rejection and shaming. You are perfect and you don't deserve to be crushed into submission!

Last, I spoke to my early twenty-something self and expressed heartbreak, sadness, and grief. I said,

> You poor, naïve, innocent, trusting Cinderella! I'm so sorry for what you are about to go through. You deserve a real Prince Charming! You have such a pure and precious heart to give, and it is about to be thrown on the floor, trampled on, and shattered into a million pieces! I wish I could warn you; I wish I could tell you who he really is!

What happened next was completely unexpected and utterly remarkable. The scene in my visualization spontaneously continued; each of my selves responded to what I had said to them, and their responses changed my life. My sweet, little, infant self reached her hands up to cradle my face and said to me,

Oh, Aidy, there was never any worry! I was never in any actual danger; I was perfectly safe the whole time and there was never any chance that I was actually going to die. I knew what I was doing; I knew exactly what was going to happen and I was up for it!

Next, with a big grin and a wink, my thirteen-year-old self said to me,

Oh, Aidy, there was never any worry! I was never going to lose myself, my authentic self! I was never going to completely conform; I was only going to bank the coals of my inner fire for a time. I knew what I was doing; I knew exactly what was going to happen and I was up for it!

Last, with a knowing smile, my early twenty-something self said to me,

Oh, Aidy, there was never any worry! The pain was never going to break me! I was never actually going to tap out; I was always going to make it through! I knew what I was doing; I knew exactly what was going to happen and I was up for it!

When the hypnotherapist brought me out of the visualization, I must have had a shocked look on my face because she anxiously asked me, "What happened?" I recounted the entire visualization, and after I shared the responses from my selves, she looked just as shocked as I felt. I sat there for a bit just absorbing the idea, the new perspective that "I was up for it." I left her office with a new insight on my whole life and everything I had suffered. The information I received was immensely valuable and had a huge impact on my life perspective.

If I really was up for it and there was never any real danger, then my whole life really could have been, and could continue to be, an adventure and not an ordeal. If I always knew what I was doing and knew exactly what was going to happen, then I must have chosen my life experiences and been in control all along. If I chose my life experiences, then they could not have been bad—none of them, not a single one.

I realized that when I was labeling my life experiences as bad, I was operating under the assumption that the bad experience was something that should have been avoided and/or removed from my whole life experience; this is how I used to feel about most of my life experiences. I was adamant that the abuse I had experienced from my parents, from the religious cult, and from my husband was bad and never should have happened. Looking at all of it from a conventional perspective, all of it was actually bad and also an injustice, and yet, looking at it from this new perspective, it was actually only an unpleasant and painful experience, albeit a *very* unpleasant and *very* painful experience, but not a truly bad experience which should have been avoided or removed from my whole life experience.

I am not trying to trivialize my experiences or invalidate myself by saying that what I suffered wasn't bad and was only just unpleasant and painful. Likewise, I do not mean to trivialize what anyone reading this has suffered, because I know that in the big picture of human suffering, what I have experienced is tame; many people have suffered much worse than I have. I have never experienced, for example, rape, torture, or murder, which many people on the planet have suffered, some of whom I have known personally. I have never been diagnosed with a terminal illness or lost a child, which many people on the planet have suffered, some of whom I have known personally.

That said, I remain firm in my conclusion that in this life, in this time and space, there are actually no bad experiences, in the sense that they should be removed from the human experience. There are profoundly painful and unpleasant experiences, and profoundly pleasurable and pleasant experiences, but they are not bad or good. The world and everything in it, including me and every single one of my experiences, is actually exactly as it should be and is truly perfect.

CHAPTER FOUR

Oh Yeah? Watch Me!

We had made plans to go to the movies together, which was weird because, at that point in our nearly twenty-year marriage, we almost never did anything together just the two of us. It wasn't because we had little children who overran our lives; it wasn't because we were gunning in our careers and had no time for each other; it wasn't because our budget was tight; it was because I had finally gotten the hint that my husband wanted nothing to do with me, and I had given up trying to suggest things that he might want to do with me (like share a life, make love, or even have a conversation). The making of these plans had not ignited in me any hope for change in the permanent status quo of loneliness and isolation in my marriage; I had only agreed to go because it was a movie that I wanted to see.

Having slept in until late morning, as I was in the habit of doing on the weekends during the years that I was clinically depressed, we had settled on going to a mid-afternoon matinee showing. As I moved around the kitchen getting my breakfast, I noticed that my husband was much more cold and irritable than normal. When I say noticed, I mean that I sensed it; as you will well know by the end of this book, I was born an empath and, as such, I experience intangible things, like hostility, just as tangibly as someone else would experience a slap across their face. My husband had a PhD in being stealthily passive aggressive; most of his loathing for me was expressed non-verbally, through impatient sighs, cold looks of disgust, pursed lips, and a constantly clenched jaw, which afforded him the convenient luxury of plausibly denying anything he was ever confronted with—slippery motherfucker! I didn't address his mood or even react—I had long ago learned that I would only be accused of being crazy or overreacting—I just kept my distance and kept my silence.

After eating my breakfast, I escaped outside to apply my choice of salve— coffee and cigarettes—to my fresh emotional blisters from yet another brush with the fire of his loathing and the ice of his barren heart. When my coffee cup was empty and my last cigarette was stubbed out, I returned to our bedroom, flopped down on the unmade bed with a sigh, and lay there just staring up at the ceiling, feeling defeated and two-dimensional.

After about twenty minutes, my husband happened to pass through our bedroom on his way to our bathroom. When he noticed me laying on the bed, he snapped, "Aren't you going to get in the shower? We have to leave soon, y'know!" I sighed and said, "I'm not going." He demanded, "Why?" and I dispassionately replied, "Because you're crabby and I don't want to be with you." He quickly shifted his tone and attitude and said, "I'm sorry I've been crabby. I'll make an effort to enjoy your company, I promise!" With a flash of inner fire that was just beginning to surface in those days, I replied, "As tempting as that offer is, I'll have to pass! I will go to the movies on another day with one of my friends, none of whom have to make an effort to enjoy my company!"

<hr />

Somewhere around my eighteenth wedding anniversary, a random, unrelated conversation with my husband wound its way around to him confessing to me that he thought he was gay (". . . *and that, Your Honor, is what we call an 'irreconcilable difference'!*"). I had begun to suspect this quite a few years prior, but hadn't investigated my suspicions because I just didn't care anymore. I had long since given up trying to have any kind of relationship with him—romantic or physical—I was only staying with him because I thought it was best for my two daughters (boy, was I wrong on that one!). I was not surprised by *what* my husband confessed, but I was very surprised *that* he confessed it; he was, as they say, "so far in the closet, he was in Narnia."

Over the next few months, we had an ongoing dialogue about his sexual orientation. Over the course of those conversations, it became clear to me that he had known that he was not straight since before we met; it also became clear to me that he had deliberately married me in order to use me as his "beard" to pass himself off as a straight man. It was at this time that he bluntly told me, "I only married you because I had to get married and you were willing." The more I learned, the angrier I got!

One night, I was hanging out with Felipe, a friend from design school who was one of my smoking buddies, and I launched into a tirade about my situation. I said, "When a gay person 'comes out,' they get a whole rainbow parade of support and congratulations; no one recognizes or acknowledges the destroyed lives that some of them leave in their wake! Where's my parade? Where's my support group? What about me?" Felipe replied, "Aidy, this is America, where there is a support group for anything and everything. There's gotta be a support group for you; you just haven't found it yet!" When I got home, I Googled, "I'm married to a gay man," and sure enough, I eventually found my way to a support group called the Straight Spouse Network. Thank God for Google!

Over the next two years, through my eventual divorce, I attended the group's monthly meetings, and they were water in the desert! It was *so* helpful to meet other people who were going through the same thing, to know I was not alone, and to be with people who understood in a way that no one else could. During my divorce, one of my girlfriends lost patience with my endless bitching and said, "Aidy, people get divorced! You are not special; get over it!" I responded with, "No, my situation *is* different! Anyone else getting divorced in a same-orientation marriage had, at least, the statistical fifty percent chance of having a successful marriage. I had a *zero* percent chance of a having a successful marriage! *At no time, under no circumstances, and with no amount of effort was my marriage ever going to work*, but I wasn't let in on that handy little detail; he knew it, but I didn't!"

It was at a Straight Spouse meeting that I learned that *mixed orientation marriage* is the official term for a marriage between a straight person and a gay person, but I started calling my marriage a "just kidding" marriage. As in, "I promise to be true to you in good times and in bad, in sickness and in health. I will love, honor, and cherish you all the days of my life . . . *just kidding!*" The men and women I met at the Straight Spouse meetings understood this implicitly, because they had all been victims of "just kidding" marriages, too.

Finding out that you have unsuspectingly married a gay person is a uniquely difficult experience because it wipes out your past, your present, and your future with that person. Having your divorce caused by learning that your spouse is gay wipes out your present and your future the same way that divorce in a same-orientation marriage does, but it also wipes out your past with that person reaching all the way back to the day you first met, because in learning that your spouse is gay, you learn that nothing between the two of you was ever true; everything reaching as far back as, "Hi, nice to meet you!" was a deception.

In a marriage between two people of the same sexual orientation, there is always a time that the two people can look back to when "it was good," before it fell apart. There may have only been five minutes when it was good, and "good" may be subject to interpretation, but nonetheless, that experience exists. For a straight spouse, no such time exists because the lie began at the first encounter; we can look back to a time when we *thought* it was good, but in the end, we realize that this good time was also a lie. This is why the experience is so unique and devastating; it is a rip off of cataclysmic proportions. The only experience that comes close is when a husband or wife discovers that their spouse has a whole other life and family in another town that they didn't know about.

Right after my divorce was finalized, I took a break from attending Straight Spouse meetings for about a year and a half. I was at a place in my life where I was trying to move forward and heal; every time I went to a meeting and heard a fresh story from a new member, I would revert back into the anger stage. Hearing about yet another closeted gay man or lesbian woman using and abusing an unsuspecting, trusting, straight person would rip open my own barely-healing wounds, and I would become enraged all over again!

Even though I wasn't attending meetings, I remained on the email list and kept in touch with several of my Straight Spouse friends, including Gloria, who had become the new facilitator for our local group. About a year after my divorce was finalized, I touched base with Gloria about how things were going in the group. She brought me up to speed with members I knew and filled me in about new members. She ended by telling me about a new member, Patricia, who was so devastated by her gay husband's recent revelation that she had tried to commit suicide twice already, and felt she was still in danger of going through with it. I was so filled with empathy for this new straight spouse because I had struggled with suicide myself.

I asked Gloria to give Patricia my phone number and tell her to reach out to me. I just did not want her to be alone!

It turned out that Patricia lived only a few miles from me. The first time we met, I went to her house because she wasn't up for meeting in public. She greeted me at the door sobbing. From our first hug, I could feel her pain; it was palpable! We sat at her kitchen table and she poured out her heart to me. She told me that both times she had attempted suicide, she had intended to be successful, but had been rescued both times—once by her sons (she had two teenage sons with her gay husband), who found her with her wrists slashed in the tub, and once by the police, who found her on a deserted roadside with alcohol and pills. Only a month after coming out to her, her husband of twenty-two years had left and moved in with his lover, a much younger male coworker who he proclaimed to be "the love of his life." She told me that she and her husband had been high school sweethearts and that she was still very much in love with him. She was finding it impossible to imagine a life without him, and was stunned by how fast he had moved on without her. To add insult to injury, her gay husband repeatedly told her that she needed to "get over it and accept that he was gay" (which is pretty common, and is code for, "Your services are no longer required; you're dismissed!").

After I shared the story of my marriage with her, including my bouts with feeling suicidal, I said something a bit provocative to Patricia. I told her,

> I'm not going to tell you to think of your sons and how many other people would miss you and be hurt by your suicide, because none of that has any meaning for you right now. But I am going to say something to you that is going to make you want to slap me; I know because I would have slapped someone for saying this to me when I was where you are . . . the thing is, you don't actually want to die . . . I know, I know! You are thinking, "Listen lady, I don't think you understand me at all! I'm not messing around here; I really want to die!" I know because I really wanted to die too, but now I realize that what I wanted more than I wanted to die was *not to feel like I wanted to*

die! I know that, more than wanting to die, you want to stop feeling like you want to die!

I went on to tell her that I was living proof that it does get better, because I was doing better than I ever thought possible. Patricia looked at me the same way that I had looked at the first straight spouse I met right after I discovered that my husband was gay, who had also told me that "it gets better"; which is to say, she looked at me in total disbelief. I said,

> What you want is to stop feeling like you want to die, and there are two ways to make that happen. The first is to commit suicide, because then you will most definitely no longer feel like you want to die, because you will be dead. The second way is to, minute-by-minute, hour-by-hour, day-by-day, travel through the time and space between where you are now to the place where you no longer feel like you want to die, and eventually, to where you feel like you want to live. I know that it is possible, and I would even argue that it is worth it, because I did it and I'm so grateful that I did.

I told her that there is no shame in feeling suicidal. To add insult to injury, society shames people who feel suicidal. When you are suicidal, you already feel more miserable than you ever have before in your life, and then on top of that, you feel like a failure, and despicably weak and pathetic for considering suicide. I have heard it said so many times that suicide is the ultimate selfish act. Although I would agree with this statement about the act of suicide, I do not agree that a person who commits suicide is selfish. A truly selfish person would never commit suicide, because they are selfish, and killing themselves would not fit their self-serving life agenda and *modus operandi*. In my experience, it is the person who has given and given and given, in an attempt to improve their life (usually through trying to please others), and has hit a dead end, feeling that their actions are useless and they themselves do not even matter, who contemplates or commits suicide—*this is not selfish; this is heartbreaking!*

I remember once discussing a friend's suicide with a mutual friend; this mutual friend angrily exploded, "I don't understand how anyone could commit suicide! It is the stupidest and most selfish thing, and I think that anyone who even thinks about it is horrible!" I said, "If you cannot understand how anyone could commit suicide, you should do two things. First, fall on your knees and thank Everything Above that you cannot understand it, because it means that you have never been so unfortunate as to feel that low. Second, keep your mouth shut and your judgements to yourself, because if you cannot understand it, then, by definition, you cannot understand it and are not qualified to pass judgement!"

As I continued to talk to Patricia, I told her what I had learned to tell myself, which is that it is okay to feel like committing suicide, but it is not okay to do it. I told her that I had laid down rules for myself to keep myself safe while I was still feeling suicidal. I told her that first, I identified my "danger zones," which were times of the day and situations in which I was most vulnerable to acting on my suicidal thoughts. For me, the worst time of day was between seven in the evening and bedtime, because seven in the evening was when my husband came home from work and walked through the door with an onslaught of criticism, loathing, and disdain for me—by bedtime each night, this put me in a very low place. Every night after my daughters went to bed, I would sit outside and smoke and drink, and these chemical influences also made me vulnerable. More than once, I sat in my car in the garage late at night with a handful of sleeping pills and the keys in the ignition, ready to go to sleep and never wake up.

The rule I made for myself was that I was not allowed to commit suicide at night. I told myself that if I still felt sure that I wanted to die when I woke up, then I would let myself go through with it. I just didn't want to die for a stupid reason, like my perspective being skewed because I was tipsy or tired! If I was going to kill myself, I wanted to make sure that it was because I truly wanted to die, and not because I made a mistake. I know that sounds crazy, but it worked for me. There never came a morning after where I felt as miserable as I had the night before; I always woke with a fresh and less fatalistic perspective, and was very relieved that I had not killed myself!! Needless to say, I now have no regrets about not going through with my suicidal plans. Not only am I grateful that I did not commit suicide, I am also extremely grateful that I went through the experience of feeling suicidal (and every other difficult experience I've ever had, for that matter), because it enabled me to help someone else through it.

As we continued to talk, I began to share with Patricia some of my life philosophy about how we choose our life experiences for the adventure they can provide us with. I could tell she wasn't any more impressed with the idea than I was when I first learned about it. I said to her,

> Let me tell you a story. I think we all know each other before we decide to come into time and space. I imagine that we all sit around with a giant menu of possible life experiences that we can pick from. You turn to me and say, "Hey, Aidy, what are you picking this time around?" I respond, with a gleam in my eye, "Oh, you won't believe the exciting adventure I am crafting for myself! Look at the parents I have picked; they're sure going to take me on a wild ride! Look at the man I have chosen to spend two decades married to; that should be interesting, right? Isn't this cool? What do you think?"

> Overwhelmed with love and concern for me (because we're best friends on the other side), you say, "Oh, Aidy, don't pick those parents! They are going to abuse and neglect you! What if you don't survive it? Oh, Aidy, don't pick that man to marry! He is going to lie to you, abuse you and disregard you! What if you become so depressed that you try to commit suicide? What if you don't make it? Aidy, you've picked too much; surely, you can't do it!"

> Upon hearing your words, fire flashes in my eyes, I set my jaw, I cock my head, and emphatically respond, "*Oh, yeah? Watch me!*"

> Then, I ask you what experiences you are going to pick this time around, and you tell me. Overwhelmed with love and concern, I respond to you with the same doubt,

"Oh, Patricia, don't choose that man to marry! He is going to deceive you, break your heart, and dismiss your pain! You are going to want to kill yourself! What if you do kill yourself? What if you don't make it? Oh, please don't pick this; surely, you can't do it!"

Upon hearing me say this, fire flashes in your eyes, you set your jaw, you cock your head, and emphatically respond, *"Oh, yeah? Watch me!"*

I am convicted by your determination, and I say to you, "I'm sorry for doubting you; I see now that you can do this, and I believe in you! I am behind you all the way, so much so that I make you this vow: in your darkest hour when you need it most, I will show up in your life and remind you that you selected these experiences from the place of your flawless non-local self, which is incapable of making a mistake. I will remind you that you knew you could and would make it through. I will remind you that, when I was foolish enough to doubt you, you said, *"Oh, yeah? Watch me!"*

She was really skeptical, but she also appreciated being able to talk to someone who understood where she was at and how she was feeling, not just about finding out that her husband was gay, but also about wanting to kill herself.

The interesting thing is that we never became friends, and had very few interactions after that first meeting at her house. She came to Straight Spouse meetings, but only sporadically. One other time she called me to come over, because she was feeling really down again and was worried that she was going to do something to harm herself (the rule that she had made to keep herself safe was that she had to call someone). After that, we kept in touch loosely through text, but after about a year, she stopped coming to meetings and I lost touch with her. About three years later, I saw her again at a meeting and learned that she had not attempted suicide again, and that once her divorce was finalized, she was able to move on and begin a new life for herself without her gay husband. I am firmly convinced that my only purpose in her life was to show up, as I had promised, and remind her that she had said, *"Oh, yeah? Watch me!"*

It makes sense to me that we would make "collaborative selections" when choosing our life experiences, because the human experience in time and space is so very interdependent and interactive. Really, the essence of life is all about relationships—relationships with our families, our friends, our coworkers, our neighbors, and even ourselves. I know that my daughters not only chose me, but for better or worse, they also chose their father. I can imagine that they were milling around at the pre-time and space party calling out,

> We're looking for a father who won't support us or put our needs first. We're looking for a father who will criticize us, be mean to us, and be emotionally unavailable. Anyone? Anyone?

. . . and their father waved them down and said,

> Hey, I'm planning on being a really selfish jerk this time around. I can fail to put you first and choose not to support you! I can criticize you and be emotionally unavailable for you! Look, this is what I'm picking for my life experience; will that work for you? Yes? Okay, cool, I'll be your father!

Since before my older daughter was born, she and I have had a very synergetic relationship; our thoughts and feelings have always been very transparent to each other. She was nearly seventeen when I filed for divorce from her father. She knew the reason why I was divorcing her father; in fact, she had come to the realization that her father was gay on her own more than a year prior to me disclosing it to her. She also knew the story of my unplanned pregnancy with her. I had told her this story from when she was little because I felt it was such a beautiful story; I always emphasized how lucky I felt that she had chosen me to be her mother, and downplayed the fact that she wasn't a planned pregnancy.

One afternoon, in the middle of a particularly difficult part of the divorce, she and I were talking on our drive home from school when I sensed her mood change. We sat in silence for a while and I began to sense what she was thinking and feeling. At a red light, I turned to her and said, "Are you thinking that if you hadn't come to me, I would have been able to leave your father years ago and I would have been spared all this pain and sadness?" She didn't say anything, but tears began to silently stream down her face. Through my own tears, I said,

> Don't you think that for a second! I am responsible for my own choices, and I would make each and every single one of them a thousand times over again just to have you and your sister! Sweetie, before the beginning of time, you and your sister said to me, "If you want us, you're going to have to be with the guy we have picked to be our father," and I didn't even give it a split second of thought. I immediately responded, "Give me the papers! Where do I sign?"

I continued by saying that I was firmly convinced that their selection of a father must have flawlessly fit in with the experiences I wanted to have in this lifetime, otherwise I wouldn't have agreed to it.

When my younger daughter was in high school, one of her teachers gave her class a "parent appreciation" assignment. The students had to write a letter to their parent(s) expressing their gratitude for everything their parent(s) had done for them. The letters were then mailed to the parent(s)' homes. My daughter's letter expressed many beautiful sentiments of gratitude, which, of course, brought me to tears. The sentence which most struck me was, "Thank you for learning the big lessons first so that you could teach them to me." Not only was I touched by her gratitude, I was also struck by her insight. She was aware of the fact that I had had no one to teach me the big lessons; I had to learn them on my own. She was also appreciative of the fact that she did not have to learn many of the big lessons on her own. I'm guessing this played into her selection of me as her mother. Unlike me, she wanted to choose a mother who could provide her with wisdom and guidance (even if I only I figured it out a few minutes before she needed it). Apparently, I must have wanted a bit more of an adventure in that department! I have reminded both of my daughters of this, as they have wrestled with the challenge their father has provided them with (to put it politely). I have said to them, "I have made it just fine with two extremely challenging and almost entirely useless parents! At least you have one reasonably useful parent. Not only will you be just fine, you will go further, much further, than I have gone!"

I think that we not only make promises to help each other make it through the challenges we have selected, we also make promises not to interfere and not to help each other too much, so that we don't inadvertently thwart the experiences we have chosen. I think we do this for two reasons; one is for the desire to do it by ourselves, like the two-year-old who shouts, "Me do!" and the other is because we actually want to have the experience of colossal failure, excruciating misery, or spectacular underachievement. This is because outside of time and space, these things are only experiences, and do not have the "good" or "bad" labels that we give them in time and space.

When my husband first disclosed that he was gay, I made him an offer that was much more than he deserved. Not only did I want to keep my family intact, my heart also went out to him. I knew how cold and rejecting his parents, and the religion they raised him in, had been to him; although I had never been rejected and vilified for my sexual orientation, I could imagine how incredibly confusing and painful it must have been for him. I told him that if he would be honest with himself, with me, and with our daughters about his sexual orientation, then I would support him in continuing to hide it from anyone and everyone else, including his family. I promised to stay and give him the best straight cover any closeted gay man could ever wish for.

At this point in our marriage, I had completely detached myself from my husband's family (they had never liked or accepted me, anyway). I told my husband that I would resume going to any and all of his family functions with a big smile on my face, be the most convincing, loving wife imaginable, and present the most convincing, happy, straight marriage. I was offering him the best of both worlds; I was willingly offering him what he had suckered me into without my informed consent when we first got married. It should have been too good of an offer to refuse, and yet he refused it. Within six months of telling me that he was gay, he was again declaring that he was straight. When I told him that I could not cope with his lies any longer, he told me, "If you divorce me, I will just find another woman that I can do this to." Clearly, he was bound and determined to have this experience, and it seems that my offer would have inadvertently thwarted the experience he wanted to have.

After the divorce, when I thought back on the offer I had made him, I was embarrassed that I had been willing to continue to make such a sacrifice, and relieved that he did not take me up on my offer! It was completely inappropriate for me to offer to accommodate him any further, and at such a personal cost to myself. I am not the only straight spouse to offer to make such accommodations for a gay or transgendered spouse; I have heard many, many similar stories from other straight spouses. I have heard even more tempting offers made by straight spouses that have been turned down by their gay or transgendered spouses. I have puzzled and puzzled over this, and I can't help but wonder if the offers of help are refused because they would inadvertently thwart the experience that the gay or transgendered spouse came here to have, even though, to an outside observer, the choice of that experience seems so bad and/or wrong.

I have learned to walk away, not only from my gay husband, but from anyone else I meet who seems to be deliberately making a bad choice, even in the face of help and advice that would guide them in a better direction. At the very least, I have learned that my continued efforts to help or advise would be a waste! I respectfully consider that they may have deliberately chosen these experiences, and they don't appreciate, nor will they accept, my interference, which only threatens to inadvertently thwart the experience they came here to have in this lifetime.

I think that people come in and out of our lives, for better or for worse, and for reasons based on pre-time and space agreements, to collaborate on and help facilitate the experiences we have selected. Sometimes we pick our parents and siblings to have a profound and lasting relationship with; sometimes the families we pick serve nothing more than to be the portal through which we get here. I came to realize that my parents were strictly portal parents; they created my physical body, kept me alive (barely), and gave me a place to stay until adulthood, but the rest I had to figure out on my own (which was according to my plan and theirs all along).

All family members, friends, coworkers, and even strangers or enemies serve a purpose in our lives, as we do in theirs. Some people come into our lives only for a moment, to perform a single, specific service and then leave. Once they have fulfilled their promise to us and it is in their plan to move on, it does not serve us or them to try and extend their time or maintain their involvement in our lives. Some people come into our lives to walk beside us and share some, most, or all of our lives with us; we do well to treasure these people and to hold them loosely.

You may remember from the story in chapter two that when my first daughter visited me in my meditations before I got pregnant with her, she had a little brother with her. You may also have noticed that my second child is a girl, and that I never had that little boy. When I was pregnant with my first daughter, I knew beyond a shadow of a doubt that she was a girl; in fact, I knew who she was in every detail. At that time, pregnant women only got one ultrasound, because it was before most doctors had ultrasound machines in their offices. I was so excited to get my ultrasound because I just knew it would confirm that I was having a girl. Well, my modest little baby girl tucked the umbilical cord between her legs and, no matter how much the ultrasound technician mashed on my belly, we could not see whether she was a girl or a boy! I was crushed and very frustrated, especially since I knew I would not get another ultrasound.

A few weeks later, a friend invited me to go see a psychic with her. I was skeptical about consulting with a psychic, but I thought that maybe I could get more information about my baby. Sure enough, the second I walked in the door, the psychic said that a little girl arrived with me and asked me if I was pregnant (this was the early '90s and I was wearing the same oversized sweater and leggings that everyone wore, pregnant or not, so my little bump was concealed). During the actual reading, the psychic brought up my daughter's little brother and told me that he did not want to come to me because my husband would be mean to little boys. I left thinking, "Well, I can't expect her to be right about everything, and she sure is way off on that one!"

Sure enough, that little boy did not come to me when I got pregnant the second time. I do not know if he decided to come in through someone else, or if my second daughter is actually the same soul who chose to come as a girl instead. Either way, I respect the change in plans because, in the end, it became very clear that the psychic was right! As my daughters grew into adolescence, their father became crueler and crueler to them; I can only imagine how much worse he would have been with a son! If our son had been born straight, my husband would have felt like even more of a failure for not being straight himself; if our son had been born gay, my husband would have been highly conflicted about whether or not to accept and support our son when his own family and religion had rejected him for being gay.

Over the years, I have thought wistfully about the son I never had, but now, with the way things have turned out, I am very grateful that he did not come to me. It was hard enough to help my daughters navigate the tricky waters of their father's deception and our divorce; I can't imagine singlehandedly trying to help a boy become a man under those circumstances! I am eternally grateful for the two amazing daughters who did pick me! Throughout their childhoods, I have regularly thanked them for picking me to be their mother; I have told them that I know they could have picked anyone, and I am honored and grateful that they picked me. During their teen years, I often teased them about picking me when I embarrassed them, or when we butted heads. I would say to them, "Right about now, I bet you are second-guessing your decision to pick me as your mother! Too late . . . hahahaha!" They would always roll their eyes, and then end up laughing with me.

Once I understood the dynamic of my ability to select and manifest my experiences in time and space, I began to see a flawless organization to my life. I began to see the mind-blowing perfection in every minute detail and in the entirety of my life, even all the parts that I had previously thought were a mistake. My eyes were opened to the omnipresent, omniscient guidance of the divine intelligence of my eternal non-local self. Looking all the way back to the start of my life, I could see countless occurrences, big and small, of guidance and intervention. It was as if chess pieces were being moved on a cosmic game board. I began, also, to see the mutual cooperation between myself and the people in my life adventure—all the people, from the most diabolical to the most divine. I could recall countless times when I crossed paths, for a moment or a lifetime, with the perfect person to provide just what I needed to continue to move forward in my adventure—someone coming into my life, just in the nick of time, with love, support, inspiration, and wisdom, and, in one way or another, reminding me that I had once said *"Oh, yeah? Watch me!"* Although, at times, I felt horrifyingly alone, I was never alone. I have had *so* much prearranged help and support throughout my adventure here in time and space!

CHAPTER FIVE

So What?

These were the darkest days of my life; in the thick of my personal battle, I was fighting desperately and ingloriously just to stay alive. To fight back the pain inside that threatened to take my life, I wielded cigarettes, coffee, alcohol, junk food, and the unconditional love so generously given to me by a few precious friends who somehow saw past my brokenness. Many nights, after seeing my daughters to bed with a kiss and a smile, I would pick up a Venti Caramel Macchiato from the drive-through at Starbucks and drive a half an hour across town to my haven: Felipe's front porch.

Felipe and I had met in design school. He was an outgoing man who had come to the United States as a teenager, when his family fled El Salvador during the political unrest of the late 1960s. He sought me out because I had the best CAD (computer aided drafting) skills of any student in our program, and because I was a redhead. He repeatedly joked with me that he loved redheads because, as he put it, "Redheads are complete pains-in-the-ass, and they're totally worth it!" His attraction to me ended at my red hair, because Felipe was gay and was honest with himself and everyone else about his sexual orientation (it would be quite a few years more before I fully appreciated the great gift a gay person gives to themselves and the world when they are out). Although he didn't know my whole story, Felipe was sensitive enough to intuit that my quick smile and gregarious laughter masked a lot of pain. He never pried; he only held a safe space for me to rest from my battle. He was also a great conversationalist, even if he was an insufferable conspiracy theorist.

This night, like so many nights, I sat in the comfortable, tattered, wicker peacock chair that liked to snag my T-shirt while Felipe's cat walked all over me, offended that I would not pet him (I am allergic to cats). I was alternately sucking down cigarettes and Caramel Macchiato and politely listening to Felipe's latest discovery that "proved" the existence of reptilian shapeshifters. Unable to provoke any response from me about the alarming presence of reptilian shapeshifters among us, Felipe fell silent. I sighed and said, "I've decided to go on an antidepressant. I hate the idea of taking a pharmaceutical medication, but at this point, it seems my only option; the alternative is suicide." I fixed my gaze on the cat in my lap, unable to look Felipe in the eye for fear of seeing shock, or even worse, judgement. When I finally looked up, I saw only compassion. Felipe quietly asked me, "Aidy, how is it okay for the wife of a psychiatrist to need antidepressants?" In a hollow, defeated voice, I replied, "I don't know."

In my late thirties, I was doing my interior design internship at a custom furniture manufacturer when I met Roxanne, the principal designer. She was a most interesting woman who made multiple valuable and curious contributions to my life education and personal growth. I will forever be grateful to her for making good on her promise to cross paths with mine in time and space, and for contributing to my journey in the way that she did! Roxanne was a smoker, and at that time, so was I; we would take our smoke breaks together several times a day. She was a fascinating person, insofar as she was a most interesting mix of base qualities (smoking, swearing, and a never-ending parade of men through her bedroom) and lofty spirituality (preaching and aspiring to the ideas of Eckert Tolle, Deepak Chopra, Marianne Williamson and the like). Over the six months that we worked together, we had some of the most interesting, provocative, and impactful conversations of my whole life, and we remained close friends for several years after my internship was over.

Like me, Roxanne was a survivor of a lot of childhood pain and abuse. She had made great strides in her personal growth, and was in the process of creating the life she wanted. By her early twenties, she was already a recovering alcoholic and drug addict; when I met her, she had been sober for nineteen years. Shortly after my internship ended, she began to date a guy who was a heavy drinker and a daily pot smoker. For some reason, she completely took leave of her senses, randomly decided that she could handle alcohol and substances again, and began drinking and smoking pot with her new boyfriend. Needless to say, she could not actually handle these substances, and began to drink to excess, at first just on the weekends, and then almost daily (she gave up the pot smoking pretty quickly after a nasty run-in with marijuana-induced paranoia). A year and a half after resuming drinking, her life took a nasty turn. In one month, she lost her job as principal designer as a result of vicious interoffice politics, she lost her uterus because of a cancer scare, and her twin teenage sons decided that they wanted move in with their father, who lived in another state. Predictably, her drinking spun completely out of control. She spent most of her waking moments in various stages of drunkenness.

It became increasingly difficult to sustain a friendship with Roxanne; it just doesn't really work to have a relationship with a person who is drunk most of the time, because, well, they're drunk. By this time, I only hung out with her once every couple of months, and always at her house so she could drink without having to drive (for which I commend her). One night, as we sat outside smoking and talking while she slowly got drunk, she broke down crying and confessed to me that her boyfriend and several other friends had recently confronted her about her drinking. She went into a tirade of self-loathing, self-condemnation, and shame for falling off the wagon after nearly two decades of sobriety. She railed at herself, saying how stupid she was for thinking that she could handle alcohol again. I politely pretended to be ignorant of how bad it had gotten, and asked her how bad it was. I was all ready to concur with her friends and boyfriend and add my own two cents, when instead, the most curious statement came out of my mouth.

When I said, "Well, Rox, how bad is it actually? How much are you drinking these days?" she said, "Aidy, it's bad! I spend most of the morning sleeping off my hangover from the night before. I start drinking in the early afternoon and I am half lit by the time my boyfriend comes home from work!" What I said in reply surprised both of us; I shrugged my shoulders and said, "So? So what?" She stared at me incredulously and weakly responded, "Whaaaat?" I repeated, "So what?" She recovered from her shock and fired back,

What do you mean "so what?" Aidy, I am a mess! I can't even get out of bed in the morning because I'm so hung over from the night before! How am I ever going to find another job? How am I ever going to rebuild my relationship with my sons? Aidy, I'm a wreck. I'm pathetic; I'm a loser!

I said, "True. All of those things are true, except for the pathetic loser part, and yet, what good is it doing you to focus on how you have failed? How does it serve you to terrorize and bludgeon yourself? Is it helping?" I paused to let that sink in and then said, "Rox, let me ask you this: does your vicious self-criticism bolster your resolve to change your life? Does your self-loathing give you the strength you need to climb out of the black hole you have gotten yourself into?" She stared at me, mouth gaping open, and slowly, meekly, said, "Nooooo, it doesn't." I said, "Let me guess . . . all your self-loathing just makes you want to drink even more, doesn't it?" She said, "Well . . . yes, it does." I said, "Well, okay then. You need to turn this ship around. You need to start building yourself up; you need to start praising yourself!" She nearly shrieked at me, "What the hell do I have to praise myself for?" I said,

You are going to have to start with the most simple and basic of things. If tomorrow you get out of bed, you praise yourself. If you build yourself up, you watch, the next day you will get out of bed *and* get a shower. You praise yourself for that, and you watch, the next day you will get out of bed, get a shower, *and* put makeup on. You praise yourself for that, and on it goes until, one day, you will find the strength to quit drinking and get your whole life back on track.

It didn't happen overnight, but by using self-praise and refraining from self-criticism, Roxanne did eventually quit drinking again, and got her whole life back on track.

Make no mistake, when I said, "So what?" in response to Roxanne's unchecked alcoholism, I was not meaning to dismiss the seriousness of the situation. She was in a very bad state! Her whole life and everyone in it was sustaining considerable damage as a result of her drinking. I said, "So what?" in order to shock her into understanding my advice about using self-praise even when it seemed ludicrous, so she could pull herself out of the black hole she was in. I had stumbled across this tool in my efforts to get myself out of my own black hole.

In my darkest days, I was the modern day equivalent of a Viking shield maiden in the throes of battle—bloodied, horribly wounded, and fighting to stay alive. I had all the signs and symptoms of someone in the middle of a battle, only my wounds did not run with blood, but rather with dysfunctional, self-sabotaging, self-destructive behaviors. Many, many times, while in the middle of my personal battlefield, I turned on myself with vicious criticism, which made my pain even more intense and my wounds even deeper. I was already in a weakened state of constant pain, and I was making myself weaker and my pain deeper by tearing myself down.

Although I didn't make the connection at the time, tearing myself down was a learned behavior from my childhood. My parents had always focused on their perception of me as defective, and they were hyper vigilant about trying to correct me. Day in, day out, week in, week out, month in, month out, for all the years I lived in their house and beyond, they nitpicked every minute flaw they found in me, set unbelievably unrealistic and ever-shifting standards for my behavior, and constantly brought to my attention the myriad of ways they felt that I was falling short of their ideal. In addition, there was my ever present sinfulness, which, as I was taught, made me so vile and abhorrent that God could not even look on me. This was my normal, and it continued uncorrected well into my adulthood, because vicious criticism and searing disdain were the trademarks of my relationship with my husband.

Living under constant criticism from my parents and my husband, it was no wonder that I held the same view of myself—fatally flawed and repugnant. What is a wonder is that there was any part of me left to voice a different opinion. Amazingly, there was; there was a small, very small, part of me, buried under a mountain of self-loathing, which balked at the negative self-perception I had accepted. There was a tiny flicker of my authentic self left which knew that I was perfect, fabulous, and mighty.

Slowly, very slowly, it dawned on me that tearing myself down wasn't helping, and I began to contemplate the idea of trying to build myself up.

Oddly enough, when I look back over my life to figure out how this small flicker of self-love was able to survive the swirling shitstorm of abuse and criticism that I grew up in, I have to give credit to my father. Even though he was a steady source of harsh judgement and physical abuse and turned a blind eye to the passive, but no less damaging, neglectfulness of my mother, he did adore me, and verbally expressed his adoration in several poignant ways, which made *all* the difference for me.

He and my mother had received their Montessori teacher training in Italy, and fluency in the Italian language had been a requirement for the year that they studied in Perugia. I grew up hearing my father regularly use basic Italian phrases with my mother, my sister, and me—like shouting, "Andiamo, andiamo subito!" when we were late for the cult prayer meetings. This loosely translates to "Hurry up!" Throughout my childhood, he consistently greeted me with, "Ciao Bella!" which means "Hello Beautiful!" The other thing that he regularly said to me (in English) was, "Aidy, you're the greatest!" My father imposed insanely unrealistic standards on my behavior and moral character, but he was always complimentary about my physical appearance. He was my port in the raging storm of my mother's relentless negative commentary about my body. I have plenty of memories from my teen years of going to him after my mother had, yet again, done or said something to make me feel fat, and asking him, "Dad, am I fat?" He always responded with, "No, of course not; you're beautiful!"

When I first considered it, the idea of building myself up was so very foreign. Not only had it not been modeled for me—just the opposite—it also seemed illogical. Just like my girlfriend, Roxanne, I thought, "what do I have to build myself up for?" I had accepted the critical statements from my parents and husband as truth about myself, and had become a walking self-fulfilling prophecy. I had been told that I was weak, lacking in self-discipline, and sinful (naturally inclined to do bad and make bad choices; unable to do or create anything good on my own) therefore I had failed in a most predictable fashion in most areas of my life. Was there anything that I could praise myself for to counteract the incessant internal litany of my faults? Slowly, very, very slowly, I began to find things to praise myself for.

I began with the simple and obvious. Sure, I was addicted to cigarettes, but I wasn't addicted to anything more serious. Sure, I was overweight, but I wasn't morbidly obese. Sure, I had a drink or two at the end of every day, but I didn't get drunk every night. Sure, I had contemplated suicide, but I had not gone through with it. Sure, I had been unfaithful in my marriage, but I had not run off with another man and abandoned my daughters. I began this practice without much enthusiasm or optimism; I just went through the motions, trying it because I had tried everything else and I had nothing to lose. It took a monumental amount of effort to speak even the tiniest positive messages timidly to myself against the deafening broadcast of negative propaganda from the critical voices in my head. Miraculously, it began to work! Slowly, very slowly, the tiny flame of my inner strength began to grow. My reserves began to increase, and as they did, I was able to double my efforts and build myself up even more. This continued to increase my reserves and gave me, in turn, the strength to praise myself even more. On it went, until the day came when I found it within myself, not only to praise myself in my strength, but to bless myself in my weakness. This was the war horse that ended up carrying me all the way through my battlefield and into my green valley.

Somewhere along the way, through my years of struggle, I came across a plaque with a quote by Mary Anne Radmacher. This quote inspired me, and at times was my only comfort: "Courage doesn't always roar. Sometimes courage is the quiet voice at the end of the day saying, 'I will try again tomorrow.'" There were many painful days when all I could manage was to say that I would try again tomorrow, but in the end, that was enough. As a complement to this quote, I created one of my own, to encourage myself: "Failure today does not preclude success tomorrow." Believing that, no matter how many times or how greatly I had failed, I could try again, inspired me and gave me the strength not to give up on myself. I came to realize that to succeed in my life, I only had to get back up one time more than I fell down; when I looked at my life this way, it felt so much more doable!

I have gotten to where I am by praising myself in my strength, no matter how little, and by blessing myself in my weakness, no matter how great, and not by forcing, criticizing, berating, or shaming myself. This is very contrary to what I was taught and how I was treated by the cult leaders, my parents, and my husband. It is also very contrary to the all-pervasive message of striving, self-denial, and self-flagellation that is found in Western religions and cultures. Nonetheless, it is the only thing that has worked for me and continues to work to this day, all day, every day.

Clinical depression is very debilitating and immobilizing. I remember comparing it to trying to run a marathon with a one hundred-pound weight tied to each wrist and each ankle; it took a heroic effort just to accomplish the simplest tasks, and oftentimes I fell short or failed completely. At this time in my life, even getting my teeth brushed every night was overwhelming. As strange as it sounds, at the end of the day, the thought of brushing my teeth was just too much. Forget anything more sophisticated like flossing or washing my face! Many nights, for years, I skipped brushing my teeth because I was just too tired, physically, mentally, and emotionally. All my energy had been used up just trying to get myself through the day, give my daughters what they needed, and keep myself alive through the evening. I can remember walking past the bathroom sink most nights on my way to bed and thinking, "I really should brush my teeth . . . ugh, I just can't . . . I'll brush them tomorrow night, I swear!"

Besides the sins of commission which I committed against myself daily, like smoking, drinking, unhealthy eating, overeating, and excessive coffee consumption, I also committed many sins of omission, like almost never exercising, rarely brushing my teeth, showering only when I had to, completely neglecting my skincare, and ignoring my toenails and foot callouses to the point of my feet looking like those of a homeless man. I would say I was a hot mess, but in reality, I was just a plain mess. Even today, to be brutally honest about how I lived my life for so many years still stings with embarrassment; I just can't believe it was that bad, and yet, it was. At the time, I didn't have the strength to look at my life honestly with eyes wide open. There were rare times when, like Roxanne, I would break down to a trusted friend and confess how much I was struggling, but most of the time, I worked hard to cover up and keep myself oblivious to what a dreadful state I was in. Looking back, I understand the wisdom of this, or at least, the necessity of it. I barely had enough strength to keep scooping water out of my sinking boat; if I had taken an honest inventory of all the leaks in it, I would surely have abandoned ship!

Needless to say, all of my struggles were lush fodder for my family and my husband in their never-ending campaign to reinforce their opinion of me as fatally flawed, repugnant, and constantly failing. They capitalized on and consistently highlighted every one of my millions of failures—perceived or actual. Their focus on how I fell short was relentless. No matter how impressive my accomplishments were, and I certainly had accomplishments, they always turned their focus to any shortcomings they could find.

As an example, one Christmas, my parents came to stay for two weeks, and my sister and her husband came for five days in the middle of those two weeks. My otherwise manageable household of four doubled in size for nearly a week during the holidays. I was singlehandedly orchestrating Christmas for everyone, including two young children aged four and eight. My standards for hosting were high, so most meals for the two weeks were homecooked (some of them very extravagant, i.e. pork tenderloin, roast turkey, lamb chops, etc.), everyone had fresh sheets and towels regularly, I ran and emptied the dishwasher several times a day to stay on top of all the dishes from cooking and serving, and I organized activities and sightseeing trips to keep everyone entertained. At the end of the visit, my mother cornered me and voiced her concern because I seemed so frenetic, criticized me for not being able to slow down and relax, and expressed her worry that I was a workaholic.

Even though I was in such a sad state for most of my thirties, I still accomplished a lot! I went back to school and got a second degree in interior design, worked for one of the most prestigious architectural firms in the world, started my own business, won four state level ASID (American Society of Interior Design) Design Excellence Awards for my work, had one of my projects selected for the feature article and front cover of my state's ASID quarterly magazine, was hired as an adjunct faculty member in the interior design department of the college I had gotten my design degree from, and had my home included in my city's ASID Tour of Designer's Own Homes. I did all of this starting from the time that my youngest daughter was only four years old, and all the while, I was still the primary caretaker for our daughters. Only rarely did I put them in after school care; only rarely did I send them to school with Lunchables or get take-out for dinner. Predictably, none of this ever impressed my husband, who incessantly criticized me for anything and everything he could find, and repeatedly told me that he didn't think I was working up to my full potential.

My full recovery from depression was very long and very slow, and then very short and very fast. As I said, I felt as if I were trying to run a marathon with a one hundred-pound weight tied to each of my four limbs; I was exerting a massive effort but not getting very far down the road. When I made the decision to divorce my husband, it was as if the weights were clipped; I was still exerting the same amount of effort, but without the weight dragging me down, I went *flying* down the road! I will never forget the day he moved out! I wasn't the only one who felt the black cloud lift! My two daughters, by then ages thirteen and seventeen, and our two corgis felt it, too. Our dogs went tearing around the house in mad hysterics—known in the corgi community as frapping—for about a half an hour. My daughters and I were mystified, since we had never seen them frap without stopping for such a long time; we just laughed and laughed and egged them on. After they had carried on for more than ten minutes, I said, "I think they know! I think they can feel the shift in energy!" It was a scene akin to that of the munchkins in *The Wizard of Oz* right after Dorothy's house fell on the witch.

When I first got married, I was not a bed maker; my philosophy was that making a bed in the morning was a waste of time because it was only going to get unmade again in the evening. As a new bride, I wanted to please my husband, and he made it clear that he considered not making the bed to be a character flaw (or perhaps he just wanted to erase the reminder of sharing the bed with me the night before). So, I eagerly adopted a daily bed-making habit. After more than a decade of fervently doing anything and everything that he said would make him happy, and never getting the love, attention, and intimacy I so desperately wanted and needed, I gave up. The things that he had said would make him happy and make him want to be with me became the very things that I refused to do in an attempt to punish him for denying me love, attention, and intimacy. Unfortunately, this only backfired on me, because it added to the already-long list of my failures, of which he kept careful account.

Although I didn't recognize it at first, making my bed again was the first sign that I was on the road to recovery. Several months after my husband moved out, a fellow designer friend, Mia, came over and noticed that my bed was made (I had a show house and the master bedroom had double doors that opened to the foyer, so it was very noticeable whether the bed was made). Mia lamented that she did not get her bed made as often as she would like to, and asked me if I made my bed every day. With a giant grin on my face, I enthusiastically responded, "I do now!"

Within just a few years of my divorce, I went from making my bed again to having every other area of my life back in order, and moving forward at lightning speed with joy and purpose. Within a different context, a few years might sound like a long time, but considering the fact that just about every area of my life had been in a state of complete disrepair for about a decade, for me, it seemed like a very short time. Ironically, making my bed wasn't even on my list of things I wanted to put back in place in my life. I only started making my bed because I began to wake up feeling refreshed and capable of facing the day. For the first time in my life, I found myself waking up thinking, "I feel fabulous! Today is going to be a great day!" Another unanticipated shift was that I, naturally and effortlessly, began to need less sleep. Prior to this time, I had needed minimum of nine to ten hours a night just to function on a very basic level, and on the weekends, I would sleep in and get upwards of twelve hours or more a night. By the time my depression lifted completely, I only needed seven to seven and a half hours of sleep each night; in fact, I had to be careful not to sleep in too much on the weekends, or I would have trouble falling asleep come Sunday night!

The top two most disconcerting and residual effects of my dreadful marriage were my smoking and my depression. As soon as I had enough strength reserves to think about tackling them, I became passionately committed to conquering them; as a matter of pride, I wanted them gone! Within two years, both issues were history! They were the result of being in a chronic state of raw pain; I was self-medicating with cigarettes in addition to the prescribed antidepressant I was taking. I knew it would be no small feat to overcome these things, but I also knew that as my pain decreased and my joy increased, they would release their hold on me.

Right after my divorce was finalized, I told my doctor that I wanted to try getting off the antidepressant that I had been on for seven years. She told me it couldn't be done. She said that the studies had shown that once a person develops a long term need for an antidepressant, they will need it for the rest of their lives. To complicate matters, I have a family history of depression. I told her I wanted to try anyway. I said I wasn't going to be reckless and try to go off the medication all at once; I wanted to decrease my 200-milligram dose by 50 milligrams every six months. I also reassured her that I definitely knew what depression felt like, and that if I had even the slightest bump in the road, I would ask her to adjust my dose back up. I had nearly lost my life to depression; I wasn't going to take any chances with it again!

By this time in my life, I had learned a bit about brain chemistry and how the brain operates; I knew that the sustained depressive thoughts and emotions I had experienced my whole life had carved neural pathways in my brain which reinforced and perpetuated these same depressive thoughts and emotions. I also knew that I could create new neural pathways by going on the offensive with assertive positive thinking and feeling, and that these new neural pathways in my brain would reinforce and perpetuate optimistic thoughts and feelings. I knew that every time I assertively chose a positive thought and/or emotion over a negative one, the old neural pathways which supported my depression would wither.

It was at this time that I read Jill Bolte-Taylor's book, *My Stroke of Insight*. Her book had a most profound impact on my understanding of my own brain, and to this day, ranks high on my list of the top ten most life-changing books I have ever read. I began to put into practice what I had learned from her experience, which was that I am the owner and operator of my own brain, not the other way around. My brain had been raised by people whose life philosophy and world view were negative, depressive, self-loathing, fatalistic, and fearful; as a result, negative, depressive, self-loathing, fatalistic, and fearful patterns of thought and behavior had been trained into my brain. In the retraining of my brain, I used the same propaganda techniques that my parents and the cult had used, but with different inputs to create a different output. I assertively spoke and behaved positively and optimistically about myself and my life (even when I didn't feel like it and even when my reality contradicted it), and I plastered every inch of my house, office, car, computer, phone, etc. with positive propaganda messages so that, everywhere I turned, my brain was being flooded with the life philosophy and world view that I wanted to become my reality.

To add support as I was slowly taking away the antidepressant and trying to retrain my brain and body, I began a yoga and meditation/ visualization practice. I found the philosophy of yoga to be very opposite from the Western philosophy of working out, and I found it to be very healing. To me, the difference between the standard workout experience in a gym and the experience of practicing yoga is that working out encourages the attitude of, "what can I make my body do for me?" (striving in opposition), and practicing yoga encourages the attitude of, "what can I do for my body?" (blessing in harmony). When I practice yoga, I come to my mat to see how I can be of service to my body, not to see how my body can be of service to my ego. Along the way, I have been blessed with many luminous yoga teachers who have emphasized that it is not about the glory of the pose; it is about honoring where my body is in that moment and what my body wants and needs in that moment, and about surrendering to the perfection of the present moment just as it is without judgement. My yoga poses will never impress anyone other than myself, but what I do each day on my mat serves my body, and that's all that matters to me.

Over the years, since the beginning of my recovery, I have practiced a variety of meditation and visualization techniques, all with the aim of replacing the negative, self-destructive images, messages, and stories that have played in my head for most of my life. My goal in meditation has been similar to the goal I learned in yoga; my meditation practice is about what it does for me, and not about pushing myself to strive for an external ideal of achieving enlightenment. I have used various techniques only insofar as, and for as long as, they have served me; at times, I have meditated for as much as an hour twice a day, and at other times, I have visualized for as little as five minutes once a day. Overall, I have found meditation and visualization, even in the smallest amounts and in any form, to be essential to my mental health, because these practices remind me that time, space, and the physical world, with all their perceived worries and pain, are an illusion—this is so key! In eighteen months, with the help of my new practices of positive thinking, meditation, visualization, and yoga, I was completely off the antidepressant and feeling more joyful and optimistic than I had ever felt in my life!

A year after my divorce was finalized and eleven and a half years after I started smoking, I finally kicked cigarettes for good! Like all smokers, I had tried countless times and countless methods to quit; the longest I ever made it was a month. As well-meaning as my intentions to quit always were, all my previous attempts had failed because I was trying to remove something that supported me without adding anything else to support me in its place, and at a time when I was still in the middle of the battlefield.

I met with a smoking cessation counselor to help me quit, and in the initial interview, she asked me why I wanted to quit smoking. She said, "I know your children have begged you and that hasn't made you quit, and I know you know all the health risks and that doesn't stop you, so why do you want to quit now?" I told her,

> If you had asked me five years ago why I smoked, I would have said (I pantomimed dragging and exhaling on a cigarette and mimicked a smoker's growling voice), "Let me tell you why I smoke! I smoke because of my fucking parents, my fucking husband, and my fucking life; that's why I smoke!" and you would have said, "Okay, I get it! Here, let me light you another cigarette!" But, if you ask me today why I smoke, I would be flat-out embarrassed; I have no reason! I am so happy, and my life is better than ever!

She laughed and said, "Okay, let's do this!" Using a combination of guided visualizations over several sessions and basic behavior modification techniques, I was able to quit for good.

Shortly after I quit smoking, when I was in my daily meditation, I just let my mind wander and a visualization began spontaneously. I saw myself five years prior standing in my kitchen. I saw how beaten-down I was—haggard, sad, frightened, and despairing. I cradled the face of my former self, lifted it up to meet my eyes, and said, "Hang on, Sweetie; hang in there, it gets so much better!" My former self, with tears streaming down her face, said weakly, "Really? Are you sure?" I said, "I promise; it will get better!" Then my mind went forward to envision the even more empowered and optimistic woman I still wanted to be. I saw her sitting on the floor in front of me where I was sitting on my meditation mat. She lifted my face and said, "Aidy, keep going; keep flying; you can go so much further! The sky is the limit; you can be every bit of the woman you have always dreamed of being! You can exceed even your own wildest dreams!"

CHAPTER SIX

The After-Market Add-On

At first glance, we may have looked like a typical group of teenagers, but if you stopped to look more closely, you would have noticed subtle differences that would have made you wonder. None of us were dressed in the gaudy clothing of our eighties generation; none of the girls were flirting with any of the boys; none of us were coupled off. It was Monday night and our weekly youth prayer meeting had just ended. To be fair, we were a jovial group, as jovial as teenagers trapped in a religious cult could be; we joked, we laughed, and we staunchly denied to our parents, the cult leaders, and even to ourselves any crushes that we had on each other.

Over the noise of platonic talk and laughter, someone yelled, "Hey, let's all go to Papa's!" Papa's was a little hole-in the-wall pizza joint, with the best pizza in the world, which we often frequented after Monday night youth prayer meetings. My first thought was, "Oh no, pizza has too many calories and I'm fat!" (Still only 118 pounds!) My second thought was, "I'll just have one small piece!" (Oh, joy!) There was only one phone in the church basement where we met for Monday night youth prayer meetings; everyone crowded around it to call their parents and ask for permission to go to Papa's. I thought, "I'll just call home from Papa's and let them know where I'm at; I know my parents trust me." I offered to drive as many kids as could fit in the little Ford Escort that had become my ride now that I was a high school senior.

Our group of nearly twenty was all seated at one long table at Papa's, and we had just placed our pizza order when I remembered . . . oh, crap, I forgot to call home! I jumped up, ran to the pay phone, and dialed home.

"Hi Dad, it's Aidy. I just wanted to let you know that a bunch of us went to Papa's after the prayer meeting."

Like a sucker punch from my blind side, my father's voice shot through the phone and nearly knocked me out,

"How dare you go to Papa's without asking first!"

"But, Dad, you've always let me go to Papa's after youth prayer meetings! The phone at the church was tied up and I thought it would be okay."

"That's no excuse! You shouldn't have gone without asking! Get home now!"

"But Dad, we just ordered pizza! Please can I stay? The youth leader is with us; we're not alone!"

"I don't care; come home immediately!"

Blinking back hot, angry tears, I returned to the table, mumbled an embarrassed explanation and goodbye to my best friend, Mallory, and snuck out hoping not to be noticed. I cried all the way home; all I could think over and over to myself was, "I don't understand; I've done everything right!"

<hr/>

I was newly married when I was first introduced to the concept of the inner critic. I had signed up for a writing class through the local community center, and found myself in a small, intimate, eclectic group of about half a dozen writers. I don't know if it was intentional or accidental, but the class ended up having a strong therapy component. The writing assignments were often provocative, and offered the opportunity for each of us to explore our personal issues to whatever degree we wanted—deep or shallow. The teacher created a safe and nurturing space for us. It was the first time I experienced a respectful sharing space. In the cult, we had multiple weekly meetings which always included sharing, but the sharing was compulsory and was always met with voyeurism, judgment, criticism, shaming, and condemnation. For the first time in my life, I had the experience of my shared thoughts, feelings, and opinions being met with nothing stronger than comments of "that's interesting" or "I can relate." I have a clear memory of a night when one of the writers talking about experiencing writer's block on that week's assignment. She shared that thoughts of self-doubt and self-criticism were holding her back. In response, the teacher spent some time talking about ways to silence the inner critic.

I had never heard the label "inner critic," and I was fascinated by this new concept! It's not that I didn't have an inner critic (on the contrary I had a huge, aggressive, and very violent inner critic!) but I never thought of it as something separate from myself. I had also never resisted, questioned, or tried to contradict it, because growing up, I had been taught that what my teacher was calling an inner critic was the Holy Spirit convicting me of or trying to keep me from committing sin. I never resisted the horrible, oftentimes violent, ways that my inner critic would incessantly bully and berate me, because I believed it to be the voice of God. I also firmly believed all the horrible things that my inner critic said about me, because I believed myself to be sinful, repugnant, and devoid of good, as I had been taught. Like a battered wife, I believed that I deserved the relentless abuse from my inner critic because I believed that I was the horrible person it authoritatively proclaimed me to be.

Little did she know it, but my teacher's casual, matter-of-fact discussion about the inner critic had a life-altering impact on me. For the first time in my life, I began to see my inner critic as "not me," and this was huge! If that voice was not me, then who was "me"? Perhaps me was nicer than my inner critic; perhaps me had a different opinion about who I was; perhaps me had a different view of my life. It would be decades before I would finally get the upper hand with my inner critic, but the process had begun.

I wasn't born with an inner critic. My inner critic was an aftermarket add-on installed first by my parents, then by the cult, and later perpetuated by my husband. I was born in a state of original perfection—not in a state of original sin, as I had been taught. I was born in bliss, perfectly content with who I was, and not needing approval to feel or know my worth; I was not born with any assumption or understanding that I would need to do something or become someone, as defined by others, to gain worth and value. I instinctively knew myself to have intrinsic worth and value just because I was. I was born knowing that just being was enough—no doing was necessary. I was actually born knowing that just being is not only just enough, it is everything! I was born knowing that my very essence is flawless, exquisite, perfect, and complete (needing nothing to be added, removed, or changed). Unfortunately, my awareness of my state of original perfection was so short-lived and so far-removed by the time I reached adolescence that I had completely lost my connection with it. I also lost any memory of it, even to the point where the truth of it didn't resonate with me for decades to come.

The loss of my connection with my state of original perfection began when I first experienced disapproval from my parents (which predates my conscious memory), which would have caused me to begin to doubt my intrinsic value and worth. Experiencing disapproval when I was still young and dependent on my parents caused my primitive brain to react with powerful fear—disapproval meant rejection, which, in turn, meant that I would not be taken care of (case in point: my first month of life), and, on a primitive level, this meant death. My primitive brain reacted on that level, as if disapproval were a death threat. Just like every other animal on this planet, I had a powerful primal drive to stay alive. Therefore, this experience of disapproval got burned into my brain and I tried desperately to avoid any recurrence of it. I would try to figure out, or I was told, what I did to incur the disapproval. Not only did I make a mental note of what I did that caused the disapproval so that I could be sure to avoid it in the future, I also tried to infer and deduce what other actions could potentially bring down upon me new disapproval, a new threat of death, so that I could avoid those, too. This experience and these mental gymnastics, after they were repeated enough times, created an inner critic in me.

I was raised in an environment of what I call violent perfectionism. Regular perfectionism is stressful enough, but violent perfectionism takes regular perfectionism to the extreme. Perfectionism is when a superhuman standard is set—a standard that is impossible to reach as a human being. Violent perfectionism is when a superhuman standard is set, and love, acceptance, or approval (all of which equate to life in childhood) are dependent on meeting that superhuman standard. Having grown up in an environment of violent perfectionism, I ended up with a supersonic, bionic, genetically mutated, uber inner critic, which was much more like an inner terrorist.

My inner terrorist was an ever-present virtual character in my head that vigilantly, unceasingly, and unfailingly monitored and mercilessly passed fear-based judgment on *every single one* of my thoughts, feelings, impulses, words, and actions, and on my physical appearance and performance. It never slept; it always had the last word at the end of every day and the first word at the beginning of each day. My inner terrorist had a machine gun primed with *"You suck!"* bullets, which it unloaded on me at the slightest provocation and to a degree which was always severely disproportionate to my "offense." For many decades of my life, my inner terrorist was so omnipresent and omnipotent that I had no idea that it was not me and not even from me. There was even a time in my life when I identified so strongly with my inner terrorist and had so little sense of myself that I even valued its presence and what it had to say about me as if I had Stockholm syndrome.

Nothing has given me insight into myself and reconnected me with the truth of who I am and my state of original perfection more than bearing, birthing, and raising my two daughters. Prompted by my writing teacher's comments, I had begun to think that my inner critic might not actually be me, but it wasn't until I became pregnant with my first daughter several years later that I began to remember and reconnect with my state of original perfection.

My husband came from just as strong of a religious family as I did, although his family was Eastern Orthodox, so we had both sets of parents pressuring us to baptize our baby long before she was born. The practice of infant baptism, which we had both been raised with, is for the purpose of removing the "stain of original sin," which Christian doctrine states that all humans are born with. The Christian doctrine of original sin states that all human beings carry, from conception, the guilt and culpability for Adam and Eve's original sin in the Garden of Eden. Just like sin committed after birth, original sin separates humans from God and precludes entrance into Heaven. Ergo, according to this doctrine, all babies are born in a state of sin separated from God and precluded from Heaven. This is why infant baptism is part of both the Catholic and Eastern Orthodox doctrines and practices.

Needless to say, my newly-budding expanded worldview and my ever-growing resistance to how I was raised caused me to question whether or not I agreed with this premise and wanted to have my baby baptized. Every time I considered it, I completely balked at the doctrine of original sin. Even though I had not yet held my flawless, exquisite, perfect, and complete (needing nothing to be added, removed, or changed) brand new baby in my arms, I knew, beyond a shadow of a doubt, that she was *not* stained with original sin. I was not yet strong enough to say no to any baptism, but I did say no to a Catholic or Orthodox baptism. In the end, we had her baptized in the Presbyterian Church, whose doctrine of infant baptism I found to be more palatable.

As my first daughter grew and her distinct personality began to emerge, I became more and more aware of the fact that she was already a finished product. Her body wasn't finished but she, who she was, was whole and finished from birth, really from before birth. As she grew, I did not witness the development of who she was the way I witnessed the development of her beautiful physical body (complete with curly red hair); I witnessed the revelation of who she was already. This perspective was reinforced with the arrival of my second daughter (also with curly red hair . . . score!) because she was so very different from my first daughter. When the ultrasound I had during my pregnancy with her showed that she was a girl, I thought I knew what to expect because she was the same sex and from the same gene pool as my first. I couldn't have been more wrong! Again, I felt I was witnessing the revelation of a complete (and completely different) person.

Observing my daughters' completeness and their state of original perfection made me realize that I must have been born that way and be that way also. As each of my daughters grew, no matter how naughty they were at times (and they were!), I just could not see them as being essentially bad or intrinsically flawed the way my parents had seen me. It's not that I never corrected or disciplined my daughters, because I certainly did; I was their mother, after all. It was my attitude that was different and made the difference. The key was that I never lost sight of their states of original perfection, and I figured out how to teach them to be self-referring.

I was unable to find a high school teaching job my first year out of college, so I went to work for my father as an assistant teacher in the kindergarten classroom of the Montessori school my parents owned in San Francisco. The head teacher, Olivia, became a dear friend and positively impacted my life for many years beyond our one year of working together. Olivia was a wise, deeply spiritual, and loving woman. Teaching young children was most definitely her calling; she intuitively understood and instinctively practiced the "respect the child" principle, which is the cornerstone of the Montessori teaching method. She was nearly old enough to be my mother, and having had a severe deficit in the mothering department, I looked up to her that way; as such, I paid close attention to how she conducted and carried herself. She was the first woman I had met in my life who I really wanted to emulate (something I never felt about my own mother or any of the other women I knew from the cult); she was not a Christian, but she was more Christian than any Christian I had ever known.

I watched how Olivia interacted with the children, especially the difficult ones, and I was shocked by her limitless kindness and patience; this was so foreign to me! There were two things in particular that she did with the children which I made note of. First, I noticed that, no matter how well behaved a child was, she never said "good *girl*" or "good *boy*," she always said "good *job*." She explained that it was very important that a child not be declared to be "good" because of something that they did. Likewise, she never said "bad girl" or "bad boy" when a child misbehaved. Her focus was solely on the impact of the child's negative behavior. For example, if one child hit another child, she would say something like, "Oh Suzie, you hit Tommy and you hurt him! Do you see the redness on his skin? Do you see that he is crying? You hurt him and that is not okay!"

I also noticed that Olivia never told a student that she was proud of them; she always just asked if the student was proud of themselves. Whenever one of her students would come to her with an accomplishment—a skill they learned or something they made—she would joyfully exclaim, "Wow!" and then she would ask the child, "Are you proud of yourself?" To this, they always emphatically responded, "Yes!" I asked her about this, and she explained that she did not want to be the point of reference for a student's pride in their accomplishments; she wanted to teach each student to use themselves as the source of their self-esteem.

Learning this new way of self-definition was huge for me! I eventually used it with my own two children, but first I began to practice it with myself. I had been raised with my parents, the cult leaders, and the Catholic church all having the sole authority to define who I was (a sinner) and the level of my worth (non-existent); the idea that I could define who I was, what my worth was, based solely on who I was and not how I performed, and proclaim my own pride in myself and my accomplishments, was just short of mind-blowing and was most definitely a game changer! I first began to gain the upper hand in my struggle against my inner terrorist when I began to practice this idea of self-referral.

For most of my life, I thought that if only I could gain the expressed approval of my parents, my sister, my husband, my friends, my coworkers, my neighbors, etc., I would finally be able to feel good about myself. Eventually, I realized that expressed approval from others didn't actually do any good; in fact, it kept me in the position of having my worth defined by others. If my worth was defined by others, then the state of my worth— good or bad—was in the hands of others, and as a result, was subjective at best and infinitely precarious at worst.

Even though she was younger than me, I grew up feeling overshadowed by my sister, who by society's standards was much more beautiful than I was. She was petite, thin, had long, thick, glossy chestnut brown hair, and could tan (which I was most envious of because tanning is a physical impossibility for me!). Being the redheaded stepchild that I was, I was in awe of her beauty and thought that all my low self-esteem and unhappiness would surely evaporate if only I looked like her; I was also certain that anyone who looked as beautiful as she did was unshakably happy and impervious to self-doubt. The bizarre irony was that even though she got almost-daily affirmation from family, friends, and random strangers, she was paralyzed by insecurity about her beauty. She would get compliments and feel good about herself only until she got negative feedback, or until there was a lull in the positive feedback, at which point she would be plunged again into a swirling vortex of insecurity.

After observing this throughout our high school and college years together, I realized that she was the problem. It didn't matter how much I, or anyone else, told her that she was beautiful; she couldn't hold onto it because she didn't declare it to be true herself. I remember telling her once, "At any given time, you can always find someone 'prettier' than you to make you feel ugly, and you can always find someone 'uglier' than you to make you feel pretty. You have to stop looking outside yourself to define your beauty." (The same goes for feeling skinny/fat, rich/poor, successful/ unsuccessful, etc.)

One afternoon, when my younger daughter was in preschool, we were driving home from school and she was telling me about her day. She got very upset as she recounted an experience from that morning with a classmate. She angrily told me, "Momma, Billy said my painting was stupid! My painting isn't stupid, is it?" After resisting the urge to make a sudden U-turn, drive back to the school, find Billy, and pulverize him, I calmly said to her, "Well, what do you think of your painting? Do you think it's stupid?" With all the indignant passion of a deeply offended four-year-old, she exploded, *"No, I don't think it's stupid! I think it's beautiful!"* I gave her a big smile in the rearview mirror and said, "Then it is, Sweetie; it is beautiful because *you* say it is beautiful!" Billy was just one of a whole host of people in my daughter's childhood who so generously volunteered to help create her inner critic. As much as I wanted to tell my daughter that I thought her painting was beautiful, which I did, I wanted even more to guide her to turn to herself for the final word on the value and worth of her work. By teaching her to be self-referring, I was empowering her to strengthen herself and weaken her inner critic.

I have come to realize that the only person who is with me from birth until death is myself. If I fail to champion myself, if I allow my inner terrorist to abuse me, what hope for success do I have? If I abandon myself, who will be there for me? If I can't count on myself, who can I count on? Every single other person in my life will come and go, but I will remain; even beyond death, I will remain with myself. I have learned to use myself as my ultimate point of reference for my own truth, my own support, and my own validation. It's not that I don't have dear friends and loved ones in my life, because I am thus richly blessed and am exceedingly grateful for their love, support, and encouragement—but they are not the constant in my life that I am for myself. When I quiet the frenzied chatter of everyone else's voices in my head—good, bad, and indifferent—I hear the voice of my authentic self, the self that does *not* judge and loves me *unconditionally.* This is the part of me that is so very proud of how far I've come against all odds, so very proud of myself for surviving so much, and so very proud of who I am today!

I found that suspending my self-judgement and self-criticism, even if only for a fraction of a second, freed me and made me feel like change, improvement, and growth were possible. When I practiced releasing self-judgement and self-criticism on a daily basis, I begin to see the evidence of change, improvement, and growth that had been there all along, but which I missed when I was focusing on the negative. As I began to transition from being other-referring to being self-referring, I increased my ability to see the truth of my state of original perfection *even when my present reality seemed contradictory to that truth.*

When I was in the darkest days of my life, my present reality was very ugly and shame-inducing. At that time, I was clinically depressed, suicidal, an adulteress, overweight, a pack-a-day smoker, a regular drinker, and subjecting myself to an abusive relationship. As a result, my present reality was that I was underproductive, unmotivated, self-sabotaging, cynical, pessimistic, had very low self-esteem, had a scarcity and poverty mindset, saw myself as limited, saw myself as a failure, felt I had little to contribute, felt I was not fulfilling my potential, felt I was not a good mother, felt I was not a good friend . . . need I go on? My present reality at this time completely disguised my true state of original perfection.

Most people in my life at this time (especially my family and my husband) looking at me from the outside, and concluded that I actually was who I appeared to be, which was a complete mess. There were a rare few people in my life who stopped to look hard and deep enough to see the truth of who I was, always had been, am still, and always will be (they were the same ones who had promised to remind me that I had said *"Oh, yeah? Watch me!"*). I did not begin my practice of self-referral when it was easy or when I had a lot to be proud of; I first seriously attempted to resist my inner critic and cultivate a practice of self-referral when I was swimming upstream against a very strong current, because my present reality at that time was very damning.

I started with the simple practice of adding the words "right now" after everything that my inner terrorist said to me. It was a small tweak to the negative statements I heard from my inner terrorist, but it had a powerful impact! The negative statement, "I am not working up to my fullest potential," which I heard regularly from my inner terrorist (and from my husband, who was the physical incarnation of my inner terrorist), was an objective and sweeping statement which passed judgement on who I was. The statement, "I am not working up to my fullest potential *right now*" was a statement about my present reality, and not about who I was. This implied that my present reality was temporary, subjective, and circumstantial. It also implied that I did have the ability to work up to my fullest potential; I was just not doing it at that time. Another version of "right now" that I also learned to add to the negative statements I heard from my inner terrorist was the word "yet." The fatalistic statement, "I'll never figure out how to leave my abusive marriage" became, "I don't know how to leave my abusive marriage *yet*"—implying that I would someday figure out how to leave my abusive marriage. Just making these small tweaks to the negative statements I heard from my inner terrorist began to mobilize resources of inner strength that I did not know I had, which amazed me and propelled me forward to even greater victories over my inner terrorist, and ultimately to a powerful new life.

When I was starting my program to quit smoking, I confided in a close friend that I was worried about failing. I said, "I have this voice in my head telling me that I am weak and weak-willed and will surely fail. I know that voice is the voice of all the horrible people in my past and it is not me, but it still shakes my self-confidence. I need to remember how much I have already accomplished! When I look at everything I have already survived in my life, I realize that I am anything but weak." She firmly said to me, "No, Aidy, you are not *anything* but weak; you are *everything* but weak!" I began to think about her comment and what "everything" meant. What was the "everything" which I was that wasn't weak? I concluded that not only was I not weak, but I was strong, whole, powerful, magical, luminous, visionary, wise, joyful, blissful, optimistic, passionate, driven, focused, guided, accomplished, successful, generous, loving, abundant, and limitless! Need I go on?

When I realized that my inner terrorist wasn't natural and wasn't actually me or any a part of me, the real me, I developed the ability to reject it unequivocally on all levels and in all circumstances. As I thought about it, I could not recall a single thing that my inner terrorist had ever said to me that was positive! I concluded that since the comments from my inner terrorist weren't positive and encouraging, then they weren't useful and didn't serve me. I decided to fire my inner terrorist and fill the vacancy with my authentic self, which was still, always had been, and always would be in a state of original perfection!

It took me many years of diligent practice to depose my inner terrorist from its position as despot over my mind and spirit. Even if I had had a mild inner critic, it would not have gone quietly or willingly; my inner terrorist violently resisted being removed and escalated its abuse of me in response to my attempts to remove it. At times, it was discouraging, but I remained committed to ridding myself of my inner terrorist, and thanks be to all deities that I did because I'm a much happier, more peaceful, more positive, and more empowered person today than I ever thought I would or even could be!

I became a huge *Harry Potter* fan after reading the books multiple times to my daughters throughout their childhoods. I came to think of my inner terrorist as a boggart, which is one of the many magical creatures in the magical world of *Harry Potter*. A boggart is a shapeshifter that has no substance or identity on its own; it assumes the shape of whatever most frightens the person it crosses paths with. I realized that my inner terrorist was no more real than a boggart, and only existed to frighten and bully me by mirroring my deepest fears.

I created several visualizations to help me rid myself of my inner terrorist. The first step was to stop positively identifying with my inner terrorist as if I had Stockholm syndrome. To do this, I gave my inner terrorist a visual image that was repulsive; this was when I first began to call it my inner terrorist instead of my inner critic, because there is no context within which a terrorist can be viewed positively. A critic can be seen in a positive light; we are taught to welcome constructive criticism, and professional critics are seen as authorities on whatever it is that they critique. I created a mental image of a terrorist who was cruel, cold, ruthless, heartless, vicious, and, well, terrorizing. When I saw my inner critic this way, I began, for the first time, to be able to reject it and what it said about me, because I could clearly see that it was not me and that it was against me.

Once I had separated my inner terrorist from myself, I gave it a terminal illness. I knew it would take time—years, not weeks or months—and practice to fully subdue it. I knew that if I visualized something quick, like chopping off its head, I would get discouraged; it would be back again the next day (or the next minute) and would mock me for failing to get rid of it. So, I gave it a terminal illness and visualized it dying slowly. I began by hearing it cough after every time it berated me; I progressed to seeing it stumble and fall with weakness and debilitation. As these visualizations strengthened me, I progressed to seeing my inner terrorist laying in a hospital bed, frail and helpless. Eventually, I got to the place where I replaced the mental image of my inner terrorist with the image of a headstone in a cemetery, with me tossing tattered flowers on its grave.

Another tool I used to combat my inner terrorist when it would say horrible things to me was to act offended and indignant. I realized that only someone who did not know me, did not know who I really was, would say these dreadful things to me about myself. I started to respond to my inner terrorist the same way I would respond if a perfect stranger walked up to me on the street and said to me what my inner terrorist said. If a stranger walked up to me on the street and said, "You have never been successful and you will never be successful!" I would be very offended and indignant! I would respond with something like, "Excuse me but *who the hell are you?* You clearly don't know me or anything about me!" When my inner terrorist would say something like that to me, I would give the same response in my head, or, if I was alone, I would yell it out loud. I also knew that if I ever heard anyone say the things that my inner terrorist said to me to either of my daughters, I would be unbelievably offended and would defend them fiercely! As I continued to combat my inner terrorist, I came to feel that I deserved to be defended against the offensive things that my inner terrorist said to me just as fiercely as I would defend my daughters from such abuse!

The more progress I made in weakening my inner terrorist and strengthening my authentic self, the easier it became. Eventually, I got to the place where I could employ the same defense against my inner terrorist that Professor Lupin teaches his students at Hogwarts to use against boggarts, which is laughter. According to Professor Lupin, the way to vanquish a boggart is to imagine it looking stupid or funny, which will make you laugh. Then, you cast the "Riddikulus" charm, and the boggart is rendered powerless. Just like a boggart, my inner terrorist could be rendered powerless when I declared it to be ridiculous and laughed at what it said to me.

I realized that ninety-nine percent of what my inner terrorist said to me was ridiculous; there was always a tiny grain of truth, which is how it used to get me, but the proclamations from my inner terrorist were so exaggerated and fatalistic that they truly were ridiculous. Take for example the proclamation, "You have always failed and you will always fail!" The tiny grain of truth came from the fact that there have been times in my life when I have failed, and there have been times when I have struggled and my success has been mediocre or short-lived . . . but *not* always and not even most of the time. When I got enough distance from my inner terrorist and enough of a balanced perspective on the truth of who I was and the truth about my life, I was able to see the proclamations of my inner terrorist as ridiculous and laugh at them. Sometimes, just to make myself laugh even more, I would respond like a second grader and say, "You're a dumb-dumb face! I have *not* always failed and I will *not* always fail! You don't know anything; you're just a big stupid-head!"

These days, it's not that I never hear anything from my inner terrorist, but it doesn't terrorize me the way that it used to—it has become much more of a weak inner critic. I no longer give it free rein, or unquestioningly believe what it has to say about me and my life; I keep it on a very, very short leash. I (my authentic self, born in a state of original perfection) am the only one with the authority to make proclamations on the truth of who I am and what my life is like. It is a much nicer way to live because I like myself, I am nice to myself, I believe in myself, and I think my life is fabulous and is getting better every day! Now my miserable little inner critic can try to say whatever it wants, and I just laugh!

CHAPTER SEVEN

It Wasn't My Fault, But It Was My Responsibility

We had been trying for second child for what felt like ages. In reality, it had only been about three months, but having gotten pregnant the first time while purposely trying not to get pregnant, I had the idea in my head that I was "Fertile Myrtle," so I became very impatient when I did not get pregnant in the first month of trying. Now, I was two months along and I was bleeding. I noticed the blood for the first time on a Saturday morning, which meant that I had to wait forty-eight hours for any answers from my doctor. I tried not to worry; I tried to console myself with the fact that many of my girlfriends had bled during their pregnancies and went on to have normal, healthy babies. Yet, I did not bleed at all with my first pregnancy, so I worried. Several times over the weekend, I tried to meditate to connect with my baby, but every time I reached out, it felt like picking up a phone that wasn't plugged in; I was expecting communication and there was only silence, which was very disconcerting.

On Monday morning, after examining me, my doctor told me that everything looked good and she didn't think I had anything to worry about. She drew my blood to check my HCG levels and told me to come back on Wednesday morning for another blood draw, to make sure that my HCG levels were rising as they should be. On Wednesday morning, she told me that my HCG levels had dropped, indicating that the baby was no longer alive. I left her office alone; my husband, disdaining me and all things female, would never have considered accompanying me to my doctor's appointments. He left me alone to find out that I was miscarrying, he left me alone to miscarry, and he left me alone to grieve. Weeks after my miscarriage, I bitterly said to him, "Well, I guess that wasn't your baby." With his trademark irritation, he demanded, "What do you mean 'that wasn't my baby?'" I shot back at him, "'Cause it sure seems like I'm the only one who lost a baby!"

Adding to my grief, a week after I miscarried, my maternal grandmother, who had been my only experience of unconditional love, died. It was February and the cold, grey, barren days of the Northwest winter mirrored my inner state of sadness and despair. In a moment of weakness, when my heartbreak was all-consuming, I reached for the phone to call him; I had not seen him in several years, and I had not talked to him in over a year. As the phone rang, I silently prayed that his wife wouldn't answer, that she wouldn't be there, that he would be alone . . .

When I heard his voice say, "Hello?" I sank to the kitchen floor, sobbing. Swallowing my tears, I choked out, "It's me; can you talk?" Recognizing my voice and hearing my pain, he said, "Yes, oh my God, what's wrong?" Between sobs, I said, "I was pregnant and now I'm not; I lost the baby." With the healing power that only love is capable of, he said, "Baby, you're not alone; I'm here for you! I wish I could crawl through this phone, wrap my arms around you, and just hold you forever!" As I hung up the phone a little while later, I remembered how he had told me when we parted that I had saved him. I thought, "Today, he saved me."

I can remember times in grade school when one of my friends would repeatedly hit me in the face with my own hand and then ask me, "Why are you hitting yourself? Why are you hitting yourself?" When I was seven, this was hysterical! When I was raised by abusive, dysfunctional parents, grew up to have self-destructive, dysfunctional behaviors, and those abusive, dysfunctional parents and everyone else in my life repeatedly asked me, "Why are you self-destructive and dysfunctional? Why are you self-destructive and dysfunctional?" it wasn't hysterical; it wasn't even funny!

By the time I reached adulthood, my inner critic and my outer critics— my parents, the cult members/leaders, and later my husband—had me thoroughly convinced that every single one of my flaws, of which they found more than I could keep up with, was solely my fault, and proof of my inherent defectiveness and sinfulness. The implication was always that I had deliberately chosen, of my own accord, to fail or fall short in the ways they claimed I had, and could just as easily and deliberately correct my failures and shortcomings.

I was thirty when my younger daughter was born, and when she was about eight months old, I had an experience with her which dramatically shifted my perspective on myself. One day, when she was crawling around on the living room floor, she crawled under the coffee table, sat up, and banged her head on the underside of the table. She burst into loud, angry tears and I scooped her up to comfort her. She continued to cry while I was cuddling her, and then she did something shocking; she looked up at me and slapped me across the face! I stared at her in shock, and then, as a floodlight switched on in my brain, I exclaimed out loud, "Oh my God, it's not my fault!"

My declaration of "It's not my fault!" was not in protest of her slapping me; it was an expression of a realization about myself. I realized in that moment that how she responded to her pain—by lashing out in anger— was how I had always responded to my pain, both emotional and physical. I also realized that there was no way, at eight months of age, that her response was a learned response. I had not *taught* her to respond to pain with anger; *she was born that way!* If she was born with this reflexive response to pain and mine was identical, then I must have been born that way also. If I was born that way, then it wasn't my fault!

Having lived with my younger daughter from her birth through her adulthood, I now understand what it is like to be on the receiving end of my own pain response. I have a keen understanding of how unpleasant it is to be slapped in the face, literally or figuratively, when I am just trying to offer compassion or help. Since I was, thankfully, granted the insight to know that it was not her fault and not her choice that she was naturally inclined to respond to pain by lashing out in anger, I didn't take it personally. On the flip side, since I took my parenting job very seriously, I knew it was my responsibility to teach my daughter how to manage her anger response to pain; I did not want to live with someone who had an unchecked anger response to pain, and I wanted her to become a fully-functioning adult with healthy, respectful, and loving relationship skills. Helping my daughter, in turn, helped me tremendously to have compassion for myself for a behavior pattern for which I had always experienced rejection, criticism, and judgment. Helping my daughter, in turn, helped me to learn how to manage my own anger response to pain. Through this process, I came to the definitive conclusion that my anger response to pain was not my fault, as I had been told for my whole life, but it was my responsibility.

Over the next two decades, this epiphany illuminated every other area of my life which I had suffered in or struggled with, the same way a single domino impacts hundreds of others, one after another after another. I came to realize that all of my not-nice personality traits, which I had been told were flaws in my character, were not my fault—they were the result of the unique DNA and brain chemistry that I was born with—but they were my responsibility. Likewise, the pain I carried from a lifetime of abuse and neglect, which made me vulnerable to making less-than-optimal choices in my adulthood, was not my fault, but those choices were my responsibility.

As I mentioned earlier, my parents endured experiences in their childhoods that were the stuff of *Law and Order SVU* episodes. All four of their parents were abusive and/or neglectful to a degree, and in a fashion, that would land them in prison today. From what I know of the four, the one who took the first prize for being the most abusive and depraved was my paternal grandmother (both of my grandfathers were very close runners-up). When I got the call, as an adult, that she had died, I literally sang out, "Ding, dong, the wicked witch is dead!" Her rampant diabolical abuse had impacted my life both directly and indirectly, and I shed no tears when she passed. Her abuse of my father impacted me indirectly; he was so crippled emotionally, psychologically, and spiritually from what she and my grandfather had done to him that he didn't have it in him to give me even half of what I needed from a father. In addition, she was directly verbally and psychologically abusive to me as a child. Neither of my parents ever did anything to defend me; in fact, my father always defended her.

I learned a lot about my grandmother's life because my father constantly used it to defend her and excuse her abusive behavior. She was the unwanted fifth girl born to parents who desperately wanted a boy. Her parents had rejected her so completely from birth that they even refused to name her; she was named by the Catholic priest who baptized her. Her parents completely ignored her and never gave her the love and nurturing that she needed and deserved. Shortly after she married my grandfather, he was diagnosed with an abdominal aortic aneurysm and was told that he could drop dead at any moment. Since she was the typical housewife of the 1940s who was completely dependent on her husband for her social status and financial security, my grandmother endured several decades of chronic worry and fear for her future. My grandfather did die when my father was in high school, making my grandmother a widow in her early forties. Whenever I complained to my father about how mean she was to me, he told me that I "needed to understand how hard her life had been and have more compassion for her," implying that she could not be held accountable or responsible for her abominable behavior, or be expected to behave any better.

One of my grandmother's closest friends was a wonderful woman named Miriam. Miriam was a German Jew who had survived the Holocaust. She and her husband had fled Nazi Germany during the war, and narrowly escaped being put in a concentration camp. Her mother and brother were not so lucky; Miriam never saw them again, and did not find out until she was in her eighties that they had both died in a concentration camp. Whenever we visited my grandmother, we usually went to Miriam's house for lunch or dinner. Even though I saw Miriam only about a dozen times in my childhood, she made a huge impression on me.

My father spent just as much time telling me about the trials and tribulations of Miriam's life as he did telling me about the trials and tribulations of his mother's life. There was one glaring difference between these two women which did not escape me, even in my youth; my grandmother was the most bitter, cruel, and spiteful woman you would ever meet, but Miriam was the most optimistic, loving, generous, and joyful woman you would ever meet! She always greeted us at the door with so much fuss you would have thought that we were royalty; she was always so excited to see us you would have thought that we were bringing her a Publishers Clearing House prize check. Her husband died a decade before she did; she had loved him deeply and missed him terribly, but her grief never dampened her outlook. She was very open in talking about her difficult life experiences, but she always ended her stories by counting all her blessings and summarizing her life's glass as being much more than half full.

I was a teenager when I first responded to my father's defense of his mother by pointing out that Miriam had experienced just as difficult, if not more difficult, of a life, and she didn't behave abominably the way my grandmother did. This stumped my father, but he just ignored my logic and persisted in his defense of his mother even after her death. Observing the night-and-day difference between who these two women were and how they responded to their life experiences was the first time I began to understand that happiness is a choice. I reasoned that if these two women could have opposite responses to a similar amount of pain and misfortune, then those responses must be their choices. If their responses were their choices, then they could have chosen differently. If they could have chosen differently, then they were responsible for their choices of response. It is true that these two women were born with different DNA and brain chemistry, which would have impacted how they responded to their similar amounts of pain and misfortune. The inclination toward a particular response, as dictated by their DNA and brain chemistry, would, therefore, not be their fault, but their choices of response were still their responsibility. Likewise, they were responsible for the consequences of their choices of response; my grandmother was responsible for how her choice of response to her own pain and misfortune impacted those on the receiving end of it.

If you slap me across the face, you are responsible for your action *and* the impact of it. You are responsible for the redness on my skin; you are responsible for the sting that I feel; you are responsible for triggering the rush of adrenaline released on command from my primitive brain, which will have perceived your action as a threat. The action I choose in response to your action is my responsibility. There are many responses available for me to choose from, including no response at all. Whether I choose to respond with a retaliatory physical assault, or with tears, or with a verbal assault, or with sulking withdrawal (the silent treatment) or with no response, these choices are mine and they are my responsibility. The inclination, influenced by my DNA, brain chemistry, and life experiences, toward a specific response (fight or flight) is not my fault, but the action

I choose is my responsibility; likewise, I am responsible for the impact of the action I choose in response to your action.

It was not my fault that my childhood experiences made me vulnerable to tragically low self-esteem, which in turn made me a perfect candidate for an abusive relationship, becoming depressed and suicidal, needing to be on medication, taking up smoking, becoming overweight, and being unfaithful in my marriage. However, as an adult, I did have to take responsibility for my choices and the condition of my life as a result of my choices. My childhood experiences helped to shape how I was inclined to behave as an adult, but once I became an adult, I also became responsible for my choices and my behaviors, as well as the impact of them.

There have been times when I have found it to be convenient and easier to absolve myself by taking the position of "I couldn't help myself," or "he/she made me do it," but I have come to the opinion that taking this position is also incredibly cowardly, insulting to my own intelligence, and disempowering. It has taken guts to own where I am and what I have done in my life, but it has also been *very* freeing and empowering; it has been the only way for me to move forward and make lasting positive changes.

One of the handy benefits that I have reaped in learning to own my choices and actions is that I have been freed from the grip of shame. Shame only has a hold on me when I am still in the place of not wanting to face what I have done; when I own (really own, not just admit, but own) what I have done, no one, not even my inner critic, can shame me. Not that other people and my inner critic don't try to shame me, but these attempts don't have any power over me. Depending on the severity of my actions and their impact, I can still feel guilt, regret, remorse, and/or sadness for what I have done, but the shame dissipates every time I own my actions and choices.

As part of the first therapy I went through in my mid-twenties to begin to sort out the craziness of my childhood, I wrote a letter to my mother detailing all the wrongs I had suffered at her hands, and holding her accountable for how she had abused and neglected me. It took me more than a year to write, and it was more than ten pages long by the time I finally sent it to her. As it turned out, I became pregnant with my first daughter while I was still in the process of writing the letter; my impending motherhood gave new significance to my own childhood experiences. I sent the letter off just before my daughter was born, and I received my mother's response when my daughter was a few months old.

In her response to me, my mother did not try to deny or minimize anything I had confronted her with in my letter. Instead, she spent her letter recounting to me all the wrongs and abuse she had suffered from her parents, much of which I knew already. She concluded her letter by telling me that she had not been capable of doing any better for me because of what had been done to her, and argued that she could not be responsible or held accountable for what she had done to me. Since I had just recently accepted the grave responsibility and supreme honor of mothering my own daughter, I had no patience for her line of reasoning. I wrote back to her, "Based on your argument, I should look into my brand new, precious, perfect baby's eyes and say, 'Sorry Kiddo . . . sucks to be you! I was abused and neglected, so you will be, too. I hope you don't mind, because I just can't help it!'" Rarely is there no reason for someone's behavior; there is almost always a reason for what someone does, but that reason is not often an excuse.

When I got married, it never crossed my mind that I would ever or could ever be unfaithful! I loved my husband truly, madly, and deeply, and had he returned my love and affection, no other man could ever have turned my head. I was completely blindsided and horrified when I first began to think about and have feelings and desire for another man. I remember telling a friend once, "I never thought I could be unfaithful, but you don't know how hungry you are until you smell the food cooking." I had no idea how much I was suffering from my husband's neglect and rejection until I experienced the attention of another man.

There was absolutely nothing I could do to spark any desire from my husband (I tried everything!). He went to such extreme lengths to avoid intimacy with me that he used to hide in our walk-in closet (foreshadowing!) to change his clothes, because he knew that if I saw him undressing, I would become amorous . . . something he dreaded. In contrast, this other man desired me naturally and fervidly, with no incitation from me. He never pressured me, but also made no secret of the fact that he found me to be incredibly beautiful and desirable, and that he thought my husband was crazy for not wanting me. I was so starved for affection and attention that eventually I chose to give in to temptation.

After the first time we made love, I was putting my clothes back on when he put his hand on my forearm and said, "Stop." I said, "What? What's wrong?" thinking, as I had been conditioned to think, that I had done something wrong. He said, "Nothing is wrong but please just don't put your clothes back on so fast; I could look at you naked all day!" This absolutely blew my mind! This was the only man, other than my husband, who had ever seen me naked; his response to my naked body contrasted so sharply with how my husband responded to my naked body that it really caught my attention! It was the first time since my wedding night that it crossed my mind that it might not be my fault that my husband wasn't interested in me, after all.

Near the end of my marriage, my designer friend, Mia, asked if I had ever had an affair. I hesitated in answering her because I wasn't sure if I felt she was a close enough friend for me to give her a truthful answer. I ended up choosing to take the risk, and I answered, "Yes, I have had two affairs." With an audible sigh of relief, she quickly replied, "Oh, thank God!" I was so surprised by her response that I burst out laughing and said, "Holy hell, Mia, of all the things I thought you were going to say, I was *not* expecting that!" She told me, "The first thing I thought when I met your husband was, 'Does Aidy know he's gay?' The second thing I thought was, 'I hope she hasn't been long-suffering!' I am so relieved to hear that you have not spent all these years completely deprived!" I very much appreciated her sympathy and support; although her response was the most emphatic, she was not my only friend who felt this way about my marital infidelity. Even so, I always owned and will still own what I chose to do; no matter how understandable it was that I ended up being unfaithful, I will never say, "I couldn't help myself!" My husband was responsible for making me vulnerable to another man's attention and affection, but cheating was my choice and my responsibility; at the time, it felt like it would have been much harder, but I could have made a different choice.

What I didn't realize at the time was that the real crime was not the cheating; the real crime was the choice to stay married to a man who was abusing and neglecting me. Having an affair makes it easier to stay in a bad marriage; it seems easier than getting divorced, but it is a coward's choice. It took decades for me to find the courage to demand a better life for myself. It wasn't my fault that I believed that I didn't have the strength to leave my marriage before I did, but staying for as long as I did and the impact of this choice were my responsibility. I do not judge and condemn myself, or have any shame for the choices I made, because own them.

I was thirteen when I lit up my first cigarette. I did not have the typical response. I did not have the response that I should have had; I should have choked, coughed, turned green, ran to the bathroom to vomit, and vowed never to light up again, but this was not how I responded. My response to my first drag on a cigarette was, "Oh, yeah!" accompanied by a total relaxation of my body as I experienced profound relief for the first time in my life. Looking back, I now know that I had suffered enough in my short thirteen years that I was already clinically depressed and had the painful physical symptoms of depression, which were temporarily alleviated by the nicotine.

Depression will occur when you are in a sustained unpleasant and/or stressful situation which you are (or feel that you are) powerless to change or free yourself from; depression is manifested helplessness. To say that my childhood was a sustained unpleasant and stressful situation which I was powerless to change is an understatement! There is, therefore, no surprise in the fact that I became depressed at a very young age. Depression does not just create a sad forced affect, it also creates a significant chemical imbalance in the body which perpetuates the sad affect and also produces actual physical pain. Given the sad state I was in and the chemical imbalance in my body, how my body responded to my first cigarette makes complete sense.

Interestingly enough, I did not become an actual smoker until twenty years later. Until I was in my early thirties, I was only a social smoker. I could pick it up and put it down at will without being snared by it. I did not know that I was playing with fire; I thought I was immune to the addiction, and for many years I was. It wasn't until my body had endured several decades of chemical imbalance from being in a state of chronic depression and my life circumstances came together to create the perfect stress storm that the conditions were just right for me to get burned and ensnared in the trap of addiction.

I had been neglected and abused in my sham of a marriage for ten years already, and we had just moved across the country. The brunt of the work for the move fell on me; I was the one who found my husband a new job, sold our house, had all our stuff moved into storage, drove 3,000 miles from San Francisco, California to Richmond, Virginia with my daughters (who were only two and six), and set up a new life for us while my husband stayed behind for several months to close his psychiatric practice. Nine months after we had gotten settled, a friend came to visit me for a long weekend. We went AWOL for some desperately needed and long overdue girlfriend therapy, which consisted of lots of shopping, movies, and dining out. My girlfriend was a smoker, and I smoked with her for the whole weekend, the way I always had, without a second thought. Several weeks after she went home, I was still smoking and still not giving it a second thought, because I was sure I could easily put it down whenever I wanted to the way I always had. Had I known then what was going to happen, I would have dropped those cigarettes like a hot potato and ran! As it turned out, I did not put them down again for more than a decade, and I did not put them down again easily!

Anxiety and lethargy are the two general ways that depression presents. These two responses are in line with the general fight (anxiety) or flight (lethargy) response that we human animals have to all our stressful experiences in life. I have noticed that people who respond to depression with anxiety seem to be vulnerable to becoming addicted to "downers" (alcohol, marijuana, heroin, etc.) because they take the edge off their permanently tripped fight switch, and people who respond to depression with lethargy seem to be vulnerable to becoming addicted to "uppers" (caffeine, nicotine, cocaine, speed, etc.) because they counteract their constant state of flight. My depression presented as lethargy—I slept at least nine or ten hours a night, napped every chance I got, watched excessive amounts of uninspiring TV, and was unable to handle the simple basics like getting my teeth brushed or my bed made. I was paralyzed by fatalistic thinking about myself and my life. When I smoked, the nicotine lifted my mood and temporarily gave me the feeling that I might be able to handle my life, especially if I were drinking coffee while I was smoking. I used to start each day with two sixteen-ounce travel tumblers full of coffee, and half a dozen cigarettes. I was in such a bad state that even this substantial dose of uppers did not make me feel happy or on top of the world; it only made me feel like I *might* be able to handle my day (in contrast to my life after depression, where just one cup of coffee can make me positively giddy).

I did not become addicted to cigarettes because I was weak-willed or lacking in strength of character; the truth is that I became addicted to cigarettes because the nicotine gave me temporary relief from my physical and emotional pain. No matter how understandable and justifiable my addiction was, it was still my responsibility. It was not my fault that I had developed a physiology that was vulnerable to addiction, but the choice to smoke was my decision; at the time, it felt like it would have been much harder, but I could have made a different choice. Just like my choice to have an affair, choosing to smoke made it easier to exist in my miserable abusive marriage. Just like my choice to have an affair, the choice to smoke was a coward's choice—at that time in my life, it seemed easier to smoke than it was to find the courage to leave my marriage. I do not judge and condemn myself, or have any shame for the choice I made, because I own the choice I made.

The epiphany that the things I had struggled with and the mistakes I had made were not my fault, but were my responsibility, was both liberating and sobering. On one hand, I was freed from the constant self-flagellation and shame—Yeah! On the other hand, it was up to me to take action to heal myself and improve my quality of life—Oh shit! If I chose not to take action, I would be responsible for that choice, as well. I spent many years crying over my misfortunes on the side of the road on my life's path, as sad and disempowered as Cinderella with her smashed pumpkin and silly little mice after midnight. It took time for me to move from the "it's not my fault" part of my epiphany to the place of "but it is my responsibility." I was still squarely in the "it's not my fault" phase when I started attending Straight Spouse Network support group meetings. One night in a meeting, I let loose a serious, "why me?" tirade, and then checked myself by saying that I knew there was much worse suffering in the world than mine. The facilitator was very compassionate and affirmed that I had every right to my suffering, but encouraged me to work on moving forward.

I made a huge leap forward in my recovery from what my ex-husband had done to me when I realized that he was responsible for what he did, but I was responsible for him doing it to me. That he did it is on him; that he did it *to me* is on me. I was not the only woman he knew at the time that he felt he had to get married, but I was the one willing to accept the level, or lack thereof, of relationship that he was offering. The fact that my self-esteem was so low, and I was so ignorant about relationships with men, that I was willing to accept how he was treating me was not my fault, but still, I was the one who chose to marry him even though he was not giving me the kind of love and relationship—not even close—that I so desperately wanted, needed, and deserved. I could have made a different choice; I could have chosen not to marry him and hold out for better. I say none of this to absolve him of his responsibility for what he did to me! The same rule applies to him—it was not his fault that he felt he had to get married to hide his homosexuality because of the pressure from his family, his church, and society, but his choice to do so was, and is, his responsibility.

It was through my friendship with Felipe, my gay classmate from design school, that my understanding of my husband's responsibility for his choices became very clear to me. Felipe came from just as strict of a religious background and just as unaccepting of a family as my husband had, but, because he was about a decade older than my husband, grew up in a generation which was even more intolerant of and ignorant about homosexuality. As a result, he did not come out to his family until he was in his mid-thirties, and when he did, his family was not accepting or supportive.

I was cautious about sharing the truth of my marriage with Felipe because I thought he would be sympathetic to my husband for choosing the path of least resistance. On the contrary, he was very supportive of and sympathetic to me as I was slowly realizing the complete truth of what my husband had done to me. In one of our many conversations about my situation, Felipe told me a story from his life which brought a great deal of clarity to my situation. In his early thirties, the man he had been secretly dating broke up with him and married a woman. In a conversation several years later, his ex-boyfriend said to him, "Felipe, you should get married, too! You gotta do it; it's so easy! All you have to do is to get a woman to fall in love with you. It makes everything so much easier; no one questions you and everyone accepts you!" Felipe told me, "Aidy, I just knew, no matter how hard it was to be gay, that I couldn't do that to another person; I couldn't lie to someone and use them like that."

Felipe's story identified a key difference between him and my husband. That was when I realized that the root of the problem was not that my husband was gay and felt pressured to present himself as straight. The root of the problem was that my husband was a cold, calculating man who seriously lacked empathy, quality of character, and moral integrity, *none of which has anything to do with being gay!* When my husband deliberately chose to deceive me in such a fundamental and all-encompassing way and use me and my life to meet his needs, he dismissed my basic humanity. To him, I was not a person with feelings, desires, needs, hopes, and dreams deserving of respect and consideration; I was merely a solution to his problem, and nothing more. Using me as a means to his self-serving ends was *not* his only choice. There were other ways he could have chosen to solve his problem which would not have involved another adult and eventually children. He could have stayed in the closet by himself instead of holding our daughters and me hostage in the closet with him.

When I was going through my divorce, I was chided by many well-meaning friends for my anger toward my husband. One of my best friends firmly told me, with great urgency, that I *must* forgive him or I would be stuck forever! This makes me chuckle because it always seems to be the people who have never gone through what I have gone through, and therefore have the least point of reference, who insist that I *must* forgive; I've never met another straight spouse who told me I *must* forgive my gay ex-husband. Even so, I did get to a point in my healing where I realized that my anger, which had been empowering me, was no longer serving me. I needed to find a way to make peace with what my husband and my family had done to me, yet I vehemently balked at the idea of forgiving them!

In the self-help and spiritual community, forgiveness is a big buzz word, but the concept of forgiveness that people talk about today is very different from the concept of forgiveness that I was raised with. In the cult, forgiveness was not voluntary; it was mandatory. As I was taught, Christ calls his followers to forgive, no ifs, ands, or buts. The forgiveness that I was ordered to practice provided little or no acknowledgement for any way that I might have suffered as a result of someone else's wrongdoing. To want the pain or injustice I had suffered to be acknowledged or compensated for was considered to be the sin of pride; it was me thinking that I was important enough for it to matter that I was wronged. I was taught that to forgive someone meant to wipe the slate clean—to pardon their offense and to absolve them of any liability of indebtedness. Furthermore, I was instructed to embrace the wrongdoer as if they had never wronged me.

Needless to say, according to this definition, I have yet to be able to forgive my ex-husband (or my parents, for that matter), and according to this definition, I doubt I ever will! I also don't feel that this type of forgiveness is appropriate for them or anyone else (myself included) who has wronged and hurt someone so profoundly. The main point of this chapter is that even if something isn't my fault, I am responsible for my actions and for the impact of my actions. Therefore, I find this definition of forgiveness to be inappropriate and unproductive.

Along the way in my ponderings over the concept of forgiveness, I was introduced to the Zen Buddhist practice of non-judgement. When I first learned about the practice of non-judgement, I confused it with acceptance—embracing the person who I felt had wronged me and saying that I was okay with them and what they had done to me—and so I struggled with non-judgement just as much as I had struggled with the concept of forgiveness that I was raised with. I now understand that non-judgement just means non-evaluation or non-assessment—not proclaiming a person and/or their actions to be right or wrong, good or bad. Non-judgement just means "no comment." For me, practicing non-judgement means to stay in a position of non-conclusion regarding another person and/or their actions. It helped when I realized that not judging someone and/or their actions to be wrong does not mean by default that they and their actions are right, or that I am okay with them and their actions.

For me, the key to being able to embrace the practice of non-judgment was understanding that, in my human state, I lack omniscience. In acknowledging my lack of omniscience, I have had to concede that it is therefore impossible for me to have all the facts necessary to qualify me to pass judgement on someone else and their actions. Even though my ego often wants to rush to pass an "off with their heads" sentence, within the confines of time and space, I just cannot know for sure that my judgment isn't flawed.

For the longest time, I felt justified in judging and condemning my ex-husband for his weak choices, born out of his need for the love and acceptance of his parents, on the grounds that I was also rejected and declared to be wrong by my parents, but I did not choose to victimize another person(s) in my efforts to earn my parents' love and acceptance. Nonetheless, acknowledging my lack of omniscience required me to concede that I don't have enough information to make an apples to apples comparison between our seemingly similar circumstances. I have gotten to the place, when I think about my ex-husband, where I can consider that perhaps, "there, but for the grace of God, go I."

For the longest time, I also felt justified in judging and condemning my parents for their catastrophic failure at parenting on the grounds that I had managed to parent so much better than they did. Yes, they had had wretched parents, but I had had dreadful parents and I managed to be a good parent despite this fact. One day, it dawned on me that maybe, *just maybe*, the reason why I was able to be a good parent was because I had *only* had dreadful parents and *not* wretched parents; perhaps, if I had had wretched parents, I would only have been able to manage being a dreadful parent.

Oftentimes, I have squandered my energy on judging and condemning others and their actions because I made the mistake of thinking that my judgement and condemnation had the power to make someone else take responsibility for what they had done to me; my life experience has taught me that they do not. I can declare someone else to be accountable for something that they have done to me—which is to do nothing more than to state the fact of their actions—but I have no power to make them take responsibility for what they have done to me. The Universe, God, karma, or whatever your word is for it has the power and does hold every one of us responsible for all of our actions—good, bad, and ugly.

To this day, I cannot tell you that I am okay with my parents and my ex-husband, or with what they did to me, but I can tell you that I feel the need to pass judgement on them and what they did to me less and less. Relinquishing the need to declare that they and what they did to me are wrong doesn't mean that I absolve them of their responsibility for their actions; even if it wasn't their fault, it is their responsibility. Likewise, relinquishing the need to declare that they and what they did to me are wrong doesn't mean that I laugh off my experience of what they did to me; my experience of what they did to me was most definitely very painful and very unpleasant! The wounds they inflicted on me are healed, but the scars remain. Nevertheless, I have gotten to the place where I can manage a pretty authentic Switzerland.

A more current and popular idea of forgiveness is to relinquish my right to hurt you in retaliation for you having hurt me. It is to release the desire and need to exact personal revenge. Another description of forgiveness I have heard is to be able to say, "what you did to me no longer matters to me." In none of these definitions is there any inappropriate letting-off-the-hook or getting off scot-free, but these definitions do contain the key component of letting it go. These definitions of forgiveness are empowering; they are the ultimate *"Oh, yeah? Watch me!"* response to being wronged. Embracing this kind of forgiveness is having the power to say, "You think I won't survive what you did to me? *'Oh, yeah? Watch me!'*" It has been said by many spiritual teachers that holding onto a grudge is like drinking poison and expecting the other person to die. Whether you call it forgiveness or something else, letting go is critical and the only way to move forward—and moving forward is the only way to get to a better place.

CHAPTER EIGHT

I May Have Been a Slow Learner, But At Least I Wasn't a "No Learner"

Sitting in the small restaurant across the table from my father at lunch, I felt miles apart from him, and this distance saddened me. There had been a time in my life when I felt affection for my father and would have said that we were close, despite how he abused me. Now there was an infinite chasm between us, and it was exhausting. In so many ways we were so alike; besides having the same curly red hair, we had the same brain wiring; our brains had the same propensity for plumbing the depths of both ponderous thought and dark mood to an equal degree. We used to see eye-to-eye on so much, but we had parted ways over a decade ago when I abandoned his faith. Like taffy, I had pushed and pulled the faith that he gave me as a child, but in the end, I could not make it stretch far enough to cover my questions. Even though my whole family had left the religious cult more than a decade prior, my father (as well as my mother, my sister, and my brother-in-law) had remained fanatical in his devotion to fundamentalist Christianity, and clung to his dysfunctional desperation for my personal salvation. He was never able to see me as just "Aidy"; when he looked at me, all he could see was, "Aidy without Jesus."

To give him the benefit of the doubt, my father must have thought that my sister's pregnancy was a safe topic for conversation. For me, my sister's pregnancy was not a safe topic, and I knew that if we talked about it, I would not be able to keep my mouth shut about the glaring hypocrisy surrounding my sister's impending triplets! My sister and I had both been taught that life begins at conception; we had both been taught that any and all interference with and manipulation of the process of procreation was a mortal sin; I was the only person in my family who no longer held and professed these beliefs. But, hey, when the needs change, the rules change, right? Having been unable to conceive naturally, my sister and her husband had used in vitro fertilization to get pregnant. Through the IVF process, more than two dozen of her eggs were fertilized, a total of ten were implanted (during multiple tries), seven didn't survive implantation, and the rest were frozen. And now, I was at lunch with my father, who couldn't keep from mooning and swooning over the miracle of my sister's pregnancy.

I sat across from him, silently pushing food around my plate and praying that the waitress would interrupt him with an offer of dessert, until I just couldn't take it anymore. I challenged him, "Dad, how many grandchildren do you have?" thinking that, surely, he would say five. He responded, "I have two grandchildren," and then corrected himself by saying, "Well, I also have three on the way." I said, "No, Dad, you have about two dozen grandchildren, but seven of them are dead!" Horrified, he demanded, "What are you talking about? How can you say that?" I said, "You are the one who defines life as beginning when the sperm fertilizes the egg, therefore, it is according to your definition that seven of your grandchildren are dead. I am not the one who says it; you are the one who says they are dead!"

To this, the man who has strongly hinted that the murder of doctors who perform abortions is God's justice, has protested in front of abortion clinics to block patients from entering, and has admitted to casting every single one of his votes in every single election based solely on the issue of abortion, responded, "Well, Aidy, you know, those fertilized eggs are really more the potential for life." I sardonically asked, "Well, doesn't that crack the door for abortion?" After a pause, he answered, "Well, I guess I'm going to have to think about that." I doubt he ever did; as deep of a thinker as he was, his need, born out of his profound brokenness, to be right, to make others wrong, and, in the process, to feel better than everyone else (even his own daughter) was deeper still. This conversation and the circumstances of my sister's pregnancy were two of the final straws that broke my relationship with my family. To be relentlessly rejected, judged, and looked down upon in the name of beliefs that weren't even actually believed after all, was, in the end, just too much for me to take.

One of my favorite quotes from the late Maya Angelou, made famous by Oprah Winfrey, is, "When someone shows you who they are, believe them the first time." It took me a long, long time to begin to master this practice in my relationships. Likely because I began my life dependent on people who abused and neglected me, I developed a habit of tolerating and accommodating people who didn't treat me well. When I couldn't leave, or choose not to leave, the multiple abusive relationships I have been in, it was easier to tolerate them when I told myself things like, "it isn't that bad; there are good times," or "he/she isn't really a bad person; nobody's perfect," or "I know he/she really loves me; he/she just has trouble expressing it." Somehow, I managed to make myself believe these lies even when my abusers were regularly presenting the contradictory truth through their words and actions. It is easier to accommodate and make excuses for an abuser than it is to leave an abuser, especially when the abuser is a parent. It has taken much more courage and strength for me to stand up for myself, declare the truth, and demand the better that I deserve. The degree to which I learned this maladaptive habit during my formative years was the same degree to which I automatically, before I treated it, repeated it in my adult relationships and with my own children. *If you don't treat, you will repeat!*

Having suffered a significant amount of abuse in my childhood, I developed a firmly established habit of clinging to false perceptions of, and making excuses for, the abusive people in my life. Unfortunately, I don't have a great track record of believing people the first time, or even the fifth, or sixteenth time, when they show me who they really are, but I am getting quicker at it, much quicker. For the longest time, I would berate myself for getting burned by the same people (friends, family, and my husband) in the same way over and over again. I would figuratively pound my forehead with my fist saying, "stupid, stupid, stupid!" I used to try and laugh it off by calling myself a "slow learner." As I made progress in reducing my self-criticism and increasing my self-praise, I put a positive twist on my statement by adding, ". . . but at least I'm not a 'no learner!'"

For me, the key to being able to believe someone when they first show themselves to be abusive has been to have a clear understanding of what constitutes abuse—physical, psychological, emotional, sexual, and spiritual. Physical abuse seems like it should be clear and easy to recognize, and yet, when I first left the cult, I wavered in calling it out and was quick to provide excuses for it. I was conditioned by my upbringing to accept my father's beatings as spankings; I unquestioningly accepted that it was his right to spank me because I was his child, and the Bible gave him that authority as my father. It took an outside observer, a therapist, to begin to correct my understanding of what constitutes physical abuse.

I had a friend who was in a "mildly" abusive relationship (is there such a thing?); her boyfriend would grip her arms tightly when he was frustrated with her. In a session one day with her therapist, she was making excuses for her boyfriend, saying, "It's not that bad. He's not abusive; it's not like he hits me!" Her therapist took the pen he was using to write his notes and threw it at her. She flinched and was taken aback. He said, "That's abuse! *Any time* and *every time* someone crosses your physical boundaries in *any way* without your invitation and permission, *it is abuse!*"

When my first daughter was just a toddler, the subject of spanking came up in a conversation with my father. I told him, in no uncertain terms, that I would not be using spanking as a form of discipline with my children. He said, "There is no way you can raise well-mannered and obedient children without spanking them!" To this, of course, I responded, "Oh yeah? Watch me!" I was just as determined not to violate my children's physical beings with the practice of spanking as I was determined not to violate their spiritual beings with the teaching of original sin. I was also committed to raising well-mannered and obedient children, so I learned about and practiced the methods of logical consequences, time-outs, and "1, 2, 3, magic"; I even created a new parenting tool for myself that I called "creative solutions."

In the end, I had the last laugh, because I was successful in raising two very well-mannered and obedient daughters who became confident, independent, self-sufficient, successful women with strong personal boundaries, not *in spite of* not being spanked or taught that they were sinful, but *because of* not being spanked or taught that they were sinful. As they grew, I became more and more convinced that I had made the right decision not to spank them. Just like every other parent, I was terrified of my children falling victim to a sexual predator. I came to realize that had I spanked my children, I would have conditioned them to accept the physical violation of their bodies, and that would have made them vulnerable to accepting the sexual violation of their bodies from such predators.

By the time I became a mother in my mid-twenties, I had corrected my understanding of what constitutes physical abuse, but my understanding of what constituted other forms of abuse did not become clear for many, many more years. I was a very slow learner in this area, but at least I wasn't a "no learner"! For a long time, I repeated the mistake of making allowances and excuses for the abusive people in my life; I stuck my head in the sand and clung to the illusions of who I wanted and needed my parents, my sister, and my husband to be, instead of believing them when they repeatedly and consistently showed me who they really were.

In our culture, we are universally taught that mothers and fathers love their children, as if shared DNA and the act of procreation somehow compel love and loving behavior. The reality is that not all mothers and fathers love their children, and not all declarations of love translate into loving behavior. Our culture also generally assumes that people get married because they love each other. The reality is that not everyone who stands up at the altar or walks down the aisle does so because of love. Unfortunately, because I believed these flawed messages for so long, I misplaced my love, loyalty, and devotion accordingly; it took me a long, long time to realize that my love, loyalty, and devotion were misplaced, and were being mistreated.

I have a history of being prematurely trusting in my relationships— romantic and familial. If someone were to tell me, "I deposited the money into your account," the first thing I would do is to check my account balance to see that the money was actually there. I wouldn't blindly trust that the money was there, and then go shopping without knowing for sure. Yet, in love and with family, I have often failed to check to see if the love is actually there before I based my behavior on it. When I have heard "I love you" from a lover or a family member, it has triggered a flood of emotions which have caused me to make assumptions on which I have predicated my loyalty and devotion, before I had sufficient supporting evidence for that love or those assumptions. In our culture, we have elevated the statement and the emotions of love to an almost mystical status. Unfortunately, in my blanket acceptance of this social norm, I had ignored the truth, which is that the statement is hollow and the emotions are useless unless they are accompanied and supported by loving actions.

Ironically, my parents, my sister, and my husband regularly said "I love you" to me; for decades, I thought that this meant that they actually did love me—even in the face of mounting evidence to the contrary. I have no idea what they actually meant when they said "I love you," but I eventually figured out that they didn't mean what I thought "I love you" meant, and more importantly, they didn't mean what I needed "I love you" to mean. In discussions about love, I used to joke that love is a four-letter word—not a swear word, but rather a word comprised of four letters that is not difficult to pronounce. It is not "supercalifragilisticexpialidocious." Just about anyone can pronounce it—nice people *and* mean people, generous people *and* selfish people, healthy people *and* dysfunctional people, loving people *and* abusive people, etc.

Of all of the excuses I hear people make for someone who is treating them poorly or abusing them, the two I find to be the most exasperating are, "I know he or she means well" and, "I know that he or she loves me." I was the facilitator for my local Straight Spouse Network support group for two and a half years, and I have heard many straight spouses make these statements about their gay or transgendered spouses, especially in the beginning when they are first trying to process the fact that their spouse is not who they thought they were.

My response to the excuse that "he or she means well" is, "Yeah, and Hitler meant well also! What's your point?" My response to the excuse, "I know that he or she loves me" is, "Yeah, and Ike loved Tina! What's your point?" My statements always get shocked looks, and then laughter, until I explain that I am serious. The truth is that Hitler did mean well; he actually did think that he was doing the right thing for Germany! The truth is that Ike Turner repeatedly told Tina Turner that he loved her (all the while beating her black-and-blue), and he believed that he loved her! Neither of these statements nor the sentiments behind them, no matter how sincerely felt or expressed, are worth anything without the reality to back them up!

During our teen years, my sister and I were polar opposites. After my one brief year of rebellion, I was completely compliant with everything my parents and the cult demanded of me. In contrast, my sister was completely rebellious in every way that a teenage girl could be. Needless to say, we had nothing in common; we fought a lot and we weren't friends. In fact, I'm embarrassed to admit it, but being as obnoxiously pious and self-righteous as I was at the time, I was viciously, relentlessly, and arrogantly judgmental and critical of her. By the time we both graduated from college, we had both mellowed.

As it turned out, I was on my way away from religion and she was on her way toward religion; for several years, we met in the middle and enjoyed a very close friendship. Unfortunately, by the end of my twenties, we had again become polar opposites on the opposite ends of the spectrum. She became the obnoxious, self-righteous Christian that I had been, and returned every bit of judgment that I had so generously given to her a decade earlier. I was well on my way to becoming the complete mess that I was for the decade of my thirties, so she had no end of opportunities to judge me! With vicious comments and hurtful actions like knives, she cut me so many times, and so deeply. Even though our close friendship was short-lived, I clung to it, and to my experience of her during our friendship, desperately not wanting to believe the new (or perhaps true) person she was showing herself to be.

I was complaining about my sister's most recent cruelty to a girlfriend one day, and my girlfriend asked me, "Would you be friends with her if she weren't your sister? If she were just a neighbor, would you be friends with her?" I said, "Oh, hell no! We have nothing in common and she vexes me something awful! But she's my sister, so, well y'know, she's family, and family is family, right?" My girlfriend just looked at me; it took many years for her observation to fully impact me and change the way I related to my family . . . but it was the beginning.

The "blood is thicker than water" creed is very strong in our culture; it is often seen as a character flaw or a sign of psychological disturbance if you draw firm boundaries with or break from your family. I have not seen or spoken to my sister or my parents in over a decade. The reactions I get when I mention this range from polite confusion and pity to blatant suspicion and hostile rejection. It took me a very long time to go against our society's "cult of family" propaganda, but eventually, as hard as I tried, I just couldn't find any logical justification for granting someone my love, loyalty, respect, and devotion, and a place in my life, based solely on shared DNA. My love, loyalty, respect, and devotion have great worth, and I no longer give them to, or make a place in my life for, anyone, no matter who they are, who has demonstrated a clear unworthiness. Today, I no longer give these things before someone has clearly and consistently demonstrated worthiness.

I never had any intention of breaking with my family. It was a last resort which I did not anticipate; not once did I ever think to myself, "One more fuck-up on their part and I'm done with them!" I tried first, and many times, to explain to my family how and why their behavior was unacceptable and hurtful to me; each time, I defined my boundaries clearly and firmly, and each time, they disregarded me and trampled all over my boundaries. Beginning with the letter I wrote to my mother when I was pregnant with my first daughter, I spent more than a decade confronting my parents and holding them accountable for how they had, and were still, abusing me. Each time, I drew my boundaries tighter and tighter and held them more and more at arms' length. Like a medieval lord, I pulled up the drawbridge, filled the moat with alligators, sealed every opening, fortified every weak spot, and placed sentries at every post. Still, by the end of each time I spent with them, they had broken through all my defenses; pillaged, looted, and damn near burned everything to the ground.

I used to devote multiple therapy sessions to readying myself before one of their visits, but they would always come at me from some new, unanticipated angle; no matter how carefully I had prepared for spending time with them, I would always end up a quivering mess by the end of it. In my final conversation with them, I said, amongst other things, "I am no match for your madness!" In the end, I had to tap out for my own sanity and to save myself for my daughters, who needed and deserved me.

Make no mistake, it was not easy, and I suffered greatly when I broke with my family and voluntarily orphaned myself; it took every ounce of strength I had and reserves of strength I didn't know I had! The tipping point came when I realized that their insidious dysfunction and continued abuse were sapping me of the precious few resources I had to give my daughters. For me to find the strength and wisdom necessary to try and be the mother that my daughters needed and deserved took nothing less than a miracle, because I had no point of reference for or experience with good parenting! One of the few kind things my husband ever did for me was to regularly compliment me on my parenting skills. I used to say to him, "I hope you know that anything I ever do right with our daughters is sheer dumb luck, because I am pulling it all clear out of my ass!"

Whenever I interacted with my family, I suffered much more than I benefitted. In the aftermath of their visits, it took weeks and sometimes months for me to build myself back up. While I was recovering, my daughters suffered. I remember berating myself to my therapist, after a particularly difficult Christmas with my parents and my sister, for not having been stronger. My therapist exclaimed, "Seriously, Aidy, how many hits do you think you should be able to take? Even the strongest person is going to go down after enough hits!"

In the years since I broke with my mother, my father, and my sister, I have missed them terribly, but I have come to realize that what I miss is something they never were. I ached for a mother, a father, and a sister that I never actually had. I longed for a mother who nurtured me physically, emotionally, and spiritually. I longed for a father who protected me and taught me that I was of great value; worth fighting for. I longed for parents who had wisdom to guide me with. I longed for a sister who was a friend, and who was for me, not against me. I longed for a family that was deserving of a "blood is thicker than water" level of devotion and loyalty.

I don't think I will ever fully get over losing my family, but I have learned to survive and, furthermore, to thrive without them in my life. In a conversation with my younger daughter, I once compared it to losing a hand in an accident. I told her, "If I lost my hand, I would always miss it and I would always wish I had it back, but I would get to a place where I was just fine without it." I have learned to create a family for myself and for my daughters from the people in my life who have clearly and consistently demonstrated worthiness through their unwavering, unconditional, non-judgmental love and support. My family is no longer predicated on shared DNA; today, it is built on something so much stronger and so much more real!

In hindsight, it was so very important for me to break with my family for the sake of my daughters. Breaking with my family contributed greatly to my ability not to repeat the abuse and dysfunction of my childhood. I came to understand that if I did not declare my abusers to be accountable for the ways that they had hurt me, I was, by default, condoning and accepting their behavior. I would have been saying that what they did to me was okay; if it was okay for them to do what they did to me, then, by logic, it would have been okay for me to do the same thing to someone else, including my own daughters.

For me, it was a critical component to the successful and effective recovery from the abuse that I suffered to find the strength to turn around, confront my abusers, and say, "What you did to me was not okay! I deserved better and you should not have done that to me!" It would not have been enough to meekly say, "You hurt me; why did you hurt me?" I needed to declare that the abuse was not okay, and to declare that I deserved not to be abused. The same goes for holding accountable the people who were responsible for keeping me safe (for example, my father should have protected me from my mother's neglect when I was a newborn). In the case of childhood abuse, oftentimes, one or both parents turn a blind eye, make excuses for an abuser, or enable the abuse; this parent is just as accountable for the abuse. *The number one responsibility of every parent is to keep their child safe, physically, emotionally, psychologically, sexually, and spiritually; any and every parent who fails to do this, whether actively or passively, is accountable for that failure!*

When my father's mother died, his sister went to the gravesite, stomped on her grave, and screamed at her headstone. My father told me, with surprise in his voice, "Boy, she's really mad at our mother!" I said, "Yeah, and you should be, too!" I remember a time in my adolescence when my father visited his mother by himself with the intention of confronting her for the horrific things that she and his father had done to him in his childhood. I have no idea how that visit actually transpired; what I do know is that he continued to make excuses for her. This leads me to believe that he was not successful in effectively standing up for himself and declaring her to be accountable for what she had done to him. Subsequently, in my adulthood, my father expected me to extend him the same kind of leniency and latitude for his abusive behavior that he had extended to his mother for her abusive behavior. *If you don't treat, you will repeat!*

In my quest to be a better parent to my daughters than my parents were to me, I spent an endless amount of time contemplating what makes a good parent. I came to the conclusion that in the broadest definition, a good parent is one who gets their child to a better starting line for adulthood than they were taken to; according to this definition, my parents actually were good parents. They did get me to a better starting line than they were taken to; the problem was that their starting line was so abysmal that mine was still pretty crappy, and was only better by comparison. I would liken my parents' success at quality parenting to what my success would be, as a redhead, if I were to spend a day at the beach with no sunscreen trying to get a tan. There is no way in Hell that I would have a tan at the end of the day; I would undoubtedly have a blistering sunburn! Nonetheless, it could be said, "Well, she did the best she could! She doesn't have a tan, but she's not nearly as white as she was when she started out."

In an effort to promote accountability in my own parenting, I encouraged my daughters to challenge me and call me out when they felt I had wronged them (I did require that they do it respectfully). I realized early in my parenting journey that my daughters did not need me to be perfect. They did not need me never to make a mistake; they just needed me to own it when I did make a mistake. Children are by nature very long-suffering and extremely quick to forgive, especially with their parents. It is imperative that parents respect this and not abuse or take advantage of it! Having reached the end of my capacity to forgive my own parents for wronging me, I knew that my daughters had a great capacity to forgive me, but it wasn't limitless. I have always considered their forgiveness to be a great gift, one that I treasure and respect!

When my older daughter entered junior high school, her relationship with her father began to crumble. Looking back, I realize that as she was growing in her ability to see through his charade, he panicked. He turned on her with cruel criticism and overbearing strictness in a desperate attempt to distract her from figuring out the truth (which was what he had been doing to me for years for the same reason). This was so painful for her! In the beginning, I ran interference, making excuses to her for his behavior and coaching him on how to relate to her. I told her things like, "You have to understand the difficult relationship he has with his parents; he was never loved or accepted so he has difficulty loving and accepting," and,

"He's your father and you know he loves you." Sound familiar? *If you don't treat, you will repeat!*

After several months of me making excuses for her father, my daughter called me on it. She said, "Mom, you are making excuses for how mean he is being to me! You are asking me just to take it! You are totally invalidating my feelings and dismissing how he is hurting me! He's being mean, and I shouldn't have to take it, even if he is my father!" I was *so* humbled; I immediately apologized to her and promised not to do it again! *It is such a blessing when you give birth to children who refuse to cooperate with your dysfunction! If you can find the strength and courage to rise to the challenge they present you with, you can experience unique and powerful personal growth!* I promptly went to her father and told him that I would no longer do damage control for him, and that from there on out, he would be solely responsible for his own relationship with his daughters. Unfortunately, since he never stood up for himself and never held his own parents accountable for how they had abused and rejected him, he continued to treat his daughters the same way he had been treated by his parents, and his relationship with his daughters deteriorated accordingly.

I was an equally slow learner in my relationship with my abusive husband—I stayed married to him for a few months longer than two decades—but in the end, I was not a "no learner." In retrospect, the truth seems glaringly obvious! It seems so obvious that I feel painfully embarrassed, at times, for not realizing that he was gay, or at the very least, for failing to see the great disparity between the kind of man he was and the kind of man I wanted (and deserved) to be with.

Do you remember the equation we all learned in our freshman algebra class? "If $a = b$ and $b = c$, then $a = c$." Looking back, I realize that I unconsciously applied this same logic to my relationship, and never thought to check my math. With no relationship experience under my belt, I had only a fairy tale vision of a boyfriend in my head. When my ex-husband was my boyfriend, I, carte blanche, applied this vision to him and ignored the fact that he in no way matched my vision. I said to myself, "If boyfriends are kind, generous, loving, attentive, supportive, passionate, adoring, romantic, etc. and he is my boyfriend, then he must be kind, generous, loving, attentive, supportive, passionate, adoring, romantic, etc." If you had asked me, when I was dating my ex-husband, why I was in love with him, I would not have given you an intelligent answer. I was the stereotypical Disney princess—I would have stared off into the distance with my chin resting in the palm of my hand and said, in a dreamy voice, "I don't know, *sigh*, I just love him!"

By the time we had reached our tenth wedding anniversary, I knew that our marriage would never work, although I didn't yet know why. I was beginning to realize that I was being psychologically, emotionally, and sexually abused and neglected, but I was not yet strong enough to demand better for myself. My daughters were seven and three, and at that time, I thought my husband and I parented well together. I thought that it was in my daughters' best interests for me to suffer through my bad marriage relationship in exchange for keeping their family intact. I now know that you cannot offer your children quality mothering when you are being torn down by their father; a good father does not tear down the mother of his children, and a healthy broken family is better than a sick intact family. When I filed for divorce, I apologized to my daughters for breaking up their family. My older daughter said, "Mom, we're still a family! It's just like cutting a bad spot out of an apple; it's still an apple!" I was saddened to hear how she perceived her father, but impressed by the strength and flexibility of her concept of family.

In my quest to become a faster learner about people, I closely studied the behavior of my family members, my husband, and other people in my life. I came to the idea that there are two general categories of people: generally nice people, or, as I call them, GNPs, and intrinsically selfish people, or, as I call them, ISPs. GNPs are generally kind, generous, open, and trusting. They practice self-reflection, can take responsibility for their actions, choices, and decisions, find joy in making other people happy, back their words with actions, and acknowledge all humans, *including themselves*, as sacred and worthy of respect.

GNPs are not ridiculously nice people (RNPs); they are not sickly-sweet, never-angry-or-sad people with perpetual smiles plastered on their faces, who are so nice they would give you the shirt off their backs. A classic trait of an RNP is that they consider all humans to be sacred and worthy of respect, *except themselves*. RNPs, although they may seem wonderful at first, can be seriously lacking in boundaries and pretty dysfunctional.

GNPs are "real" people; they are perfectly capable of being mean and selfish on occasion, but that is not who they are at their core.

Opposite to GNPs are ISPs, who are mean, selfish, stingy, and suspicious of others. They are lacking in empathy and self-reflection, find no joy in making others happy, and rarely take responsibility for their actions, choices, and decisions. Rarely do their actions match up with their words, they have a pervasive disregard for the sacred humanity of others, and they see and use others as means to their own selfish ends. ISPs can be mistaken for GNPs; they are capable of appearing nice, especially when others are looking, but that is not who they are at their core. If you look closely, more often than not, you will find that their moments of niceness are primarily self-serving and for show.

The trusting and open nature of GNPs can be their greatest stumbling block because they are quick to give others, deserving or not, the benefit of the doubt. It is a classic GNP mistake to assume that everyone who they come into contact with in their lives is also a GNP and operates with the same general niceness. Unfortunately, GNPs are easy prey for ISPs, because they can be very slow to believe an ISP when the ISP shows who they really are. Most slow learners are GNPs. ISPs are generally "no learners"; the lack of self-reflection inherent in ISPs retards learning and growth.

Several months before I filed for divorce, my younger daughter, who was in seventh grade, came to me with a vocabulary word that she needed help defining. Right in front of her father, she asked me, "Mom, what does 'conscientious' mean?" I said, "It means caring how your actions impact other people. For example, if I am hungry and I open the refrigerator and see your cupcake there, I will want to eat it, but I know that if I eat it, you will be sad and angry, so I don't. Actually, it means more than just caring how your actions impact other people; it means choosing *not* to do something when you know that it will hurt someone else, *even if* it will benefit you." GNPs are regularly conscientious; ISPs will only give the appearance of being conscientious when others are looking.

In the final year of my marriage, my eyes were opened to just how much of an ISP my husband really was, and it was a brutal realization! At this point, I had been clinically depressed and suicidal, to one degree or another, and on an antidepressant for about five years. When I first came to my husband, who was a psychiatrist, and told him that I was feeling suicidal and had a plan to kill myself, he brought home some antidepressant medication samples and gave me the name of another psychiatrist to see for a prescription. I asked him, "What is another psychiatrist going to do for me that you can't?" He said, "They will listen to you." At the time, I laughed and said, "Well, that about sums up our relationship!" I remained unaware of how complete his callousness toward my basic humanity was until years later.

Right before filing for divorce, in a last-ditch attempt to help my husband accept himself and to salvage our family, I asked him to join me in a therapy session. Over the course of the session, it came up how indifferent he had been when I disclosed that I was suicidal. He looked upset about it in a way that he never had before; I was puzzled because, as many times as I had gotten angry at him for this in private, he had never been significantly moved.

Several days later, it hit me like a ton of bricks! He was not upset over the possibility of me killing myself or remorseful for his apathy about it; he was upset because he was being exposed in front of another therapist as being a therapist who did next to nothing when he knew that his wife was suicidal! Had I been his patient, by law, he would have had to take action to help me, more than just to give me some medication samples and the name and number of another psychiatrist who would listen. Unfortunately, I was not his patient; I was only his wife and the mother of his children!

When I realized that what he really cared about was not me, but rather his own embarrassment and the possible professional ramifications, I was stunned! Right in the middle of angrily confronting him about this realization, I burst into hysterical laughter. He looked at me in amazement, sure that I had completely cracked and finally lost my mind. Through my laughter, I said, "I am telling a selfish man that he is selfish! I am telling a man with no moral fiber that he has no morals! By definition, you don't care! You have no conscience to be pricked; you have no moral standard that you care about falling short of! What a waste of my breath!"

I had a roommate in college who studied music. As a part of her course, she had to "learn" a lot of foreign languages in order to be able to sing songs in those languages. I put the word "learn" in quotes because she didn't have to actually learn all the languages she wanted to sing in; she only had to learn the correct pronunciation of the words she wanted to sing. For example, in order to master singing an Italian opera, she had to learn how Italian words are pronounced, but she didn't need to learn anything more than just pronunciation. I found this to be so curious; how strange to be able to pronounce words correctly and convincingly without having any knowledge of their meaning! Years later, I drew a correlation between her studies and why it had always taken me so long to believe it the first time someone showed me who they really were.

It dawned on me that ISPs are often very good at pronouncing English (or whatever language they speak) without understanding or even meaning what they are saying. An ISP, who is only good at pronouncing English, will speak their words and execute their actions not to communicate the actual meaning of those words or carry out the intrinsic intention of their actions, but rather to facilitate the expression of their dysfunction and the fulfillment of their selfish needs; oftentimes, the words and actions themselves are irrelevant and randomly selected—they just say and do whatever they think will get the job done.

For many years in our marriage, my husband jerked me around, misleading and deceiving me with his words, which were so contrary to his actions. Every time I would reach the place where I was just about to make my peace with our relationship not working and move forward for myself, he would have an emotional epiphany and say that he "really did love me and really did want to make our marriage work!" I fell for it time and time again because I believed his words, and to be honest, also because for a long time, it seemed easier to fall back into my dysfunctional relationship with him than it was to forge ahead with new personal growth for myself. Conditioned as I was from childhood to make excuses and accommodations for people who abused me, I constantly gave him the benefit of the doubt. For so long, I closed my eyes to who he really was; I used to say to him, "You're a good man, you're just not good with me," as if the problem were with me and not with him.

The first time I rejected his plea for us to try again, I said, "It won't work. The reason why is no longer relevant; there's always a different reason but every time we end up at the same dead end. I don't want to try again because it won't work." Mind you, I came to this conclusion even before I knew he was gay (which he knew all along), which unequivocally ruled out any possibility of our relationship ever working despite effort or desire. He was shocked and angry that his tried and true method of reeling me back in and keeping me in the service of his selfish needs wasn't working. In an attempt to undermine the truth of my statement that our relationship had never worked and could not ever work, he retorted, "Well, that's your opinion!" I calmly replied, "No, that is not my opinion; that is my *experience*." Strangely, he continued say "I love you" to me even after we were divorced. My automated reply became, "Saying it doesn't make it so; you have to do it!" To this day, he has never been able to comprehend my reply, further substantiating my claim that he, like so many ISPs, is good at pronouncing English but does not actually understand it.

If I had picked parents with more love, guidance, and wisdom to offer me, and subsequently a husband with more honesty, integrity, and authenticity, I would not have been such a slow learner in so many areas of my life, and it wouldn't have taken me so many years to figure so many things out. One of the most healing and beautiful experiences in my life has been to see how much more quickly my daughters have been able to make progress in their lives than I was able to; they have been able to take what I have learned and build on it. They are so much further along in their personal growth than I was at their ages. I am thrilled to see how much better my daughters are at not being slow learners! I feel no shame for being as much of a slow learner as I have been as a result of the life experiences that I picked for my adventure; I do, on the other hand, take great pride in not being a "no learner"! There is no shame in being a slow learner, *no matter how slow you are*, as long as you are not a "no learner"!

CHAPTER NINE

I Am Hurt

I was once again sitting on Felipe's porch alternately sucking down cigarettes and Caramel Macchiato, but tonight I was commanding the conversation, leaving no space for speculation about reptilian shapeshifters. Although I was not yet fully aware of it, the battle I had been waging for the salvation of my authentic self and my human form had begun to turn, ever so slightly, in my favor—and I was feistier because of it.

"Felipe, I'm telling you, I know he's gay!" Although Felipe knew my husband and had hinted that he wondered about it, as a gay man, he was not impressed by a straight woman flippantly labeling someone as gay who had not labeled themselves as gay; he was in agreement with the unspoken rule that only a gay person has the authority to say whether or not they are gay. His eyes were skeptical and critical as he dragged on his cigarette. Challenging my declaration, he asked, "Well, I don't know but tell me this, have you ever noticed him checking out other men?" Raising my voice, I shot back, "Felipe, I've seen him check out so many men so many times that I can tell you his 'type'!" Stumped but not convinced, Felipe said, "Hmmm . . . well, that's not good, but it doesn't prove anything."

Several nights later, much to Felipe's discomfort, I continued the conversation. "Felipe, the other day I remembered something else and after I tell you this, I rest my case! A couple of years ago, my husband and I were taking a bath together in our soaking tub. Never mind the fact that we were naked together in the tub for over an hour and he didn't even touch so much as my big toe, much less my big tits!" Seeing the look of distaste on Felipe's face at the mention of touching tits, I said, "Yeah, I know, you're not into tits! But that's my point!" Not impressed, Felipe asked, "That's your point?" Forcefully exhaling cigarette smoke and waving it away with my hand, I continued,

> *No, that's not my point! There's more! While we were naked in the tub for over an hour with him not touching me, I said to him, "I didn't grow up with brothers, so I didn't run around naked or take baths with little boys in my childhood the way some kids do, and so the naked male body sometimes still looks funny to me. Don't get me wrong, I love your cock and balls but sometimes they just strike me as odd!" Then I asked him, "What do you think of when you look at my pussy?" He said (and get this!), "When I look at your vagina (he would never say 'pussy'), I just see an undeveloped phallus."*

Felipe took a deep breath, preparing to offer a counter-perspective on the story I had just shared, then exhaled dramatically, dropping his shoulders and throwing up his hands, as he conceded, "Aidy, I got nothing! That's just weird!" Laughing, I responded, "Yeah, I know, right?" Then, Felipe's face began to tighten and twist as tears sprang to his eyes, and his whole body began to shake with sobs. Alarmed, I reached out, placed my hand on his knee, and practically yelled at him, "Oh my God, Felipe, what's wrong? What's wrong?" When his sobs subsided, he said, "Aidy, he was telling you that there's something wrong with you, and there's nothing wrong with you!"

When I was about six years old, I had a sleepover with a friend from school. When my parents came to pick me up the next morning, my little suitcase was bursting with stuffed animals which my friend had given me to keep. Before we left, to my extreme horror, my parents made me give them all back! In response to my vehement protest, they let me pick one to take home. I got in the car absolutely indignant and furious with them; my friend *said* I could have *all* of them! I sulked in the back seat of the car all the way home. When we got home, I ran to my room, yelled, "When I grow up, I'm going to have a boyfriend who will give me all the stuffed animals I want!" slammed my bedroom door, and threw myself on my bed crying (I was a passionate child). As an adult, I find my declaration to be curious and hilarious! I don't know why, at age six, I designated a boyfriend as my future source of satisfaction and happiness (and stuffed animals); perhaps it was because I was already keenly aware of how lacking my parents were and I already knew they could not be relied on for what I needed and wanted. Who knows?

All I know is that as far back as I can remember, I have wanted a boyfriend. But, as you know, I was born a redhead. From grade school through high school, I was neither the cute blonde nor the beautiful brunette, both of whom registered with the boys; I was the redhead (one of only four percent of the total US population) for whom the boys had no category. To compound the problem, I had a mother who did nothing to help me with my physical appearance. She was a hippie, and as such, she rejected just about all personal hygiene and grooming for herself and her daughters. She didn't shave her legs or her armpits, she rarely cut her hair or took us to get our hair cut, and she bathed us only once a week. That last one proved to be very problematic when I entered junior high; as you might expect of kids that age, my classmates were mercilessly cruel about my very greasy, five-day-old hair! I very quickly learned to shower and wash my hair more frequently; the rest of my personal care—hairstyle, makeup, and clothes—took me a lot longer to learn, not just because my mother had no guidance to offer me, but also because most of the mainstream color palette offered in clothing and makeup, back then and even now, doesn't suit redheads.

As I was self-taught, my success in putting myself together was very hit-and-miss, and I didn't fully master it until I was about halfway through college. Just like the quintessential ugly duckling, in my youth and adolescence, I was teased, overlooked, and rejected by boys my age. Per the mandates of the cult teachings, my parents forbade me to date or have a boyfriend in high school because I wasn't old enough to be ready to move toward marriage. As it turned out, it was never an issue because I was never asked out, not even once, nor ever given a second look from a boy; I was invisible to boys all the way through high school. It didn't help that my graduating class at the conservative Baptist high school my parents sent me to had a grand total of nineteen students, only five of whom were boys!

Thankfully, just like the ugly duckling, once I came into my own as an adult, I began to turn heads easily. By the time I entered college, I had no trouble attracting men; unfortunately, I only ever liked the men who weren't interested in me. I was so used to getting no response from any guy I ever liked that I didn't know how to respond to a guy who did express interest in me. Perhaps I subconsciously thought, "You like me? Well, that makes absolutely no sense; there must be something wrong with you." To complicate matters, no one in the campus branch of the cult was supposed to be dating, so any and all attractions were clandestine and stymied.

By the time I met the closeted gay man who became my husband, I was so thoroughly convinced of my unattractiveness and undesirability and so sure that I would never have a boyfriend, much less a husband, that I was flat out *stunned* when he showed interest in me. I thought a miracle had occurred; not only did a guy who I liked like me back, but he was also one of the best looking and most desirable guys in the pool of guys available to date in the cult at that time! Little did I know that his interest in me was not for the reasons I thought, and not for the reasons he led me to believe. As it turned out, marrying him was the culmination of years of repeated experience with unrequited love. As a straight woman, you can't get love much more unrequited than by trying to have an emotionally and physically intimate relationship with a gay man. For years, I gave him my love generously and lavishly, and for all those same years, he responded to my love with revulsion, rejection, and disdain. The pain of this unrequited love was unbelievable and unbearable and yet, time after time for so long, I continued to lay my love at his feet; in the ways of love, as in so many other areas of my life, I was a slow learner, no doubt.

After nearly two decades of suffering under the unrequited love of my closeted gay husband, I made a quantum leap forward in my slow learning in the ways of love. This leap was the result of a profound dream which, as it turned out, was so much more than the average dream. At this time in my life, I was deeply and chronically depressed, and as a result, I slept a lot. On this day, I had dropped my daughters off at school, and having returned home with no urgent business to attend to and feeling unable to face the day, I crawled back into bed. I immediately fell into a deep sleep and had the most vivid, intense, powerful, and cathartic dream of my life.

As the dream began, I was stretched out on my stomach with my hands firmly covering my face and my body pulled tightly into itself, in anticipation of something unpleasant. I was not lying on anything—this whole dream took place far out among the stars between the planets—but there was a solidness beneath me. I had a dull, nebulous feeling of dread; I knew that something was coming. It was something that I instinctively knew would be uncomfortable, but I also knew it was necessary and inevitable.

A massive paw, with long, thick, dull claws, longer and thicker than my fingers, enclosed my right shoulder and gently rolled me over. I did not want to roll over, but it was immaterial. With my body holding tightly onto itself, I was rolled over stiffly and settled onto my back with a soft rocking thud. My hands were still rigidly covering my face, trying to avoid what was coming. My eyes under my hands were tightly squeezed shut, and all the muscles in my face were tense. I was not afraid, but I was not looking forward to what was coming, although I did not know what it was. The massive clawed paws gently and authoritatively pried my hands from my face and pinned me down at the wrists with the energy of a loving parent resolved to do something for a child's own good.

I opened my eyes and saw, above me, the largest bear I have ever seen. He had the body size and color of an Alaskan brown bear, with the face and snout of a polar bear. The bear leaned his face close to mine and began to lick inside my mouth. As he licked, he began to draw something out of me, which he took into himself. I could feel something being pulled out of me, beginning at my throat and then coming from deeper and deeper inside my body, until finally, it was being pulled from near the very bottom of my spine. Whatever it was, it was being pulled out of me in one continuous, heavy thread, like a thick rope, and the bear was taking it into himself.

It wasn't until the tail end of the "rope" had reached my mouth and nearly exited my body that I became cognizant of what the bear was pulling out of me. The long, continuous, heavy thread was the sequence of relationships, spanning decades of my life, with men whom I had loved, but who did not love me in return. The thread was in reverse order, beginning with my husband and ending with the very first memory of an experience of unrequited love from junior high school. I felt all the memories of these experiences being pulled out of my body as if they had a physical form inside of me. I felt them physically vacate my body, and once they were out, I could feel the space that they had inhabited, now empty.

Once the bear took the last memory of these experiences from my body and into his, still pinning me down at the wrists, he lifted his head and bellowed. He bellowed so loudly that the entire firmament shook. He bellowed, *"I . . . am . . . hurt!"* I understood his meaning to be twofold— he was feeling my hurt (he was hurt by my hurt), and he had become the physical embodiment, the personification, of "hurt" (much like a poet might say, "I am sorrow"). The deafening bellow from the bear, combined with the power and shock of his statement, startled me awake. I was completely exhausted and felt as if I had gone through a very intensive therapy session. The rest of the day, I walked around in a daze, feeling physically depleted but also strangely peaceful.

This dream was a significant turning point in my quest for a healthy relationship; one which would bring me love, joy, peace, and strength, not pain. Although it would be several more years before I was divorced and free to seek a better relationship, the groundwork was being laid. Since I had this dream, I have not suffered under unrequited love. That is not to say that every man for whom I have felt my affection grow has loved me in return; it is to say that I have not since *suffered* under unrequited love.

In the times since that dream that I have encountered a man for whom I have felt my affection grow, but from whom I have not received affection in return, I have been able to walk away from him before the suffering could begin. I have learned to make the number one requirement for any man who I might think is The One that he also think that I am The One. Keeping this requirement firmly as my top priority, I am no longer enticed by any man who meets many or even all of my other requirements, but doesn't think I am The One. I now know that any man who might spark my interest but who does not think that I am The One is, by definition, *not* The One. Establishing this premise as the starting point for my pursuit of a new and better relationship prevented me from repeating the heartache of the unrequited love that I had suffered under in all my previous relationships!

Larry was the first man I dated after my divorce. He was a lawyer who was younger than me by five years, and only taller than me by a few inches (which didn't bother me unless I wanted to wear heels). He was straight and was over the moon for me, which was notable progress, but he also had a mean streak that was eerily similar to that of my ex-husband.

The first time he said something cruel to me, I brought it to his attention with all the appropriate, "I feel . . . when you . . . because" dialogue, and he was very apologetic and remorseful. About a month later, it happened again, and I brought it to his attention again; again, he was remorseful and apologetic. By this time in my life learning, I was very clear on what constitutes emotional and psychological abuse, so when it happened a third time, I broke up with him.

In the aftermath of this relationship, I was discouraged at first when I realized that I had been attracted to yet another man who ended up treating me unkindly and in such a familiar way. Then, I decided to look at the cup as half full; it took me twenty *years* to break up with the first man who mistreated me, but it took me only twenty *weeks* to break up with the next man who mistreated me. When I realized this, I thought, "Now that's a learning curve I can be proud of, and that's a learning curve I can work with!" I went from feeling discouraged to feeling very encouraged; I nearly broke my arm patting myself on the back in congratulations for my progress!

The other encouraging fact of this first post-divorce relationship was that I could break up with Larry without legal action, without tens of thousands of dollars in lawyer's fees, without the division of property, without allocation of child custody, etc.! All I had to do was sit him down and say, "This isn't working for me." It was *so* freeing when I realized that I never again had to stay in a relationship that was causing me pain! I came to the conclusion that, even though I still wanted a boyfriend and to be in a relationship just as much as I ever had, being single was definitely preferable to being in a bad relationship!

The lesson I took from dating Larry is that when someone mistreats, abuses, or neglects me in a relationship, whether it is a coworker, a friend, a family member, or a lover, they are implicitly asking me if I am okay with being mistreated, abused, or neglected. *I have learned to think very carefully about my answer!* It is not enough for me to answer them with my words; for my answer to have truth, I must answer them with my actions. Just as I need to believe someone when their actions show me who they are, I also need to show who I am and define what I want with my actions. It is an old, worn-out cliché, but it is true: actions speak louder than words! For decades, I told my husband that I would not tolerate his abuse of me, and yet, for decades, I did. Which was the truth? The truth was that I *would* tolerate his abuse, no matter how many times I emphatically stated it to the contrary, *because, in reality, I was tolerating his abuse.* My declaration that I would not tolerate his abuse *only became true when I actually stopped tolerating his abuse.*

Even though Larry was a marked improvement over my ex-husband, his treatment of me still did not meet my ideal for a loving, healthy relationship. When he was not capable of, or not willing to, change the way he was treating me, even after I had repeatedly brought it to his attention and told him verbally that I was not okay with how he was treating me, I had to make my statement with my actions. When he implicitly said with his actions, "This is the kind of relationship I am offering you, are you okay with it?" my response, emphasized loudly through actions which backed up my words, was "No!" Many times during my marriage, I asked myself, "Why does my husband treat me so badly when I love him so much?" What I should have been asking myself was, "Why do I love him when he treats me so badly?"

Back before I realized that the root problem in my marriage was the fact that I have girl parts and my husband preferred boy parts, I dragged him to several marriage counselors. After once spending a session articulating and expressing my needs, I remember coming to the realization that he would have to pretty much become a whole different person for me to get what I needed and wanted in our relationship (little did I know how true that was!). I also knew that I was tired of compromising and settling for less. I had tried for years to re-work myself so as not to need and want what he wasn't giving me, and it wasn't working—I was becoming more and more frustrated and depressed. At the end of the session, I expressed my epiphany to him. I said, "I don't have the right to ask you to be someone other than who you are—no one has that right—everyone should be honored for who they are just as they are, but I also do have the right to need and want someone other than who you are." Unfortunately, the road from where I made that statement to where I finally drew my line in the sand and refused to settle for less was long and painful.

The pain of going through a breakup or a divorce, and the awkwardness of adjusting to being single again, holds many people back from ending a relationship that no longer meets their needs. In our culture, we have a stigma attached to failed relationships, especially when that failure happens multiple times. We admire people who have been married for great lengths of time, as if somehow the value of the relationship is inherent in the number of years, instead of in the quality of the relationship. When I hear of someone celebrating their fiftieth wedding anniversary, I don't think, "Wow! That's impressive!" I think, "I wonder what their relationship has been like? Have they been loving to each other for those fifty years, or have they become stony roommates coexisting in a prison of their own making?"

When my parents reached their fiftieth wedding anniversary, they renewed their vows in their church. I wasn't there to witness it, but when I heard about it, I thought, "What vow did they renew? The vow to spend every waking moment and all their available energy destroying each other? Because that's the only vow I ever saw them keep!" Yet, they are admired for being a shining example of an enduring marriage; they even mentor engaged couples in the church! It's not that they never tried to have a better marriage, because they went to multiple counselors, individually and together, for years, but they were unable to fix the damage they had done and persisted in doing to each other. What they have been for me is a shining example of the disaster that happens when you are not willing to admit relationship failure, walk away, and try again for better. I do not consider my divorce to be a relationship failure; I consider it to be a relationship success! Without my divorce, I would have had no hope of a successful relationship!

There were many reasons why I stayed in my unhappy marriage for as long as I did, not the least of which was the shame of a failed marriage and a broken family. When a couple breaks up or gets divorce, we are conditioned to say, "Oh, how sad; what a shame!" When people offered me sympathy and condolences when they heard that I was getting divorced, I would cheerfully respond, "Oh no, it's a good thing, and something I should have done a long time ago!" Going through the divorce process was definitely stressful, and I appreciated others' sympathy for that, but I always corrected any pity for or sadness over the ending of my marriage relationship—for me, it was the beginning of a new beginning, which was long overdue!

Nowadays, when I hear about someone getting divorced, I think, "Good for them for having the courage to recognize a dead end when they have reached it, and for having the strength to begin again!" After all, the only way to get what you want, exactly what you want, in life—relationship, career, standard of living, etc.—is to have the strength, the courage, and the willingness to walk away from anything and everything that is not what you want, and to keep going until you arrive at exactly what it is that you want. It is not easy to be single, but being single is the only way to be available for the right person when he or she comes along. We worry so much about finding the man or woman of our dreams, when what we really should be worried about is wasting our precious days, weeks, months, and years with the man or woman of our nightmares!

After my divorce, to fill my time while my design business was slow, I volunteered at a thrift store. While volunteering there, I was blessed to interact with many retired senior women who also volunteered there. While sorting through the donations, we would chat. It was such a gift to hear the life stories and experiences of these women, who were much further along on life's journey than I was! I developed a particularly good rapport with one woman, who, over time, opened up to me and shared very personal stories about her loves and heartaches over her nearly eighty years. She had four children by three different men, none of whom she married. She confessed that she was always attracted to the "bad boys" who made her heart pound, but who couldn't be faithful as lovers or dependable as fathers.

While we were sorting through donations one day, I confided in her that, having recently broken up with my boyfriend, I was finding my newfound state of celibacy to be irksome. She surprised me by telling me, "Oh, I closed the door on that over thirty years ago. I realized that I was confusing sex with love, so I decided to give up sex." Knowing what a passionate and feisty woman she had been (and still was), I was a bit dumbfounded that she would make and stick to such an extreme resolution. I stuttered my surprise in a few awkward, half-started sentences, and she responded with, "Well, I clearly didn't know how to pick 'em, so I just gave up on all of it altogether!" I fell silent because I didn't want to risk saying something that would offend her, but inside I was very saddened and disheartened by what she shared. Her decision really made me think hard about my past experiences with relationships, and how I wanted to approach relationships going forward. On one hand, I totally understood her decision, and with a few more experiences of failed relationships, I could see myself possibly coming to the same place. On the other hand, I was horrified by her decision, and terrified by the thought that I could potentially make the same decision.

It is not easy to pick yourself up after a relationship has ended; what's even harder is to have the resiliency to get back in the saddle and attempt another relationship! After my first post-divorce relationship ended, I sat myself down and had a serious "come to Jesus" meeting with myself; I thought long and hard about whether I wanted to keep going in my pursuit of a healthy, loving relationship, knowing that even though my slow learner pace was improving, it may take some time and multiple tries before I found what I was seeking. I thought about the repeated disappointment and heartache I would likely encounter if I continued to seek my ideal relationship and did not stop or settle until I found it. I considered the alternative choice to forgo the gamble of continued dating in favor of the security of keeping my heart safe. After careful consideration and thoughtful deliberation, I decided that I would rather brave the perils of the journey to love than endure the dull, unending ache of an isolated, albeit safe, heart. To create a positive and optimistic perspective on my journey and its potential perils, I decided I could view each ended relationship as a learning experience which would serve to better prepare me for the ultimate relationship I was seeking. From there on out, whenever a relationship ended, to ease the heartache and help myself move forward, I created the mantra, "He was The Lesson, not The One."

When my older daughter was two, she had this adorable way of expressing her desires; with her whole body singularly focused, she would point at whatever it was that she wanted, and calmly but firmly insist, in her broken toddler English, "Have it; want it!" Children have no shyness about confidently and clearly stating what they want; it never occurs to them that they shouldn't want what they want or that they won't get what they want. It's not until they hear the messages of doubt ("Yeah, right, good luck getting that!"), shame ("Who do you think you are to ask for that?"), and guilt ("Don't be so greedy; you should be happy with what you have!") that they falter in their singular desire for and pursuit of what they want. Unfortunately, by the time most children reach adulthood, they have internalized these messages, and have become adults who think that they cannot get what they want, or are not deserving of what they want (or both).

As I thought about the love relationship I had always wanted (which had, thus far, eluded me), it dawned on me that it was my prerogative to state what I wanted, exactly what I wanted, in a love relationship, no matter what anyone else thought of it. This was an idea that was very contrary to the messages I was raised with. I realized that I had been operating on the premise that I could not get what I wanted and was not deserving of what I wanted in a love relationship, therefore, it was no surprise that, thus far, I had not gotten what I wanted in a love relationship. With my resolution firmly decided, to keep going until I found the love I wanted, I got practical and made a very detailed list of exactly who I was looking for and what I wanted in a relationship. I covered every category—personality, spirituality, physicality, etc.

It should be noted that my list, which ended up more than a page long, did not describe a perfect man. By this time in my life's journey, I had figured out that striving to correct every weakness in myself or others was a futile pursuit and one with no intrinsic value, because that's not why I am here. That said, I knew that there were some weaknesses in others that I found to be more troublesome and irritating than others; I figured that others probably felt the same way about my particular collection of weaknesses. I concluded that it would be good to look for someone whose weaknesses were reasonably compatible with my own, and whose weaknesses inspired compassion in me, and not disdain. My list was comprised of character qualities, not personality perfections. For example, nowhere on my list did it say anything like, "doesn't fart or leave dirty socks on the floor." My list was comprised of statements like, "is committed to and has a life-long habit of pursuing personal growth" and, "is peaceful, loving, and kind."

I grew up hearing both of my parents regularly, almost daily, call each other names—"shit-head" was their favorite—which is a very ineloquent and unkind way of expressing anger and dissatisfaction with someone else, to say the least. When I got married, I vowed that there would be no name-calling between us. Not surprisingly, my husband was the first one to fall short of this standard; he called me stupid for insisting that we bring our three-month-old daughter's car seat on a flight to visit my grandmother in Hawaii, because he thought it was too much trouble and a bother to the other passengers. I'm not proud of it, but by the end of our marriage, I had called him plenty of names.

I realized that as a result of my exposure to the hateful relationship that my parents modeled for me and the abusive relationship I had experienced in my own marriage, I valued kindness above all; I had developed a zero-tolerance policy when it came to unkindness! That is not to say that I keep a sweet smile plastered on my face and never raise my voice, nor do I expect or even want this from a man. It is entirely possible to express anger, hurt, dissatisfaction, frustration, disappointment, etc. without unkindness! The English language affords us many, many words with which to eloquently articulate our feelings without being cruel.

As a child, I found my parents' relationship to be so confusing; they acted like they hated each other, but they said they loved each other. Did they hate each other, or did they love each other, and if they loved each other, what did that mean? I remember once, when I was in high school, my father was away on the hunting trip that he took every fall. I came into the kitchen just before dinner and found my mother crying over the food she was cooking. When I asked her why she was crying, she sobbed, "I miss your father!" I didn't say anything out loud, but in my head, I thought, "Really? 'Cause you act like you wish he would drop dead when he is here!" In an attempt to puzzle out the mystery of their relationship, I once asked my mother, "Do you love Dad?" She only added to my confusion when she responded, "Yes, I always love him, but I don't always like him."

As an adult, when I would talk to friends about what I wanted in a relationship, one of the things I would say is, "I don't want 'but . . .' love." This, of course, would elicit stifled and embarrassed giggles! More times than I can count, I have heard someone say, "I love my husband/wife/ boyfriend/girlfriend, but . . ." That is what I mean by "but . . ." love, and I didn't want it. Believe me, I'm not naive enough to think that there exists a man with whom I will never have a chronic frustration, or who will never have a chronic frustration with me! I have found that practicing kindness, compassion, generosity, and humility (which is the awareness that others suffer under my faults just as much as I suffer under theirs) can circumvent just about any "but . . ." statement in a relationship. When I encounter one or more "but . . ." statements that won't go away, I have learned that the relationship should probably be reevaluated.

After I clarified my vision of what I wanted in a relationship and strengthened my resolve to keep going until I found it, I let my intention go out into the Universe and trusted in my adventure. I knew that I had developed enough strength and balance to keep my heart both open *and* safe through the potential hazards of my continued journey to love. After all, my journey to love is just one part of the whole great life adventure that I have selected, and which I am totally up for!

Scotty was the second man I dated after my divorce. Aside from the fact that he was a towering six foot six, which meant that I could wear my highest heels and still feel petite, he was just absolutely wonderful! He was the first man in my life that I did not break up with because he was a jerk. Although Scotty and I were highly compatible and I experienced a beautiful love with him, his life was not compatible with my life, and more importantly, his life was not compatible with where I wanted my life to go.

When we first met, we instantly felt a very powerful attraction to each other. At this time, my younger daughter was eighteen months away from her high school graduation, and Scotty's three children were five, six, and seven. He also lived two hours away in a much smaller town (with no Sam's Club!), and he was not free to move anywhere else until his youngest graduated high school because of his joint custody agreement with his ex-wife. On our very first date, I was upfront with him that I had reservations about dating a man with children so much younger than mine who lived in such a small remote town. I explained that my life would be shifting very dramatically in the near future when I no longer had children at home, and that I had big plans for where I wanted my life to go (there was no small town or young children in my vision for my future).

Scotty and I agreed that we would just date casually and "see where it goes." I do not recommend this! It was about as brilliant as if I had said, "I'm just going to run around this hay barn waving a flaming torch; surely, nothing will catch fire!" Very quickly, where it went was in the direction of the two of us falling head over heels in love with each other! Before I knew it, I was making plans to move to his small town after my daughter graduated, and partner with him for another round of raising children. As I enthusiastically continued to make these plans, plans which were very contrary to what I actually wanted for my life, the stress mounted in me, and subsequently, in our relationship. In the end, I broke up with him because it came to my attention that I was not telling the truth to myself.

Telling the truth has become very important to me, probably because I have been surrounded for so much of my life by people who have not told the truth. When I say telling the truth, I don't mean never telling a lie. There is a difference between actively telling a lie and passively not telling the truth (and, of course, I have been guilty of both at times in my life). A friend who tells me that they cannot meet me for coffee because their child is sick, when their child is not sick, is a friend who is lying to me. A friend who repeatedly finds truthful reasons for why they cannot spend time with me, all the while saying that they value our friendship, is a friend who is not telling me the truth. Obviously, flat-out lies are hurtful and damaging. Likewise, not telling the truth, even if you are not actually lying, is just as hurtful and damaging, sometimes even more so because not telling the truth has the effect of making the other person feel crazy.

This was my experience in my marriage to a closeted gay man; he regularly looked me straight (no pun intended) in the eye and told me that he loved me and wanted to make our marriage work, while at the same time, did not want to spend any time with me or touch me at all. I have heard it said that the cruelest thing you can do to another person is to lead them to believe that you care about them more than you do; it's not only cruel, but eventually, that level of not telling the truth will drive a person crazy.

I have noticed that not telling the truth to myself will also eventually drive me crazy, and can manifest in physical symptoms. I have learned that when I am unable or unwilling to tell the truth to myself, I force my body to tell the truth for me. Usually, it does so in ways that are blatantly symbolic! As Scotty and I continued to date, and I continued not to tell the truth to myself about what I really wanted for my future, I began to experience back pain. When I ignored the back pain and plunged ahead with my untruthful plans for my future, I ended up with a pinched nerve in my spine between my shoulder blades. It was so painful that I could barely talk for several days! I described it to a friend by saying, "Imagine if someone grabbed your shirt in between your shoulder blades, twisted hard, and yanked you back. That's exactly what it feels like except it's not my shirt, it's my muscles!" When I described it out loud that way, I made the connection; my body was yanking me back because I was headed in a direction that I did not truthfully want to go.

In hindsight, I ignored my intuition about the incompatibility of our different life circumstances because Scotty and I had such an amazing compatibility between the two of us as people. The more I got to know him, the more I saw that he had so many of the qualities that I had put on my list of what I wanted in a man and in a love relationship. In addition, there were many bonus things that we had in common, like the fact that he was a college professor and I had taught both at the high school and college level. At that point in my life, our relationship was the best and only truly good relationship I had ever had, which is what made it so tempting and easy for me to ignore the voice of my intuition when it quietly but firmly told me the truth: "He's not The One."

Ending that relationship was incredibly painful and heartbreaking for both of us. I cried rivers of tears, missed him dreadfully, and spent many months mourning the ending of our relationship. Nonetheless, through it all, I had a peace in my heart knowing that my path was once again in alignment with *all* my heart's deepest desires, not just *some* of my heart's deepest desires. Not surprisingly, the pinched nerve between my shoulder blades released as soon as I began to tell the truth to myself.

These days, I am less and less frustrated and heartbroken when my path refuses to accommodate any of my mistaken desires, born out of my own shortsightedness and temporary inability to trust in the flawless perfection of my life's path. I have learned to be grateful for precious time not wasted on people and experiences that, no matter how wonderful, are not aligned with all of my heart's deepest desires and intentions. I am thrilled that my heart's deepest desires and intentions are strong enough to push for what I truly want, need, and deserve, and to protect me from settling for anything less!

CHAPTER TEN

The A-Man

I had passed by the kitchen once already this morning and noticed that my mother was on the phone. This was unusual, since my mother, having no real girlfriends to speak of, was not one to be found chatting on the phone. When I passed by the kitchen a second time, I stopped long enough to try and figure out who she was talking to. My mother noticed my curiosity, covered the mouthpiece of the phone, and loudly whispered, "It's Aunt Betsy!" Aunt Betsy was my mother's second-youngest sister, who lived halfway across the country. When I passed by the kitchen a third time, I sat down shamelessly at the kitchen table to listen to my mother's side of the conversation, and to try to deduce my Aunt Betsy's side. Normally, my mother's few-and-far-between phone conversations never sparked my curiosity, but this morning, she had been on the phone for over an hour and I just had to know what it was all about! See, my mother portioned out minutes for long distance phone calls with the same stingy exactitude that she portioned out calories, and she never let herself indulge for this long!

I was seated at the kitchen table for only a few minutes when my mother began saying her goodbyes. After hanging up the phone, my mother dramatically plopped down in a kitchen chair and said, "Well, that was interesting!" With all the body language and tone of voice that indicated wonderful news, my mother announced that my Aunt Betsy was leaving my Uncle Mark, who she had been married to for several decades, for another man. To say I was confused doesn't touch it! Besides the fact that in my short decade and a half of life, my Aunt Betsy and Uncle Mark had been a staple in my family experience and to think of them getting divorced was just weird, I just could not reconcile my

141

mother's statement with her disposition in delivering it. This was the same woman who, as a devout Christian and fanatical cult member, had adamantly preached to me throughout my whole life about the evils of divorce, the tragedy of a broken family, and the mortal sin of adultery; here she was announcing with obvious glee that my aunt had gotten involved with another man, was leaving her husband, and breaking up my cousin's family!

Even after she had divulged the full circumstances leading up to my aunt's decision (my uncle was an alcoholic and their relationship had become abusive), my mother could see that I was unbending in my allegiance to the letter of the law that she had drilled into me. As I glared at her, daring her to undo her rules (which had become mine), my mother sighed and said, with what I would later come to understand was divine inspiration, "Aidy, sometimes God writes straight with crooked lines." My mother was not unlike the Harry Potter character of Professor Trelawney, who was, for all other intents and purposes, completely inept except for the rare moments when she uttered something entirely brilliant, keenly insightful, and completely true.

———⟶⟨⟶———

Like most modern people, I have been conditioned to put more stock and faith in the world that I can process with my five senses than the world that is intangible, ethereal, elusive, and beyond the parameters of time and space—the non-local realm. However, the more time I spend in time and space, the less stock I put in time and space; more and more I have found the strange to be completely plausible, and at times it makes even more sense than the normal. At the very least, I am much quicker to sit up, take notice, and pay attention when a fluke situation happens. In my experience, once the event has finished unfolding, it will have shown itself to have been no fluke after all, but instead, an event that was actually carefully planned, fully guided, and flawlessly executed by unseen forces in the non-local realm. Such was the case of The A-Man.

It began with a car accident that was as much not my fault as it possibly could have been (and still may have been) my fault. It was the afternoon of Saturday, June 5, 2010, and I was running late for my girlfriend's daughter's second birthday party. I was hungry because I had skipped lunch. It was a forty-five-minute drive to my girlfriend's house and I knew that she would be serving only toddler fare at the birthday party. As I neared the last traffic light before I got on the highway, I remembered that there was an Arby's on the corner. I would have to make a left turn and then swing back around to get back on my way to the highway. I glanced at the clock, did a quick mental calculation in regards to the time, quickly fabricated an excuse in my mind for being late, and decided to go for it. As I approached the intersection, moving into the far left of the two left turn lanes, the red light turned to a green arrow, and the half a dozen cars waiting to turn left began to move forward. The timing was perfect! With a tiny burst of extra speed, I would have no problem making the light, swinging into Arby's, and getting back on my way with a minimal loss of time.

The light had turned green and all the cars had begun to move forward, so all the cues were go; I had no reason to think that we would be stopping. I did not have my radio on and I was not talking on or looking at my phone; my full attention was focused on the road and my driving. I have *no* idea why I didn't hear it, but approaching the intersection, from a little way down the cross road, was an emergency vehicle. Since I was in the process of approaching the intersection and wasn't quite there yet, I did not see the emergency vehicle. The other cars in front of me, who had begun to move, saw it and came to a stop instead of proceeding through the intersection. When I realized what was happening, I literally stood on my brakes, but still ended up rear-ending the car in front of me.

The reason I emphasize that this accident was as much not my fault as it possibly could have been (and still may have been) my fault is not because I don't want to take the blame; I was at fault and I am not squeamish about admitting that. What I want to emphasize is the fluke nature of the accident. I cannot find a mundane cause for the accident; I cannot point to an obvious cause. I cannot say, "I was distracted by my phone" or, "I was rocking out to my music full blast" or, "I was driving recklessly."

The car that I hit was a yellow Toyota Tundra truck with a ball hitch on the back bumper. Right after impact, I immediately jumped out of my car and began apologizing profusely. Two men got out of the Tundra—the driver/owner and the passenger, who was the driver's father. Having stood on my brakes as hard as I could, the impact was minor, but it did knock the ball hitch off (after punching a hole in my front bumper). I was standing outside my car apologizing and the two men were beginning to assess the damage when the father noticed the ball hitch laying on the ground. What happened next happened very quickly.

The father exploded and started coloring the air blue with profanity over the broken hitch; I started shaking, backing away, and crying, while still apologizing. A police officer, who *just happened to be* one of the half dozen cars in the two left turn lanes, and who had witnessed the whole accident, got out of his car, protectively stepped in between the father and me, and began to try and calm the father. He said, "Sir, it was just an accident; there's no need to get so upset. Please calm down!" The son, the driver, just stood there observing. The police officer directed all three of us to get back in our cars, complete our left turns, and pull in to the parking lot on the far corner so we could sort everything out.

In the short amount of time that it took us to get parked in the lot on the far corner, the father had calmed down. When we all got out of our cars again, I reiterated my apologies, and the father offered his own apology for his reaction. He explained that he had just spent three hours that morning installing the ball hitch, which they were planning on using the next day to haul their camper for a week-long family camping trip. I told him that I completely understood his frustration, and that if I were in his position, I would feel the same way. The police officer collected our insurance information and was filling out the report while we stood around in awkward silence.

It was at this time that I noticed the license plate on the truck: THEAMAN. I turned to the son, the driver, and said, "I'm guessing your name is Aiden?" He said, with surprise, "Yeah, how did you know?" I said, "Your license plate. My name is Aideen and I know that we (Aiden and Aideen) get 'A' as a nickname. For some reason we get it, and Alberts, Ashleys, Adams, Abbys, etc., don't." That broke the tension and soon we were chatting easily. His father said that he and his son's friends tease him and call him "Thea Man," because the plate could be read that way instead of "The A-Man."

When the police officer finished his paperwork, he came over and told us that there would be no report and no ticket, because the damage was so minimal and we both had good insurance. He gave us forms with each other's information and said we could settle it ourselves between our insurance companies. As we had all calmed down and become friendly by now, we all shook hands and said goodbye. I got back on the road to the birthday party without Arby's, but now with a legitimate reason for being late.

Not getting a ticket (and no points on my license) for an accident that was so clearly my fault, which I had owned up to, and furthermore, had been witnessed by a police officer was my first tip-off that there was something bigger at play. At the time, this unusual occurrence did nothing more than make me think, "Hmmm . . ." Now, I know it to have been the genesis of the greatest surge of personal growth and life evolution I had gone through to date. Now, looking back, I can see the guidance clearly, like a hand moving pieces on a chess board. I was carried, cared for, and guided . . . flawlessly. So many people, friends and strangers, showed up and made their contribution to my cause, beginning with The A-Man.

It was a year prior to my accident with The A-Man that my husband had confessed to me that he was gay. His confession set in motion a chain of events that took the next several years to fully unfold, and which took my life in a new and unanticipated direction. Unfortunately, about six months after his confession, my husband recanted everything he had admitted to me and fled even deeper into the closet, insisting, against all evidence and admission, that he was straight.

In the months prior to me rear-ending The A-Man, my husband's behavior had become more and more erratic. He began to withdraw from our family, and was chronically irritated with and harshly critical of our daughters, often to the point of cruelty. I confronted him with this change in his behavior, but he was oblivious to it and denied that anything was different. An alarm went off inside me and I went searching for answers. Intuitively, I knew that what was going on (although I didn't know what it was) was a problem, a big problem. Instinctively, I knew that what I didn't know could and would hurt me and my daughters.

I learned that my husband had gotten involved with a female colleague (fifteen years his senior and married); their relationship had progressed to a level such that, had he been straight, they would have been having sex already. (He used her marriage as a safeguard to avoid sexual intimacy with her, insisting that he didn't want her to be unfaithful.) I also discovered more information about his true sexual orientation, which even further confirmed to me that he was gay. Even though what I had uncovered was very alarming and should have been enough to make me call a divorce attorney, I still wavered.

Most of my friends who knew the true state of my marriage regularly urged me to get divorced. I would always protest with a standard list of reasons, and at the top of that list was my daughters and my desire to keep our family intact. I would always say that even though my husband was an epic failure as a husband, I thought he was a good father and parenting partner. I was complaining on the phone one day to my girlfriend, Mia, about how detached from our family and cruel to our daughters my husband had become. She said something to me that stopped me in my tracks. She said, "Aidy, you've always said that the only reason you were staying with him was because he was a good father. If he is no longer a good father, why are you still staying?" I was speechless and found myself unable to "b . . ., bu . . ., but . . ." my way out of her confrontation. I was stunned and could not ignore the truth of what she said. I realized that she was right; I no longer had a single reason to stay, but I also had no idea how to leave.

Almost two years prior to hitting The A-Man, I had been rear-ended by someone else in a minor fender-bender accident which caused very little damage, just a small crack in my bumper. I had never bothered to get it fixed because I intended to drive my car into the ground, so I wasn't worried about it looking good for resale. I had a Toyota Land Cruiser that I had done all the scheduled maintenance on, and I knew I could drive it forever before it would die.

At the time that I hit The A-Man, I was ninety percent convinced that I was going to file for divorce; I was still holding out hope that I could confront my husband with what I had learned, and that he would come to his senses and care enough about our family to face his issues. That never happened; I confronted him, but he was unmoved, and having already secured a new woman to use for cover, he was unconcerned by what I had discovered. His top priority was to remain closeted, so he had already lined up a new beard, as he had said he would. He no longer needed me or our daughters to front for him, therefore we were no longer a priority for him.

I started thinking about all the million and one details that had to be considered and handled if I were going to file for divorce. I began to re-think my vehicle, which at that point had over two hundred thousand miles on it. I was completely unsure of what my financial situation would be as a divorcée, and it occurred to me that I might want to secure a much less used vehicle because I had no idea when or if I would be able to afford another car again.

I took my car to a body shop to get a quote for the damage from the accident with The A-Man, and asked about the rear bumper, as well. The owner of the shop told me that if I would get both fixed, he could discount my deductible. I agreed because conveniently, by having the rear bumper fixed, which was from an accident that was not my fault, I could get a rental car to drive that would be covered by the other driver's insurance. I also asked the body shop owner what it would cost to remove the bumper stickers covering the back door of my Land Cruiser; my daughters and I, being *massive* Harry Potter fans, had covered every inch of the back of my Land Cruiser in Harry Potter bumper stickers (which had made us quite famous in our little town). He said he could make it look like new for about one hundred dollars. So, I left my Land Cruiser with him and got my rental, thinking I would be back in about a week to get my car.

Several days after I left my car at the body shop, three massive hail storms hit in one day—if I had still been in the cult, I would have thought that the apocalypse was upon us! The first one was around nine in the morning, the second one was around noon, and the third was around three in the afternoon (very apocalyptic!). I was at home for the first one, but got caught in the second two. The hail was the size of walnuts, and from inside my car, it sounded like I was caught in machine gun crossfire.

Those hail storms were an early Christmas present to every body shop owner in the entire area, because almost every car that got caught out in them suffered severe body damage; many cars looked like Mafioso henchmen had gotten ahold of them. It was a freaky experience for me, but my rental car suffered no damage from either hail storm I was caught in, and my Land Cruiser was safely inside the shop during the storms. The biggest impact that those storms had on my life was to delay the work on my Land Cruiser for six weeks! I don't know why my car got dropped down to the end of the list when the body shop got inundated with cars needing repair from the storm damage, but it did.

At first I was patient, because in the meantime, I had gone and bought myself a much less used car. After a month, I began to lose my patience, and in the end, my clearly and firmly expressed dissatisfaction with the service from the body shop was heard. When I went to pick up my car, the shop owner ended up completely covering my five hundred-dollar deductible and charging me nothing for the removal of the bumper stickers. He told me that he had made such a killing on the storm damage business that he could afford to compensate me for the inconvenience he caused me by not having my car ready for six weeks. I was thrilled, especially since the work he had done, although delayed, was flawless and my Land Cruiser, with more than two hundred thousand miles on it, looked brand new!

A few weeks after leaving my car at the body shop, I had decided that, in preparation for my inevitable divorce, I definitely needed to get a much less used car, and had figured out a way to get one without raising suspicion from my husband. My older daughter was sixteen and just learning to drive. We had planned on getting her a reliable clunker, as you do for teenage drivers. I knew that the condition of the car we would be getting her would preclude us from getting financing for it; we would have to pay cash, which we did not have readily available at that time. I proposed that I get a newer used car, which would be eligible for financing, to replace my Land Cruiser, and use the cash from the sale of the Land Cruiser to buy a car for my daughter. My husband agreed, and I began to investigate a newer used car for myself.

I was a Sam's Club member and had heard that Sam's Club offered perks to car buyers. I looked into it online, and ended up filling in my contact information when prompted. Almost immediately, my phone rang and I was contacted by the nearest Toyota dealership. I happened to have some time that afternoon, so I made an appointment to meet with an internet sales rep. When I got there, the rep asked me what I was looking for and I confessed that I hadn't really thought that far yet, that I was really there just to learn about how the buying program worked.

The rep was very kind and friendly, the kind of guy you could find yourself opening up to and trusting—kind of atypical for a used car salesman. He explained that the buying program was for certified used cars only, but that they also had as-is cars on the back lot. When I divulged my budget, which was very modest, the rep politely suggested that we start by looking at the as-is cars. There were about half a dozen cars on the back lot, all in various conditions. One, a little white Camry, caught my eye. It was everything I was looking for: lots of perks (leather seats, nice sound system, burled wood trim, etc.), and the mileage was about half of the mileage on my Land Cruiser. The price was right but I hadn't come ready to buy, so I told the rep that I would think about it and get back to him.

Knowing that the car would go fast, I only took a day to decide that it was the right car for me. I went back the next day and started all the paperwork with the rep. As I said, the rep was the kind of guy you could find yourself opening up to, and sure enough, as we chatted our way through the paperwork, I found myself telling him my story. His first marriage had ended in divorce (although not for the same reason) some years back, and he was sympathetic. When the issue of income to be considered for financing came up, it became apparent that my income (which was meager as a result of new design projects having dried up during the economic recession) compared to the size of my monthly mortgage payment (which was substantial) was not going to get approved for financing. The rep informed me that I would have to have my husband cosign the loan. I was discouraged and explained that I did not want to have yet another thing owned jointly that would have to be divided in the divorce. I said that once the divorce was final, I knew I would be able to count the part of my husband's income that I would receive as spousal support as my income, and asked if there was some way to handle the paperwork taking that into consideration, so that the car could be put in my name only. The rep said, "Let me see what I can do," and left to confer with the guy in finance. When he came back about fifteen minutes later, he said, "It's all taken care of. You can finance the car in your name only." To this day, I have no idea what kind of magic that rep worked for me. All I know is that he helped me multiple times over, far beyond the purchase of my Camry.

After I got my Land Cruiser back in "like new" condition, I put it up for sale. It took a few weeks, but in the end, I got a very good price for it; enough money to pay cash for a car for my older daughter. With the cash now in hand, I contacted the rep and told him to start looking for a car for my daughter. I stipulated the budget and told him that it needed to be a reliable make; my daughter asked for a coupe and the color red. We weren't in any hurry, so I told the rep just to call me when something came in that fit the bill. I did not get a call from the rep for another four months.

In the meantime, I filed for divorce. My husband and I had both agreed (or so I thought!) that we needed legal representation, but also that we wanted a bloodless divorce and that we would put our daughters' needs first. With this understanding, I went looking for a lawyer who would be fair and reasonable. I found one, through the internet, who I felt comfortable with, one who seemed very moderate and matter-of-fact. As it turned out, my husband was referred to his lawyer by the new woman he had gotten involved with. She was very well connected to the family law community through her work and knew just about every divorce attorney in the area. She also had an agenda, and I was the wife of the man she was in love with. As you might guess, she did not refer my husband to a moderate and matter-of-fact divorce attorney; she referred him to a bloodthirsty pitbull of a lawyer who had just gotten divorced himself, and consequently had an axe to grind.

It wasn't until our first court appearance that I met my husband's lawyer. By this time, I had already retained my lawyer and gone through the initial paperwork after filing. Just on body language alone, I could tell that there was a huge difference between the lawyer I had selected and the lawyer my husband had selected, or rather, his new beard had selected. It was very clear by the end of our first court session that my lawyer was no match for his lawyer, and this was not going to be a fair fight. Needless to say, I left the courtroom full of anxiety and fear, with no idea what to do, sure that I was going to get destroyed by this divorce.

About a week later, I got a call from the rep at the Toyota dealership saying that he had found the perfect car for my daughter that was exactly what we both wanted. I went straight over to see the car, and sure enough, it was perfect! It was a ten-year-old red Toyota Corolla coupe with about one hundred thousand miles on it. It was in spectacular condition; the cloth interior looked like it was only a few years old. The price was right, so I snatched it up.

In the process of buying the car, I had to call in to my insurance agent to verify coverage for the new car. We had been with the same agent for over a decade; she was a very feisty older woman with whom I had clicked instantly. Although we only talked about once a year, I had always felt a special simpatico with her. In recent years, she had been transitioning her agency over to her son so that she could retire. She was rarely in the office those days, and most of the time when I called, I spoke with her son. I had spoken with her son just after I filed for divorce to ask about separating our auto policies, so he knew that I was getting divorced and had shared this with his mother. On the day that I called about coverage for my daughter's new car, I spoke with her son. In saying goodbye at the end of the conversation, I told him to tell his mother "hello" for me. He said, "She's here; would you like to tell her yourself?" Since I was still in the middle of all the car-buying paperwork, I asked if she would still be there if I called later, and he said she would be.

When I got on the phone with her later that day, she told me that her son had informed her that I was getting divorced. The first thing she said was, "Are you okay?" When I explained that this divorce was long overdue, and in the big picture, was a very good thing, she said, "Okay, good. Now, do you have a good lawyer?" I said, "Well, I thought I did, but . . ." and filled her in on the situation. She said, "Well, that won't do! Here is the name and number of my good friend, who works for one of the best divorce attorneys in town. Call her tonight and she will get you going in the right direction." I was thrilled, relieved, and felt a flicker of hope. I called her friend later that night, and she gave me a wealth of advice and guidance (way more than my own lawyer had provided me with) and told me to call the office the next day to set up a consultation. I hung up thinking, for the first time, that I might not get destroyed by this divorce after all.

The next week, I met with the new lawyer, and I knew right away that I was in the right place. It was clear, from our first handshake, that she would be an equal match for my husband's lawyer. The first thing she told me was that, on principle, she never takes on a case that has already been started by another lawyer, but that she had agreed to meet with me because her aide had told her of my plight. She told me that she knew my husband's lawyer very well and had been up against him in court many times. She also confirmed my doubt about my current lawyer. She said, "I don't want to disparage him because he is a good lawyer, but he is not aggressive. Let's just say that when your husband's lawyer saw who you had representing you, he wasn't the least bit concerned." After talking with her for about an hour, I decided to retain her and let my first lawyer go.

This decision was a clear turning point in my divorce. With my new lawyer's guidance and representation, I was able to secure a favorable settlement which gave me the financial security I needed to see both of my daughters through high school without worry. In the years between my divorce and my youngest leaving for college, instead of worrying about putting a roof over our heads or food in our bellies (during the economic downturn which had caused my design business to all but dry up), I was free to focus my attention and energy on my daughters and on putting myself back together physically, psychologically, emotionally, and spiritually . . . all because of my accident with The A-Man.

Although I have had many extraordinary experiences in my life (small and large), it's not often that I have had an experience, like this one with The A-Man, where I can so very clearly see the chess pieces being moved for me on the chess board of my life. The A-Man has come to symbolize and represent to me the assurance that I am guided, aided, and cared for. Just to add amazement to wonder, The A-Man continued to show up in my life at times when I needed a reminder that I am not alone, and that my life is not random.

One Sunday, halfway through my divorce, I was on my way to pick my daughters up from their father's house, where they had been for the weekend. It was at a point in the divorce when everything was still very much up in the air, and in fact, at that point, it was not looking very good for me. As I drove, my mind obsessed over the details and the many possible outcomes, most of them negative. Anxiety and dread engulfed me, and I felt hopeless and helpless. At that moment, even with my new lawyer, I was more convinced of a negative outcome than a positive one. Glancing around while stopped at a red light, my eyes fell on the license plate of the vehicle in front of me; my mouth fell open when I saw "THEAMAN." It was quite a coincidence, and one that was not lost on me! I remembered the intricate and carefully orchestrated sequence of events, starting with rear-ending The A-Man, which led me to my new lawyer, the one who gave me a fighting chance. I immediately felt my fear dissipate, and I was comforted with a knowing that everything would be alright. (And, to answer your question . . . no, I did not rear-end him a second time!)

It was late spring when my divorce was getting wrapped up. It crossed my mind that I was coming up on the one-year anniversary of the day I rear-ended The A-Man. I began to think how wild it would be if my divorce got finalized on that exact date one year later. Out of curiosity,

I looked at the calendar and realized that the fifth of June was going to fall on a Sunday, which would make it impossible for my divorce to be actually finalized on the one-year anniversary, because the courts are closed on Sundays. I didn't give it any more thought until early June, when my lawyer called with the news that our consent decree had been recorded by the courts and my divorce was officially final. She called me on Thursday, June 9, 2011. She said, "Good news! I got the notice today that your consent decree has been recorded; it is officially over! Actually, it was signed by the judge on Sunday, the 5th, but it takes several days for the court to record it." I said, "I'm sorry, would you repeat that? Do you mean to say that my consent decree was signed on a Sunday? What was the judge doing in chambers on a Sunday?" She said, "I don't know, but the report says that it was signed by the judge in the late afternoon on Sunday, the 5th of June, 2011. The judge must have been in chambers to catch up on paperwork . . . I don't know." I was blown away, and it doesn't stop there!

With the finalization of my divorce, I turned my energies toward healing myself and becoming more positive, empowered, and optimistic. My sense of purpose and enthusiasm for life increased exponentially. I began to be able to see the big picture of my life, and I began to think that there was a purpose after all to all the pain I had gone through in my childhood and my marriage.

One day, while driving down the highway, I was suddenly overcome by feelings of doubt and futility, the likes of which I had not felt in several years. I was thinking thoughts along the lines of, "There is probably no real purpose to life, Aidy. You are just deluding yourself with your positive life view of guidance and purpose. All of this optimism is probably just a smoke screen to shield you from the depressing truth, which is that there is no purpose, everything is random, and all of life is a meaningless crap shoot!" I don't know why my mind was thrashing about in this cesspool of negativity and cynicism, but it was.

In a routine check of my rear-view mirror, I noticed that the driver behind me was following very closely. I thought, "Geez, buddy, get off my tail!" The traffic was not heavy, I was driving slightly above the speed limit, and there was no reason for him to be tailing me. He then sped up, swerved around me, got in front of me, and put on his brakes! I was alarmed, and then stunned . . . it . . . was . . . The A-Man! By this time, I was no longer driving the Toyota Land Cruiser that I had hit him with, and I doubt he recognized me from the back through my rear window several years later! I have no idea why he crawled up my tail, sped around me, and then slowed down! All I know is that at a moment of doubt in my life, he showed up again to affirm to me that my life is not random; it is very full of purpose and I am guided! I started laughing and crying at the same time. I threw my hands up in the air and said out loud, "Okay, I give up; I believe!"

CHAPTER ELEVEN

Following Felix

Somehow, I had known this was coming. Something had been off from the moment I had arrived two weeks earlier, after selling everything I owned and leaving behind everyone I knew in Richmond, Virginia, where I had lived for the previous sixteen years. I had driven cross-country to move in with my cousin and his wife so that I could be closer to my younger daughter, who had just started college in California. I had been tormented all day by a dreadful premonition which I had tried desperately to ignore and to combat with positive thinking, which I had mastered; now it was unfolding in gory detail in real life, and I felt as if no amount of positive thinking could possibly save me from the terror that ripped through me.

I was sitting at the dining room table answering some work emails while the dinner I had started for the three of us was cooking on the stove. My cousin, Darryl, and his wife, Bertha, were upstairs changing clothes after their workday. I heard them coming down the stairs, and with each footfall, the nebulous fear that I had been fighting back all day mounted. They came into the dining room and sat down together across from me. Darryl spoke first: "Aidy, we need to talk; this isn't going to work. You have to leave."

The levy burst, and fear rushed over me like a tsunami; beginning to shake and blink back tears, I tried to calmly ask, "Why? What's wrong?" Bertha spoke up, "Darryl's health hasn't been good and the doctor has said that he cannot have any disruptions in his life right now. I don't know if you know this, but he's had several mini-strokes since his stroke last year. I hope you understand!" I said, "Of course, I understand; I just wish you had told me!" thinking to myself, "If I had known that, I never would have agreed to move in with you

155

despite your enthusiastic insistence that it was a great idea!" *Completely devoid of empathy or any sense of responsibility, Bertha callously and dismissively said, "Well, you said you wanted to move West anyway." In a flash, fear turned to anger, and I shot back, "Yes, I did want to move West, but I wouldn't have sold everything I owned!" Knowing that I was about to completely lose my shit, I left the house, got in my car, drove aimlessly for several hours, and did not return to their house until I knew they had gone to bed.*

As I drove, sobbing and hyperventilating, all I could think over and over was, "I'm all alone! I don't know anyone here! And I'm homeless!" I couldn't sleep at all that night; around two in the morning, I reached for my phone to check the time and saw a Facebook notification for an inane post about pugs that Bertha had posted only a few hours after she and Darryl had H-bombed my life. I took it as further confirmation of her complete lack of awareness of or concern for how their actions had impacted me, and it enraged me; with an impulsive surge of childish pettiness, I unfriended both of them.

I left the house very early the next morning to go apartment hunting. By early afternoon, I had signed a lease for an apartment several towns away, purchased a mattress, and settled myself into the corner of a coffee shop with free wireless to try and get some work done. My phone buzzed with a text from Darryl; he wrote, "I see you have unfriended us on Facebook. I will take this to mean that you want nothing more to do with us. You have forty-eight hours to get your stuff out of our house. Anything left after five o'clock on Sunday night will be taken to the dump." Paralyzing fear turned into mobilizing terror as I spent the next forty-eight hours making five two-and-a-half-hour round-trip hauls between their house and my new apartment; they hid alternately in their bedroom and the basement to avoid me while I single-handedly moved out everything that I had, just days earlier, unpacked into their house.

Late Sunday night, eating takeout on the floor of my empty new apartment, exhausted and covered in bruises, I caught my first bird's eye glimpse of what had just transpired. I spontaneously thought to myself, "This is perfect; I don't know how yet, but I know that this is perfect."

<hr />

Friends who know me now and learn about my upbringing often tell me, "Aidy, I just have a really hard time picturing you being a fundamentalist religious fanatic; that's just so not who you are!" I say, "Well, I've got the photos to prove it!" I pull out my old photo albums, show them pictures of me in my *Little House on the Prairie* dresses, with bows in my waist-long hair and a Bible tucked under my arm because I'm on my way to a prayer meeting, and their faces go blank with complete confusion! Their next comment almost always is, "Well, how did you go from there to where you are now?" I laugh and say, "How much time do you have?"

I will never forget the last cult prayer meeting I ever went to. At the end of it, I walked outside into the parking lot, looked up at the sky, and said out loud, "I don't know what I am going to do, but I know I can't do this anymore." I was twenty-two years old, I had just graduated from college, and was only months away from getting engaged. I wasn't consciously aware of it, but I had been outgrowing the religious construct I was raised in for several years already. Like a high school senior trying to fit back into a pair of jeans from freshman year, I had reached a point where I just couldn't force myself into it anymore.

I had put a monumental amount of effort into trying to deny myself, reject myself, and fracture myself, striving to achieve a one-sided, unbalanced, unhuman existence, one with only holiness and no sinfulness. After a decade of valiantly trying and miserably failing, I started to question the goal. I puzzled and puzzled over the disparity between who I was and who I was told that I was supposed to be. I began to think that if I knew myself to be essentially a good person (as I only tentatively did at that point in my life) but I could not "fix" myself to meet their ideal, maybe the problem wasn't with me; maybe the problem was with their ideal. Putting my own spin on the adage, "If it ain't broke, don't fix it!" I came up with, "If it can't be fixed, then maybe it's not broken."

I had wholeheartedly believed what I had been taught, which was that these efforts of nearly-monastic depravation and devotion would produce the promised reward of a better, happier, and more peaceful life, but they did not. Instead, I was plagued by relentless internal discord as my authentic self cried out against the persecution it was enduring and begged to be acknowledged as perfect and complete (needing nothing to be added, removed, or changed). In the end, as I was unable to silence the urgings of my authentic self, I knew I had to find a different way to live; a way to live that would *actually* bring me peace and happiness. It was a very strange place to be. I had been so completely devoted to the cult's ideology and dedicated to their way of life, and since the age of eight, I had known nothing else. I knew that it wasn't where I belonged anymore, but I didn't know where I did belong; thus, I began my journey away from where I began to where I belonged.

One of the control tactics used in the cult, which is typical of every cult, was to isolate us from and create fear about anyone and anything that was outside of the cult. Piggybacking on this tactic was the message they preached to us that we couldn't make it if we left the cult. Of course, they told us that if we walked away from our faith in God, we would come to certain ruin and end up in Hell, but they also told us that it wasn't possible to sustain a real, "on fire," and committed relationship with God without the structure and support of the cult (this circumvented any thinking that attending a regular church was sufficient). We were often warned with stories about members who had left and the misfortunes which befell them. These were presented as proof positive of God's judgment on them for leaving the cult. We were also instructed to shun anyone who left; they had questioned the wisdom and authority of the cult leadership, which spoke for God, and if we interacted with someone who had left, we would be in danger of falling away, as well.

In my years as a devout Christian, I attributed any good fortune I ever experienced, small or large, to the fact that I was a Christian and a committed member of the cult; God rewards his faithful, and we were the most faithful, so I was taught. A small example occurred when my husband (then boyfriend) and I were dating; I wanted to make a nice dinner for us but I did not have the money for groceries, so I prayed, and an hour later I found a twenty-dollar bill on the sidewalk (which, at that time, was plenty enough money for groceries). A more significant example happened when my younger sister was a senior in college and downed sixty Tylenol in an attempt to end her life. Within an hour, I had found out about it and called my friends to hold a prayer vigil. The ER doctor later reported that in the same hour that we were praying, my sister's toxicity levels fell to normal at a rate that was medically inexplicable. At that time, I believed that these happenings, and any others like them, were indisputably answers to prayers and blessings directly from God, in reward for my belief and devotion to Him and His chosen people—the cult.

During my years in the cult, I wholeheartedly believed that I would forfeit all these blessings and aid if I were ever to leave, or, worse yet, lose my faith in God. Even as I walked away from the cult, I was sure that I was leaving all of these benefits behind. Much to my great surprise and delight, these blessings did not cease, and to date, have not ceased (case in point, The A-Man) even though I have walked away from not only the cult, but also any faith or belief in any God, Christian or otherwise. *I do not say this to imply that this proves that God does not exist; only that it provides evidence for me* that, *for me*, these phenomena are independent of a belief in a God.

As I started on my journey away from where I began, I realized that I had this massive bag of beliefs which had been given to me (more to the point: beliefs which had been forced on me). I had not chosen these beliefs voluntarily; I had only accepted these beliefs out of fear and a primal need for self-preservation and familial belonging. I realized that I did not know what I actually believed. I thought that figuring out what I didn't believe out of what had been given to me to believe was a good place to start. As I continued to walk down the road of my life's journey, one by one, I pulled out the beliefs I had been given, examined each one closely, and one by one, left each by the side of the road. It took more than two decades to empty my bag, and in the end, it turned out that there wasn't a single belief that I had been given to believe which I actually believed on my own. As I was figuring out what I didn't believe, I was also trying to figure out what I did believe.

The first place I started to try and figure out what I did believe was New Age spirituality, as it was called at the time. Olivia, the woman who I had gotten to know just out of college while I was her assistant teacher in the kindergarten classroom of my parents' Montessori school, was deeply into New Age spirituality. I was struck by how peaceful, loving, and kind she was; having come from a family and a religious community devoid of these qualities, I was drawn to her like a moth to a flame!

As I talked with Olivia about the multitude of beliefs I had been raised with which no longer fit me, she began to share the ideas she had come to embrace on her life's journey. She was the one who gave me my first meditation tapes (yes, they were actually *tapes* back then), along with the books and audio programs of Wayne Dyer, Deepak Chopra, Ram Dass, Krishnamurti, and Thich Nhat Hanh. I approached all of it initially with skepticism, and then with curiosity which quickly turned to enthusiasm; I had, of course, been taught by the cult leaders and my parents that the New Age movement was the devil's work, and these voices were still loud in my head.

During this time, I got married, moved to Las Vegas, Nevada, where my husband was doing his residency, started teaching high school, and had my first daughter. I was caught up in a whirlwind of change, and my attention span for my rapidly changing belief system was limited. When my husband had completed his residency, we moved to Lynden, Washington, where he took his first job. By this time, I was in my late twenties and a young mother of a toddler; I decided to be a stay-at-home mom for the time being, since we wanted to try for another child in the near future. I threw myself into homemaking and being a wife and mother, which kept me busy but did not occupy my intellect, which was left to roam free and contemplate the new ideas I had been introduced to.

The majority of the population in Lynden was Calvinist Dutch Christian Reformed, and as such, was strictly conservative, exceedingly judgmental, self-righteously exclusive (their saying is, "If you ain't Dutch, you ain't much!"), and tragically dour (the Puritans were Calvinists). There was also a strong, albeit small, community of spiritual seekers in our area. During the next five years, I explored New Age spirituality by connecting with this small community of spiritual seekers through various writing classes, meditation classes, and spiritual retreats.

The tenets of New Age spirituality seemed to offer a safe and supportive space for my newly and tentatively emerging authentic self; a space that was encouraging, positive, non-judgmental, and empowering—so very unlike the tenets of the Christian faith I had been raised with. Unfortunately, the community of spiritual seekers that I connected with was strangely similar to the community of fundamentalist Christians in the cult that I had just walked away from; it was just the vocabulary that was different. Instead of striving for righteousness and holiness, they were striving for detachment and enlightenment; the main problem for me was that they were still striving, which, given my experience in the cult with striving, unnerved me, to say the least! They related to each other within the same framework of competition, comparison, and fear-based judgment as the people I had known in the cult. They were just as driven by fear, the same fear of not getting it right, only their solution and reward were different.

One of the people I met in the New Age community in Lynden was an absolutely wonderful woman named Emma, who was a Trager body work practitioner. We had a lot in common; we were both young mothers of toddler daughters, we were both from San Francisco, and we were both redheads, but Emma had been raised Buddhist. Emma provided me with Trager body work for the five years that I lived in Lynden, and became a dear friend. She was a luminous soul who truly lived the tenets of the Buddhist tradition she followed. Over the course of my sessions with her, I confided in her that I had been unfaithful in my marriage. I had broken it off with the man I had been unfaithful with and was trying again to put all my efforts into making my marriage work. It was very difficult and emotionally painful to shut the door on my feelings for and my relationship with a man who had given me love so freely and lavishly, and walk back to a man whose love was meager and stingy at best. Needless to say, the whole process took its toll on my body, and Emma noticed.

After a session one afternoon, Emma told me that Tibetan Buddhist monks were in town and emphatically recommended that I attend one of their lectures. So, I happily went. At the end of the lecture (of which I have no recollection), there was a question and answer period. Someone asked a question about adultery, and the response given by the Buddhist monk could have just as easily come out of the mouth of a fundamentalist hellfire and brimstone preacher! It was harshly judgmental and devoid of the loving kindness that I had thought was one of the cornerstones of Buddhism. I got up, rushed out as fast as I could, and by the time I got to my car, I was sobbing and gasping for air! I had already been tortured mercilessly by my inner terrorist and the shame conditioning still in place from the cult since the very first minute I even thought of being unfaithful; to be condemned again from yet another camp, and one where I was trying to seek asylum, was devastating!

The next time I went in for Trager, Emma asked if I had gone to hear the monks speak, and inquired as to whether I enjoyed it. With palpable distress, I recounted my experience. She responded with profound sadness and true loving kindness. She said, "Oh, Aidy, I'm so sorry you had that experience! That is not what the Buddha would have said to you; the only response the Buddha would have to your adultery would be to say (and she cradled my face in her hands), 'Oh, My Child, I see that you suffer; I don't want you to suffer!'" Her pure compassion, without any judgment, was exactly what I needed; her response was such a gift, so healing, and I have never forgotten it! Unfortunately, as I came to realize, the way she practiced her New Age spirituality was atypical compared to most of the New Age people I met while living in Lynden; after enough experiences that were too uncomfortably familiar, I walked on from the New Age community just as I had walked on from the Christian cult.

While I was walking away from the conservative Christianity that I was raised in, my sister was walking toward it. Along the way, she and I had many, many discussions about life, faith, God, belief, Heaven, Hell, etc., which became increasingly tense as we were becoming polarized once again. I remember one time, when we had come to yet another awkward impasse in one of our many discussions, she said to me in exasperation, "Can't we just agree to disagree?" I said, "That works for me, but I don't see how it will work for you when it is a core tenet of your belief system to believe that you are right and I am wrong, that your creed is true and mine is false, and that you are going to Heaven and I am going to Hell."

One of the many beliefs I found in my bag-o-beliefs that I was slowly unpacking was the belief that I was right and anyone who didn't believe the way that I believed was wrong. The first fissure in the concrete form of my naive narrowmindedness occurred in a world history class discussion group during my freshman year of college, when we were talking about the Roman Empire. We had just finished reading about the bestiality, incest, and homosexuality that were commonly practiced during the time of the Roman Empire. In accordance with the only moral code I had ever known, I expressed my arrogant and self-righteous disgust. The TA (graduate student teaching assistant) who was leading the discussion very calmly and matter-of-factly said, "Well, Aideen, before Judeo-Christian morality became dominant, none of these things were considered to be deviant or even wrong." Little did he know it, but my TA's simple statement cracked open my skull and spread my brain on a cracker like pâté! It was the first time I considered the fact that my moral code might be nothing more than just that: *my* moral code.

While at UCLA, I crossed paths with other students of many different faiths—Christian (outside of the cult), Muslim, Jewish, Hindu, Orthodox, etc.—who were just as devout as I was, and as such, were just as convinced that they were right and I was wrong as I was convinced that they were wrong and I was right. When I grasped for proof (other than "because I said so") that I was actually the one who was right and they were wrong, I came up emptyhanded. I had a god; they had a god. I had a savior; they had a savior. I had a holy book; they had a holy book. My religion had a history; their religion had a history. My religion had a moral code; their religion had a moral code. My religion had an afterlife with reward and punishment; their religion had an afterlife with reward and punishment. My religion declared itself to be the one true religion and denounced all other religions as false; their religion declared itself to be the one true religion and denounced all other religions as false. In the end, I concluded that if there was actually just One Truth, then there would be only one truth, and not so very many truths all claiming to be true to the exclusion of all other truths.

This is not to say that I think there is no truth and that we cannot know anything. It is to say that I have released the belief that I can be or am right, universally right, or more right than someone else. As tempting as it is for me to indulge in the comfort of being right, I cannot declare myself to be right without first making someone else (or everyone else) wrong, and this itself is wrong; to nullify and make wrong another person's belief system, world view, or life philosophy is an act of violence, and violence in any form undermines peace, love, joy, and strength, which are the things I desire for my life.

Growing up in the cult, God was defined for me as a specific entity, and by default, what was not God got defined for me, also—similarly to how Hell can be defined as not Heaven. According to the concept of God, as it was defined for me by the cult, the most "not God" thing in existence, after Satan and his fallen angels, was me with all of my vile sinfulness! This judgement of myself as divided from God was very painful and confusing! It was the most painful and confusing when I was young and still had some shred of self-love that resisted this judgement. Of course, I was taught that my salvation through Jesus Christ "undivided" me from God, but I never really felt undivided from God because I still sinned. When I was a practicing Christian in the cult, I had rare moments of feeling connected to and loved by God, but they were few and far between; most of the time, I keenly felt that I was very much "not God."

After five years of living in Lynden, which included the birth of my younger daughter, we moved to Richmond, Virginia. By this time, I was in my early thirties and at the beginning of the darkest decade of my life. Not surprisingly, it didn't take long for the pain and stress that I was suffering under to turn me off to anything spiritual; I had become very bitter and I had lost all faith in everything, including myself. On a practical level, I just didn't have any extra attention available to contemplate spiritual mysteries, or any energy reserves to attempt any spiritual or personal growth; I was under siege and had gone into survival mode. God, religion, spirituality, the meaning of life, etc. were still my favorite subjects to talk about, but my take on them all had become much darker and more cynical.

I remember angrily declaring myself to be an atheist while smoking with a friend one night, and I was very taken aback by her response. She said, "You may say you're an atheist, Aidy, but you don't sound like an atheist and you don't act like an atheist." Like a belligerent child, with arms folded across my chest, I retorted, "*Well, I am!*" and then asked, "What do you mean I don't sound or act like an atheist?" She said, "I can tell that you don't believe that there is nothing out there; you just don't talk or act like someone who believes in nothing." Her observation really made me think, and prompted me to continue to clarify what I did believe.

I came to the conclusion that, at the very least, I was not comfortable saying that I *believed* in something, or anything. In the process of defining of my spirituality, given my experience with fanatical religion, I found the concept of belief to be problematic. As I was raised, to believe in something requires faith, and this meant putting my trust in something that I had little or no evidence for. Although I acknowledged that this worked for many other people, this no longer worked for me. My past experience of putting my trust in something that I had little or no evidence for was not a positive one; in fact, it was a disastrous mistake!

I am much more comfortable using the word "know." There are things that I feel confident saying that I know based on my experiences, and therefore, I feel comfortable that I have evidence to support my knowing. My knowing, being based *only on my experiences*, is most definitely not universal truth, and I would never proclaim it to be. For example, I know that there is a much greater reality than my experience of the physical world in time and space; I know this because I have had many, many experiences with a reality beyond my five senses and the physical world. I do not need to have faith in or believe in a non-physical, non-local realm, because I have had many, many experiences with it (many more than I have included in this book). These experiences have provided me with all the evidence I need to support my knowing that it is real. Establishing this construct of knowing over believing really served me; it gave me a solid platform to build on which I could be at peace with.

Interestingly enough, I would still call myself an atheist, although I'm only eligible for membership in this group on a technicality. Traditional atheists believe that there is nothing beyond what can be experienced in time and space and through the five senses, and therefore, they believe that there is no God and no experience after death. As a result of having entirely too many experiences outside of time and space and beyond what I can perceive through my five senses, I cannot dismiss the existence of a non-local realm. I also experience this non-local realm as divine, insofar as it has qualities which the non-divine local realm lacks, such as omniscience, omnipresence, omnipotence, infinite correlation, infallibility, immutability, etc.

Ultimately, I would agree with my girlfriend who said that I am not really an atheist, but I still call myself an atheist because, technically, I do not have any defined person, personality, or entity of God as a part of my spiritual practice. I have been told, in many a conversation on the subject, that what I call the divine non-local realm is, in fact, God. I have no problem with this, because I do think that it is all the same regardless of the vocabulary used to define it—but I choose not to use the word "God" in my own vocabulary. Nevertheless, I am still quick to point out that my concept of the divine non-local realm is not one of a defined person, personality, or entity; I prefer to think of God as a verb (action, state of being, or relation) rather than a noun (person, place, or thing).

The experiences I have had, which have caused me to conclude that there is a non-local realm, have also provided me with evidence that I am guided from the non-local realm and that my non-local self orchestrates people, places, events, and things in my local reality (as it did with

The A-Man). I have learned from my experiences with guidance and intervention from the non-local realm that when I pay attention and follow with as little questioning and analyzing as possible, even when it looks like it makes no sense, I will much more quickly and effectively arrive at the result I am aiming for, be it small or large. This has been called many things: following your gut, your intuition, your spirit guide, the voice of God, your guardian angel, your higher power, the Holy Spirit, etc. I call it "following Felix," because, in case you haven't noticed yet, I'm a crazy Harry Potter fan (yep, I'm one of those).

In *Harry Potter and the Half-Blood Prince*, the sixth book of the *Harry Potter* series, Harry is given a difficult but vitally important task by Dumbledore, the headmaster of Hogwarts School. He tries every clever and logical thing that he and his two best friends, Ron and Hermione, can think of to accomplish this task, but he remains woefully unsuccessful until he decides to use the Felix Felicis potion (liquid luck). After taking the potion, Harry feels certain that accomplishing this difficult task will be, "not only possible, but positively easy." He then announces that he is going to visit Hagrid, the groundskeeper, which is just about the most unlikely route to success and makes absolutely no sense to Ron and Hermione, who strongly question Harry and express doubt about the efficacy of the potion. Harry laughs off their concerns and says, "Trust me . . . I know what I'm doing . . . or at least . . . Felix does." What unfolds next is the most unlikely and most flawless sequence of events, which effortlessly produces success for Harry in a way that none of the three of them (especially Hermione, who relies heavily on her human brain) could have either orchestrated or even anticipated. When I first read this story, it struck me that it was a perfect allegory for the workings of guidance and aid from the non-local realm that I have experienced throughout my whole life.

I have found several dynamics of non-local guidance illuminated in the story of following Felix. The first dynamic is that the human brain is a very poor tool for figuring out how to achieve complex life goals, such as how to meet a soulmate, or find a dream job, or accomplish the task Dumbledore has given you; these feats are orchestrated at the non-local level, outside of time and space, where the human brain is not located. By the time Harry uses the Felix Felicis potion, he, Ron, and Hermione had already spent several months and tried multiple tactics to accomplish the difficult task

Dumbledore had given Harry; any tactic they had tried, which they had thought up using their human brains, had been a complete failure.

My human brain is great for executing the tasks of my daily life; it keeps my whole body, which is my vehicle for operating in time and space, running beautifully without me having to think about it, and it also organizes all the details necessary to get me from point A to point B as I move through the mundane events of my day. My brain is also very good for daydreaming about my ideal life, which inspires me to reach for it. What it is woefully inept at is figuring out the grand orchestration of the people, places, things, and sequence of events necessary to bring about my ideal life; this is far beyond its capacity. Omniscience and infinite correlation are required in order to effortlessly and flawlessly orchestrate a biggie like a dream job or a soulmate; omniscience and infinite correlation are qualities of the non-local realm, and not of the local realm or the human brain. I have learned not to try and affect a cosmic solution with my finite human brain; it's the wrong tool for the job!

I spent years dreaming of being free from my abusive marriage, and made plans with my human brain to start a new, more lucrative, career as an interior designer in order to be financially independent enough to divorce my husband without being at his mercy. These plans failed completely when the economy crashed and flattened the housing market, and along with it, the interior design industry, leaving me with no earthly way to get divorced on my own terms. Enter the flawless guidance and aid from the non-local realm through my accident with The A-Man, and I end up at the exact place I had been dreaming of after all (actually better than I had ever dreamed of), but in a way that was so much more effortless and flawless than what I had concocted with my human brain.

The second dynamic of non-local guidance in the story of following Felix is to trust the wisdom and guidance from the omniscient non-local realm even when it makes no sense, or seems to be the most unlikely route to success. Under the influence of the Felix Felicis potion, Harry has no idea why going to visit Hagrid is the right thing to do, and it certainly makes no earthly sense. As J.K. Rowling describes it, Harry "could not see the final destination . . . but he knew that he was going the right way."

I have a brain that likes to work similarly to that of the character of Hermione, who approaches everything academically and logically. I am a fairly intelligent woman and have had a good amount of success in my life with puzzling things out pragmatically; logic has been a staple go-to for me. The problem is that logic uses time and space as its point of reference, and wisdom and guidance from the non-local realm, which is flawless, are outside of time and space and therefore don't always appear to be logical within time and space. In fact, this wisdom and guidance rarely appear to be logical within time and space.

It made no logical sense for me to divorce my husband at the time that I did; I was not financially self-sufficient, as I had planned, my daughters were not through high school, as I had planned, the economy was in the toilet, as no one had planned, and we were severely upside down in our mortgage, which we certainly had not planned. The situation in my marriage had escalated through none of my own doing and put me in a position where, for my daughters' sake as well as my own, I needed to get out and stop waiting for the perfect time to do so.

I knew that I was ready to get divorced, regardless of the circumstances not being what I had hoped and planned for them to be, when my answer to every fearful question became, *"I don't care!"*

"What if I lose the house?"

"I don't care!"

"What if I never have any money to retire on?"

"I don't care!"

"What if . . . ? What if . . . ? What if . . . ?"

"I don't care! I don't care! I don't care!"

When the price for staying became unaffordable, the cost of leaving became negligible. As I liked to say it at the time, "He decided to board the bus to Crazy Town, and I decided that we were not going with him." As it turned out, I divorced my husband at the exact right time, not a moment too soon and not a moment too late, all because I trusted and followed the non-local guidance I received.

As strange as this sounds, I have discovered that my greatest tool for connecting with the wisdom and guidance of the non-local realm is my physical body. This seems to be paradoxical, because the physical body is only local, but the physical body also does not lie; it is an accurate indicator of our intuition and therefore is an infallible source for truth. This is why we say, "I have a 'gut' feeling." I have learned to go to my physical body for the answer when my Hermione brain reaches a dead end.

When I made the decision to file for divorce, I had complete peace in my body; I knew in my gut that it was exactly the right thing to do, and that it was the right time to do it even though it made no logical sense. That is not to say that going through the divorce was a peaceful experience or that I wasn't worried about my future; on the contrary, I was terrified! It is to say that I had an inexplicable, rock-solid confidence about my decision. There has never been a time when I have turned to my physical body, my gut, for an answer and it has led me wrong; I cannot say the same thing about my human brain, as much as I love, value, and appreciate it.

In Latin, the word "felix" means happy, in addition to meaning lucky (which is how J.K. Rowling uses it). In my experience, guidance from the non-local realm always directs me toward what makes me happy. Coincidently, I have found that choosing to do what makes me happy is also what brings the greatest amount of luck my way! As you might guess, this is very different from what I was taught growing up about following God's will for my life. I was taught that God would test my faithfulness and devotion to Him by requiring me to make choices for my life that I would not enjoy, and would not want to make. This translated to meaning that if I wanted something, it must mean that it wasn't God's will for my life, and if I didn't want something, it must mean that it was God's will for my life. Um, that's a pretty serious mind-fuck! I've seen this concept on a much broader scale in our culture, as what I would call the Should Commandment. For example, "I should go to college," "I should get a sensible degree," "I should have a family," "I should stay married," "I should play it safe," "I should follow the herd," etc. (I had a girlfriend who used to jokingly say, "Don't should on my day!"). We are not often encouraged to ask ourselves, "is this what I want to do?" or, "will this make me happy?"

After graduating from college, my older daughter was in a quandary about the next step she should take in her life (as is so common at that age and juncture in life). This was the first time in her life that she was truly walking out on her own as an adult, and she was really feeling the enormity of it all! As we talked about it, I could tell that she was feeling a lot of pressure to figure it out and get it right. She was torn between continuing in the sales job she had worked at during college and going back to school for her master's degree. She felt like she should pursue her master's degree, because that would take her farther along on her career path. She felt as if she would be compromising on her career goals if she stayed in her sales job. Although her job wasn't something she wanted long term, she also felt a lot of resistance when she thought about applying for graduate school. She told me, "Mom, it just doesn't make any sense because the master's program is perfect for me, but every time I think about filling out the application, my heart sinks!"

I told her that if the thought of grad school made her heart sink, then that was a surefire sign that it must not be the right thing for her to do at that time. I encouraged her to follow her heart, even if where her heart was leading her didn't appear to be sensible, or to be the right thing to do. I told her, "Sweetie, trust your path! You don't have to have it all figured out right now; just do the next thing that feels right. Just start off down toward Hagrid's hut, and everything else will fall into place flawlessly!"

Several years after my divorce, the economy began to improve, and with it, the interior design profession. Slowly but surely, all the tradespeople (contractors, upholsterers, cabinet makers, lighting designers, etc.) and designers who I had worked with when business was booming reached out to collaborate with me again. I felt like I should be thrilled, and should aggressively pursue any and all of the new design opportunities that were now available to me. The problem was that my heart was no longer in it; as much as I had loved and been inspired by interior design when I started out, it now left me cold. Unbeknownst to me, a new passion had taken ahold of my heart.

During the lull in my interior design business, I had begun to write, dabble unofficially in life coaching, and try my hand at public speaking (an easy transition from teaching), and these were the things that now made me happy and sparked joy in my heart. The idea of being able to help people design their lives, not just their homes, thrilled me so much that I could barely breathe when I dared to dream about doing it full time! I was caught between what I thought I should do and what I really wanted to do. I *should* pursue these new design opportunities, right? After all, didn't I spend five years of blood, sweat, and tears (not to mention, money) getting a second degree and professional certificate in interior design? I *shouldn't* let my degree or my business go to waste! Plus, I was single now and in my mid-forties; I really *should* be sensible and stick with the career I already have instead of pursuing yet another new career!

Thankfully, the Universe has my back and believes in me and my path, even when I doubt myself and my path. As I dutifully pursued the new design opportunities, as I thought I should, everything I touched turned to dust. It was pretty spooky! Even the most promising slam-dunk projects that I began went belly-up for one reason or another, despite all my hard work and dedication. After this happened a handful of times, it caught my attention, and I began to wonder if doing what I thought I should do instead of doing what I really wanted to do was the wrong choice after all. So, once again, I took a gamble on following Felix . . . grounded in knowing, I let go of the known and walked into the unknown with both fear and excitement in my heart.

Not long after my divorce, I attended a lecture given by Deepak Chopra during which he spoke about the "wisdom of uncertainty," which is the idea that the amount of possibility in any given situation is directly proportional to the amount of uncertainty in the situation. He said that when his children were younger, he used to say to them every morning, "Let's hope and pray that today is even more unpredictable than yesterday!" When I heard him say this, I had an actual physical anxiety response—my stomach tightened and my heart began to race!

Like most people, it is not my natural inclination to welcome uncertainty; on the contrary, it is my natural inclination to dread uncertainty. Having just survived the wildly uncertain circumstances of my divorce, I was beginning each day hoping for predictability, not unpredictability! Yet, the more I thought about it, the more I could begin to understand the wisdom of uncertainty. To offer an obvious example, winning the lottery would be a wildly unpredictable event that most people would welcome. I realized that although I had responded to the unpredictability of my divorce proceedings with great anxiety, it was out of the very same unpredictability that my favorable settlement was procured. Had the outcome of my divorce actually been the predictable outcome, I would have suffered much more anxiety and long term hardship! It's a work in progress, but I am learning more and more to embrace the wisdom of uncertainty, and to begin each day hoping that it will be more unpredictable than the day before.

Learning to trust the wisdom of uncertainty and follow Felix served me well when my cousin Darryl and his wife ungraciously and unceremoniously kicked me out of their house and gave me forty-eight hours to find a new place to live. Although my initial reaction was incredibly fearful, I was very quickly able let go of the certainty of what I thought was going to happen and embrace the uncertainty of what had actually happened. Several weeks later, after I was settled into my new place, I was reflecting on the whole ordeal over the phone with my younger daughter. I said, "I now know, without a doubt, that I was never actually supposed to live with Darryl and Bertha; I was always meant to live where I ended up but, if I'm being honest, I don't know if I would have had the guts to move clear across the country if I didn't think that I was going to land with people and in a place that I knew."

Several years ago, I was talking on the phone with my adoptive dad— an older friend who, intuitively sensing that I was basically an orphan, had taken me under his wing, and along with his wife, has given me the guidance and nurturing I never got from my biological parents. He was telling me that he was finding it awkward adjusting to retirement. He said, "I'm having a hard time figuring out what my 'job' is now that I don't have a job." I started laughing and said, "Oh, Dad, I have long since given up trying to figure out what my 'job' is; I just do what the day requires, and when the sun goes down, I go to bed."

My response was indicative of the fact that my life has not at all followed the predictable path that I thought it would when I started my journey just out of college. I have had so many unexpected twists and turns; so often, just when I thought I had something planned out and it was going to stick, my life would take a sharp left. So many of the things that I thought I was planning and doing for the face value of the thing— like getting a second degree in interior design in order to be financially independent from my husband—turned out to serve a purpose which had nothing to do with the thing itself.

I feel certain that all these twists and turns have served to bring my awareness to the constant, ever-present guidance I am blessed with from the non-local realm. Having rarely had any of my own plans work out, but having had my life, thus far, turn out to be better than I ever planned, anticipated, or imagined with my finite human brain, I now trust and rely on the guidance from my non-local self much more than I do my local self. I still make plans for my life, short term and long term, and I still have goals, hopes, and dreams, but I hold them very loosely. I practice listening carefully and watching closely for guidance from the non-local realm; I am ready to embrace the wisdom of uncertainty and follow Felix anytime, anywhere.

Looking back on the path that I have traveled from where I started to where I am now, I see a flawlessly organized spiritual quest, and I have found where I belong. I no longer strive to placate a deity, I no longer strive to please a savior, I no longer strive to conform to another's creed, and I no longer strive to gain enlightenment. I only desire to be at peace, because it is only from a place of peace that I can have anything to offer anyone else—which after all, is why I am here. Twenty-five years ago, I was in a state of merciless torture; I was tortured by my inner terrorist, my religion, and the multitude of abusive people I had yet to remove from my life. Today, I am at peace with who I am and what I have gone through; I am at peace with myself, inside and out.

CHAPTER TWELVE

My Exquisite Purple Life

One afternoon, shortly after my divorce was finalized, I had a curious experience in the middle of an afternoon nap. At this time in my life, I worked from home and ate my lunch from my own kitchen. On this day, I had a slow-growing migraine headache, which was unusual for me. After eating my lunch on the couch while watching some TV, I decided to lean into the corner of my sectional and rest my head for the fifteen minutes I had left before I needed to leave to pick my daughter up from school. I instantly fell into a deep sleep; a few minutes later, I sat straight up, eyes open and wide awake, and exclaimed out loud, "I will live an exquisite purple life!" I then immediately fell back into the corner of the couch and went right back to sleep. When my alarm woke me up to leave to get my daughter from school, I remembered what had happened. I went straight to my office, wrote down what I had said, and pinned it up on my note board. However, I phrased it in the present, rather than future, tense: "I live an exquisite purple life!"

On the drive to my daughter's school, I got on the phone with my friend David, who was a Reiki master and an aura reader. Dispensing with greetings when he answered the phone, I blurted out, "David, I just had the weirdest experience!" He laughed and said, "Aidy, your whole life is full of weird and wonderful experiences! What is it this time?" I recounted the experience to him and then asked, "David, what does this mean? Tell me everything you know about the color purple!" He replied, "Oh, Aidy, this is good; this is really good!" Excitedly, I demanded, "Tell me more!" He said, "Well, the color purple is associated with the highest chakra, the crown chakra, and represents cosmic consciousness, universal energy, and connection with divine spirit!" Even though I was driving down the highway (going the speed limit, of course!), I let go of the steering wheel, threw my hands up in the air, and shouted, "Whoo-hoo! I'll take it!" Later that afternoon, I did some more of my own research on the internet. I found out that across cultures, the color purple is associated with royalty, abundance, and a life of ease (again, I'll take it!).

When I turned to Merriam-Webster for the precise definition of the word "exquisite," this is what I found: "carefully selected, choice, accurate, marked by flawless craftsmanship or by beautiful, ingenious, delicate, or elaborate execution." All of the words in that definition were fabulous, but the ones that jumped out at me the most boldly were the first words: "carefully selected." What a completely different characterization of my life from the perspective that I had held onto for so long! For so long, I had seen my life as a random, chaotic, harrowing ordeal; I had viewed myself as a helpless victim of unfortunate circumstances and bad experiences which were beyond my control. As a result, I perceived much of my life and my experiences to have been a mistake, and I constantly longed for a do-over, even to the point of being suicidal at times. But no! I have lived, I do live, and I will continue to live an exquisite purple life—a life of cosmic consciousness connected to divine spirit with abundance and ease, one which I have carefully selected and ingeniously executed. What a blissful change of perspective on my life!

I think everyone has memories from when they were a child of saying things like, "When I grow up, I'm going to be . . ." or, "When I grow up, I'm going to do . . ." or, "When I grow up, I'm going to have . . ." The identity, action, or object changes, usually from fantastical to realistic, as we pass from childhood to adulthood, but the desire to fulfill a future dream remains constant, because that is a universal characteristic of the human experience. By my early twenties, I had a clear and detailed picture of who I wanted to be and what I wanted my life to be like. I don't know if this is universal or not, but in my mind, I unconsciously set forty as the age by which I wanted all the details of my life picture to be in place. Perhaps I settled on forty because I thought that this would provide me with ample time to achieve and acquire it all; perhaps I settled on forty because at age twenty-dumb I thought forty was *really* old, and I sure as hell better have it all together by then, because my life would pretty much be over after that.

Needless to say, as I neared my fortieth birthday and took stock of my life, it was not even close to being what I had wanted or planned for it to be; likewise, who I had become was not only not the woman I had wanted to be, but would also have been completely unrecognizable to my twenty-something self! I also realized that everything I had set my sights on from the start—a loving marriage relationship, a strong family unit, a happy, healthy, and successful self—was just as far out of my reach at nearly-forty as it had been in my early twenties. I was nowhere near where I wanted to be, and where I found myself was somewhere that I had never wanted to be. True to myself, I had a long, glorious, and overly indulgent Cinderella moment crying in the dirt on the roadside of my life, and then I had a serious come-to-Jesus meeting with myself, after which I rolled up my sleeves and got down to business.

Somewhere in my early twenties, my father was diagnosed with bipolar disorder, although what he primarily suffered from were bouts of depression, not mania. I have vivid memories of my father's bouts of depression during my childhood, when his mood would turn extremely dark and angry for months at a time. I remember several times, during my teen years, seeing him shake his fist at the ceiling, angrily shouting curses at God (this terrified me because he had raised me to take the wrath of God seriously and literally!). In my adulthood, I was less impacted by, or even aware of, his mood swings, because I no longer lived with him.

The year prior to when I broke with my family was an anomalous time in my relationship with my father. One mid-October afternoon, I was on my way to the fabric store to get supplies for my interior design homework when I got a call from my father. I chatted with him all the way to the door of the store, and I was about to tell him that I had to go when he launched into a tearful apology for the many ways that he had abused and failed me in my childhood. It stopped me in my tracks, literally—I never made it into the fabric store! Over the next few months, we continued to have conversations in which he welcomed me to share all the grievances I had with him. I started out small and then began to push the boundaries as he continued to respond with humility, remorse, and a constancy of love that I had rarely experienced in the nearly forty years that I had known him. In the end, I had laid it all out on the table, even all the ways I had been and still felt abused by his practice of his Christian faith, and he continued to respond with humility, remorse, and love. I was amazed! In that year, I experienced a quality and depth of relationship with my father that I had never experienced before. Unfortunately, it was not to last.

The entire time that I thought my father and I were rebuilding our relationship, there was a little voice in the back of my mind saying, "Be careful, Aidy, be very careful; don't let your guard down!" I remained cautious and skeptical for nearly a year. After nearly a year, and after testing the strength of our new relationship more than I ever imagined I could, I felt I could believe that what I was experiencing with my father was real, and I let my guard down. Unfortunately, as I later learned, my father had been in a hypo-manic state for the whole time that I thought we were rebuilding our relationship. A month before he and my mother came to visit for Christmas, he slipped into a deep depression; my mother had neglected to tell me of either his hypo-manic state or of the depression that he had slipped into. The father who came to visit me for the last time was the dark, angry, abusive, judgmental, and critical man with whom I was all too familiar.

Over the two weeks of my parents' visit, I tried to talk to my father multiple times, but each time, I hit a brick wall. In our final conversation on the last day of their visit, I pleaded with him, saying, "Dad, talk to me; you said that reconciling with me was the greatest gift of your life!" When he remained unmoved and was unwilling to address any of what had transpired during their visit, with tears streaming down my cheeks, I warned him, "'Fool me once, shame on you; fool me twice, shame on me.' Dad, this is your last chance; I won't be fooled again!" Without a word, he turned his back on me and walked away.

It was the most unbelievable and unbearable two weeks I had ever spent with my parents! Their boundary-less, abusive, and dysfunctional behavior towards me and each other raged out of control and went unchecked until the last day, when I snapped and threw them out of my house, luggage and all. It was a horrifying scene, and although I make no apologies for nor do I regret the drastic action I took, I was not particularly proud of my behavior.

For several months afterwards, I was a quivering mess! I have never had my house wiped out by a hurricane, but on an emotional and psychological level, it felt similar. Like a hurricane survivor, I began my recovery in shock, just surveying the damage, and then slowly, I resolved to rebuild. I remember sitting outside one night, self-soothing with cigarettes and alcohol, and thinking to myself, "I may make a complete mess of it, but as God is my witness, I will do *something different* from what my parents have done!" My parents were the very definition of insanity; doing the same thing over and over and over again, and every time, expecting to get a different and more improved result. I had no idea what to do to create the life I wanted, but thanks to their appalling example, I sure as hell knew what not to do; I figured that just doing something different, *anything different*, had to be a step in the right direction.

During my come-to-Jesus meeting with myself, one of the things I seriously asked myself was whether or not I wanted to keep aiming for the lofty goals I had thus far set my sights on, but which I had not even come close to reaching; I considered the option of dialing back my dreams and goals in exchange for the reassurance of knowing that lesser dreams and goals would be more attainable. After much pondering, I concluded that I was not interested in living a life of compromised dreams and goals. I resolved to continue to reach for my dreams and goals for the rest of my life, so that when I came to the end of my life, I would either have succeeded or I would still be trying. From this resolution came another one of my life mottos: "succeed or die trying."

I call my "succeed or die trying" resolution my Scarlett O'Hara vow. When I look back on myself at that time in my life, I can clearly see, for the first time, the rise of my mighty self, fist shaking in the air, declaring, "As God is my witness, I will succeed or die trying!" Shortly after reaching this point in my life, I came across a quote from Brian Tracy which summed up my Scarlett O'Hara moment: "I have found that every single successful person I've ever spoken to had a turning point, and the turning point was where they made a clear, specific, unequivocal decision that they were not going to live like this anymore. Some people make that decision at fifteen and some people make it at fifty, and most never make it at all."

When I reached this point and made this vow to myself, I went one step further and made myself a promise, which ended up being much like the ruby slippers given to Dorothy to protect her as she pursued her dream of getting back to Kansas. I promised myself that *I would not judge or criticize myself for how long it took me to reach my goals, or for any time*

I stumbled along the way. Just like Dorothy's ruby slippers, this promise ended up keeping me and my dreams safe from any violent terrorist attacks from my inner critic, or any outer critics I came across on my journey to success.

When I tell people my "succeed or die trying" mantra, they often look a bit alarmed, thinking that I am a vigilante who is willing to die for the cause. This might be in part because I have "succeed or die trying" tattooed on the inside of my left wrist; people can be so funny about tattoos! This is not at all what I mean by "die trying." I do not mean to imply that I am willing to die for success or the realization of my goals. I have no intention of sacrificing my life, my integrity, or my authenticity to achieve what I want in life. What I mean is that I will never give up on my goals and dreams, and I will never compromise on the highest vision I have for my life; I will continue to actively pursue my dreams until I either succeed or I die.

If I set my sights on a goal or a dream, be it short term (losing ten pounds) or long term (getting a degree), there are three possible outcomes: one is success, one is giving up, and one is that I come to the end of my time in this physical realm (I die) before I succeed. Failure is an illusion; there is no such thing as failure. What I might call failure, is, in reality, me giving up on the pursuit of a goal or a dream, and therefore, it is my doing and I am responsible for that choice. I am *never* a victim of circumstance. It is a victim mentality that says, "I tried but I failed," implying that I was vanquished by forces greater than myself. The truth is that I did not fail; I gave up. The truth is that there are *no* forces greater than me, no matter how difficult my circumstances are!

I have endless compassion for misfortune and suffering, but I have no pity for helplessness (except for the truly helpless—children and animals) because helplessness is an illusion. If I die before I succeed at a goal or a dream that I set my sights on, I did *not* fail; I only ran out of time! Chances are, if I had had more time, I would surely have succeeded! One of my favorite quotes, which echoes this idea, is from Thomas Edison in regards to how many tries it took him to invent a working lightbulb. He said, "I have not failed; I have just found ten thousand ways that won't work." In the end, he was successful because he refused to give up!

There is always room for reevaluation of the goals and dreams that I have set my sights on. There are goals and dreams I had when I was younger that I grew out of, or when I learned more about them, lost interest in. On the other hand, there are goals and dreams that have never left me, and my desire for them has only intensified over time. These are the goals and dreams that I hold in my focus when I commit myself to "succeed or die trying." These are the goals and dreams that I will *never* compromise on and *never* give up on!

For me, a key element in the pursuit of my goals and dreams has been the practice of the Law of Detachment, which is one of the spiritual laws of success discussed in *The Seven Spiritual Laws of Success* by Deepak Chopra. Learning how to let go of my attachment to my goals and dreams has been a very long study for me. I remember that I was somewhere in my twenties when I first heard about the Law of Detachment, and I did not get it at all; I could not understand how you could desire something and also be detached from it! Surely, the two states of desire and detachment were mutually exclusive! I mistakenly thought that detachment meant saying and feeling that I didn't care about getting what I desired. In my twenties and thirties, I was not getting pretty much anything that I deeply desired, and I very much cared about the fact that I wasn't getting what I so deeply desired.

In my thirties, my first misguided attempts at practicing my limited understanding of the Law of Detachment looked something like this: "I can't get what I want? Fuck it! I won't need or want what I can't get; I'm fine without it!" This is not actually the Law of Detachment; this is, in fact, the Law of Denial! Practicing the Law of Denial in my life was what caused me to turn to self-destructive ways of numbing the pain I felt from not getting what I wanted and needed. Ultimately, practicing the Law of Denial was completely unproductive and actually prolonged my pain.

In my early forties, I found the strength to pursue my goals and dreams again long before I had manifested any of them, which brought me back again to trying to practice the Law of Detachment. After much puzzling over the seeming contradiction between the state of desiring something and the state of detachment from that thing, I had an epiphany. Detachment doesn't mean that I don't want it anymore, or that I don't care whether or not I get it; it means that I let go of the angst and fear that arises when I think about not getting what I want! It means that I stay in the pure "Have it; want it!" (like my daughter when she was a toddler) state of desire, which exists without angst and fear, because angst and fear corrupt pure desire. Once I figured this out, I found it much easier to practice the Law of Detachment!

I often still find it challenging to keep myself in the state of pure desire and not let myself get pulled into angst and fear. For me, there is a direct correlation between how unattainable the object or circumstance of my desire seems to be and how strongly I will feel the pull into angst and fear. It is a daily, if not minute-to-minute, discipline, but it gets easier and easier because, as I have come to experience, the state of pure desire is *so much more* enjoyable than the state of angst and fear!

Fear and angst will rush in, corrupting my pure desire, when I can't see how the thing or circumstance that I desire could be possible; this happens when I make the mistake of using my finite human brain to try and orchestrate a cosmic solution. When I realized that asking how, and trying to figure out how, brought on a tsunami-level of fear and angst, I decided to stop asking and stop trying to figure out how. The culmination of this handy-dandy aha moment resulted in the creation of yet another very powerful mantra that I use all day, every day: "I can, and I don't ask how!"

In my experience, saying "I can, and I don't ask how" makes all the necessary hows appear in time and space as surely as expressing a need three times outside the Room of Requirement makes it materialize for any Hogwarts student. Side note here: if you are lost with all these *Harry Potter* references because you haven't read *Harry Potter*, may I ask why? Why haven't you read *Harry Potter*? Never mind, I don't care why you haven't read *Harry Potter*! Just go read *Harry Potter* . . . now! Yes, I mean right now! Yes, I mean *all* the books! You can finish this book after you've read *Harry Potter* . . . it's that important!

As hows have appeared throughout my life, I have been tempted to attach to them out of relief: "Oh thank God, now I know how I am going to get this thing or have this experience!" Can you hear the underlying fear and grasping? This is a trap of attachment that I have fallen into many times. As I have discovered, the tricky thing is that there are two kinds of hows: facilitator hows and endgame hows. If I attach to a how that shows up, I run the risk of attaching to a facilitator how, which has only shown up in my life to facilitate the endgame that I really want. I don't want to settle for a facilitator how when my heart's desire will only be manifested in the endgame!

A perfect example of this was my relationship with Scotty. In so many ways, he matched my heart's desire for an intimate and romantic relationship, but not in all ways. When he showed up in my life, my response was, "Oh thank God, now I will finally experience the relationship I've always longed for!" Can you hear the underlying fear and grasping? Instead of trusting that I could have *all* that my heart desired in a relationship, I fearfully attached to a relationship that was only *most* of what I desired. As it turned out, my relationship with Scotty was only a facilitator how and not an endgame how. I am grateful that I found the strength to detach from that relationship and let it be the facilitator how that it was always and only meant to be. Scotty was the first man in my life to love me without abusing me in any way, and having that experience with him facilitated me leaving abusive love behind for good, just as effectively as my "I am hurt" dream facilitated me leaving unrequited love behind for good.

The mantra I have discovered that safeguards me against attaching to hows as they show up in my life is: "this or better." When a how shows up in my life and I feel relief from the fear of uncertainty about getting a thing or experience that my heart desires, I remind myself, "this or better." It helps my fear to release what has shown up from its desperate claws of attachment. When I tell my fear "this or better," it abates because the underlying worry that triggers my fear is some variation of, "this better work out because it could be my only shot at love, success, security, happiness, etc." Suggesting "better" to my fear impresses upon it that this how is not the only way that I can get a thing or have an experience that my heart desires, and it opens the door for me to the limitless potential of the Universe. It works as magically as giving a crying child a lollipop; my fear immediately stops crying and starts smiling!

A lot of my motivation not to give up on my dreams comes from knowing that my dreams are backed by a force and a source much greater than just me. I know that if I have something to offer, it is because someone, or many people, need what I have to offer. I know that anyone and everyone who needs what I have to offer is pulling for me, whether they know it or not. Their cry, prayer, or petition for help, which can be met by what I have to offer, mobilizes and orchestrates all the people, places, things, and events necessary to support and facilitate me being able to bring forth what I have to offer. With that kind of backing, why would I give up? With that kind of backing, how could I possibly fail?

My daughters had been sternly taught in school about the wickedness and dangers of smoking, and had dutifully adopted a fanatical abhorrence for smoking and a merciless "off with their heads" attitude towards smokers. Feeling certain that I would be unable to endure their disappointment and judgment, I didn't have the guts to tell them when I became a smoker; I hid it from them for many years. Eventually, by the time they each reached junior high, they each caught me at different times, and I confessed. Each time, they were upset and worried, but loved me too much to be mean to me about it, for which I am eternally grateful. As they moved into high school and became more cognizant of how miserable I was, they were more understanding of why I smoked, although they still hated it.

I remember one day, in the middle of my divorce, I had just come inside from smoking a cigarette and my older daughter wrinkled her nose at the smell; this always made me feel terrible about my smoking! In guilty response I said, "Trust me, Sweetie, as soon as I have made it through this divorce, I will quit smoking for good!" Her reply just about knocked me on my ass! She said, matter-of-factly and with no judgment or harshness, "Yeah, Mom, 'cause then what will your excuse be?" *Out of the mouths of babes!* After I picked my jaw up off the floor, I said, "You're right, Sweetie! I swear I will make this divorce work for me, and I will become a happier person, and my life will get better! I refuse to be one of those people who says, 'I struggle because my life sucks,' and then somehow still has the same struggles even when their life doesn't suck anymore, or who finds some new way for their life to suck to justify their continued struggling."

I had reached a point where I realized that I was responsible for my whole life; all of my actions and inactions, no matter how understandable or justifiable, were my responsibility even if their causes weren't my fault. Moving forward, I knew that I would be responsible for taking action to change my life. I also knew that choosing to do nothing was an option and it is an effective option, insofar as it does work. It will produce the predictable outcome: do nothing, change nothing. If I make no changes in what I am doing, there will be no change in what I am experiencing. As crazy as it sounds, doing nothing is a choice that I am entitled to make, but it is one that I have learned I don't want to make.

For much of my life, I have hated my life circumstances and I have been angry and depressed. I used to think that I was angry and depressed because I felt powerless to change my life circumstances. I now realize that what was actually making me crabby was that it was on me to change my life circumstances and I knew it, but I didn't want to accept the responsibility. At that time, it felt easier to claim that I was powerless to change my life circumstances than it was to take responsibility for my life and move into the power that is my birthright. When I chose to step fully into my power and take action to change my life circumstances, I discovered that the source of my power is in my ability to respond—my response ability.

For so long, I thought that I stayed in my abusive marriage because I didn't have the strength to leave. I have only recently realized that, in truth, I left because I no longer had the strength to endure the abuse and misery—I literally couldn't take it anymore! Instead of becoming stronger, I actually became weaker, and in the process, it actually became easier to leave than to stay. I know this seems like it doesn't make sense, but hear me out . . .

When I was in my abusive marriage, I was not the only person I knew who was in an abusive marriage. In fact, the majority of my friends were in unhappy marriages that were abusive, to one degree or another (misery loves company), and some of them were in even worse marriages than mine. My friends' abusive marriages seemed normal to me when I was also in an abusive marriage, but once I was out of my abusive marriage, the truth and reality of my friends' abusive marriages became *so* glaring. What also became glaringly obvious to me was just *how much* hard work and strength it takes to stay in an unhappy, abusive marriage. From my new vantage point, I witnessed my friends putting a *monumental* amount of time, attention, energy, emotion, and resources into sustaining their bad marriages. Looking at my friends through this new lens, I now saw them as some of the strongest, most tenacious people I have ever known! I was flabbergasted—here I had been thinking that they were weak, too weak to leave their bad marriages!

The more I pondered this new perspective on strength versus weakness, the more I realized that I have actually been strong my whole life, although I have harshly judged myself (and been harshly judged by others) to be weak many, many times. In fact, I'm beginning to wonder these days if I am not actually getting weaker and weaker with every passing year (but in a really good way!). Again, I know this sounds confusing, but bear with me . . .

In the early days of transitioning to my third career of life coaching, public speaking, and writing, I was quite often terrified and gripped by a nearly paralyzing fear of the unknown. My inner critic aggressively questioned my sanity, and screamed insecurities over a loud speaker in my head all day long, oftentimes leaving me completely exhausted by the end of the day. If I had not been so consumed by a passion for the work that I now believe is my true calling, I would not have persevered. Even though I was persevering, I felt weak because it was a daily struggle to keep moving forward in the face of my fear.

One day, as a part of my gratitude practice, I was reflecting on how grateful I was for the life I now lived, because even with all the fear and uncertainty, I was so much happier. In comparison, I remembered what my life was like in my abusive marriage, and I felt even more grateful! I thought to myself, "I would rather face the challenges of my life now instead of having to face the challenges of my life back then any day!" I laughed and said out loud, "I'm not strong enough anymore to face such misery again! I've developed such a weakness for joyful living; I'd even go so far as to admit that I'm a joy junkie!" I now understand that I have never, ever been weak, not ever. I've only been misguided in where I have chosen to apply my amazing strength.

I can be so very prone to judging myself (and others) when I choose not to make changes, fall short of the changes I attempt, or don't make progress as quickly as I think that I (or others) should make. The implication in this judgment is the idea that the purpose of life is to "get it right" (and to do so as early in life as possible). The campaign to get it right falls apart when I try to define "it" and "right." The argument that I am here to get it right is only valid when and if it and right can be defined universally and objectively. How can I say what it is and when it has been gotten right? Do I use a religious or moral code to define it and right? Unfortunately, there is no universal agreement between religions or codes of morality. Do I use the general consensus of culture or society to define it and right? Cultures and societies agree no more than religions do on the definition of it and right. Not only is the definition of it and right subjective within religions and cultures, it is also ultimately subjective within time and space; we all know the saying "you can't take it with you," and yet such a huge part of the definition of "getting it right" in many cultures is based on the accumulation of wealth, which ultimately has no meaning outside of time and space.

I have been socialized to look at a homeless person and think, "he/she is not doing it right," or think, "he/she must have done something wrong along the way." I might look at someone like Oprah, who is exceedingly materially successful, and pass the judgment that she got it right. Or, perhaps, if I were to consider self-discipline to be a greater hallmark of success, I would pass the opposite judgment that she has not gotten it right, because despite her phenomenal professional success and great wealth, she has continuously struggled with her weight.

Any and all of the judgments that I may pass on myself and/or others are ultimately irrelevant and useless, because they are subjective based on my own personal, racial, cultural, religious, and even time and space biases. Time, space, and all biases contained therein are a subjective illusion; therefore, to be judgmental toward myself or another person is to reveal myself to be fooled by the illusion, however temporarily. I don't think that I am here to get it right or do it right; I think I am just here to have the experiences I want to have, which are only good or bad within the subjective context of the illusion of time and space. The question remains: *"What experiences do I want to have, and am I having the experiences I want to have?"*

As I neared my fortieth birthday and realized that I was not having the experiences that I wanted to have (not even close!), I knew that I would have to begin again; I had reached a dead end in just about every aspect of the life I had envisioned for myself when I was in my early twenties. Since I had decided that I wasn't willing to give up on or compromise what I wanted, I knew I was going to have to start over again with a new game plan. It was a daunting prospect to consider beginning again with nearly half of my life behind me already; as I pondered the prospect, I came to the conclusion that to begin again is to begin a gain. With this positive shift in my perspective, I set my sights on all the gains that I desired to begin.

In the pursuit of my aspirations, it has been very tempting to follow someone else's path, someone who I perceive to be "doing right" the "it" that I desire or aspire to. This has been a life-long temptation for me; one of my life lessons has been to stick to my path, my unique path which is perfect for me, and defer only to my unique truth. Every time and in every way that I have taken a detour in my life, it has been, in hindsight, because I was following someone else's path or deferring to someone else's truth; following someone else's path or truth is, essentially, sacrilegious, because doing so demotes your truth and your path, which are inherently sacred and perfect.

When I have been tempted to follow someone else's path, it has often been out of fear and insecurity about my own path, because I am in the middle of my path and the end of it is still unknown or unclear to me. The ancient wisdom from the *Bhagavad Gita* says that "It is better to live your own destiny imperfectly than to live a perfect imitation of somebody else's life." I would argue that to live my own destiny is intrinsically perfect, no matter how imperfect it is judged to be by someone else who is being temporarily fooled by the illusion of time and space.

In my late twenties, I had my aura read by a woman who made an observation about me which stayed with me. She said, "Aidy, you struggle with being here in this human experience. You find the perceived imperfection of your experience in time and space to be very frustrating, and you reject your humanity as being flawed. Just remember that we are here for a reason; this human experience has something valuable to offer us, or else we wouldn't have chosen it." For the first time in my life, I began to think about relaxing into my human body and embracing my choice to be in time and space, although it took several more decades for me to fully engage in the time and space human experience that I had chosen.

The challenge of my human experience has been to submerge myself in the illusion of time and space as fully as I possibly can without losing my understanding that it is an illusion. I am not supposed to believe that it is real, but I am also not supposed to reject it or try to withdraw myself from it. My experience in time and space has value, and my being here is no accident; there is a value in being human.

I am just a regular old, real, live, luminous, and eternal being of light operating in the illusion of time and space through a very human body and a very human brain; as such, I am just as vulnerable to being fooled by and caught up in this illusion as anyone else! If you don't believe me, just cut me off on the highway sometime; you'll see just how fooled by the illusion I can be, and trust me, it won't be pretty! Out of habit and humanity, I still get fooled and have many of the unpleasant experiences of this illusion: the worry, the fear, the doubt, the anxiety, the sadness, the hurt, the loneliness, and the attachment—all of it. I am still learning the balance between participating in the illusion of time and space in order to benefit from all of the experiences it has to offer, and not losing sight of the fact that it is an illusion, so that I don't fall into the experience of pain and confusion that believing in the illusion brings.

My personal growth and life changes did not happen overnight, not even close! I did not make my Scarlett O'Hara vow and then never stumble, doubt, or regress into a Cinderella moment again; it was a back and forth process, very much like making bread. When you make bread, you mix as much flour into the dough as you can in the bowl with the spoon, but there comes a time when the dough will not accept any more flour with just the stir of the spoon; that is when you have to turn the dough out onto the board and knead the rest of the flour in. The insights and epiphanies I have had on my journey only sank in so far when they were just realizations; there came a time when I had to roll up my sleeves and knead the truths of my insights and epiphanies into my brain, my behavior, and my life. Then, like bread dough, I let my progress rise; when life punched my progress down, I kneaded it some more, let it rise again, and so on.

These days, I am much less of a slow learner, but my progress can still often be "two steps forward, one step back." I am comfortable with this and have no judgement for myself for where I am, or my pace of progress; in fact, I'm soundly impressed with my pace of progress these days, especially when I remember that there was a time, not too long ago, when my pace of progress was much more along the lines of, "two steps forward, one and seven eighths steps back"! I have learned to trust in the flawless perfection of the Universe and to lean into the flawless perfection of my own life.

The truth of my experience was that at no point along the journey of my struggles did I know that I was going to make it, and yet I continued to wage my battle of personal growth. To be honest, I am more proud of myself for not giving up in the middle of my battlefield than I am for reaching my green valley, because it was the act of not giving up that got me to my green valley! I have learned that, as Martin Luther King, Jr. said, "You don't have to see the whole staircase, just to take the first step." When I find myself on the first steps of yet another staircase that I cannot see the entirety of, I am proud of myself for stepping!

I believe in life after misery, and I find happiness to be so very easy now! Like Walt Whitman in "Song of Myself," with effortless joy, "I sound my barbaric yawp over the rooftops of the world!" Like the character of Jean Valjean from Victor Hugo's *Les Miserables*, having spent so many years in prison for just as guileless of a reason, I will never take my freedom or my happiness for granted! Having been at a place in my life where I struggled so greatly to find any source of joy, I now find joy in everything and in the simplest of things; just the simple act of making my bed in the morning or flossing my teeth at the end of the day puts a smile on my face, because I am blissfully aware of the fact that I am no longer so sad that I cannot manage to do these simple things. One Saturday several years after my divorce, my daughter asked me why I was putting on makeup when I was only going to the grocery store. With a huge grin, I responded, "Just because I feel like it!" I am so grateful to feel like doing even the extra things these days, instead of having to heroically struggle against not wanting to do anything, even the basics!

One of the millions of positive messages I have plastered all over my house is, "No journey is too great if you find what you seek." Although I am still moving toward some of the specific particulars of my goals and dreams, I have no hesitation in saying that I have found what I have been seeking, and the journey has not been too great! I have found myself, I have found love, I have found joy, I have found peace, and I have found strength! I have a magnet on my refrigerator that says, "Life doesn't have to be perfect to be wonderful." There was a time when I thought my life needed to be perfect to be wonderful; I now know that because my life is wonderful, it is perfect! From where I am now, I unwaveringly feel that *I am well and truly pleased with the adventure I have chosen for myself*; I am pleased with *every* single detail of it, pleasant and unpleasant, pleasurable and painful! As I see it now, my life is, and always has been, exquisite and purple in every sense of those words!

Epilogue

Raw and fragile, like overly tired toddlers who had missed their naps, we silently and wearily filed back into the large conference room after our break. We had spent the morning journaling about the people in our lives who had hurt us the most deeply, and we were all emotionally quivering. Although no one spoke, I felt certain that there was not one of us who was actually looking forward to the upcoming exercise; I know I sure wasn't! The chairs had been rearranged into pairs facing each other, and we had been instructed to sit down with someone we did not know, which was going to be easy for me since I had come to this retreat alone. Only a little of what we were going to do next had been explained to us. From what I understood, we were going to briefly share the story of how we had been hurt, and by whom, with our partner, and then go through a healing and release process that had not yet been fully detailed. I was feeling equal parts "Get me the hell outta here!" and, "Fuck yeah, let's do this shit!"

I had just entered the room, and was looking for the right chair to sit in across from someone I did not know, when I heard it. As plain as day, I heard my maternal grandmother's voice in my head say, "Aidy, I take responsibility for how I failed your mother and I apologize for the painful and damaging impact that it had on you; I'm sorry." The room did not go dark, the ceiling did not open, no beam of heavenly light shone down, and there was no scene cueing angelic music. It was such an unremarkable incident that it almost escaped my notice, and yet it was the most impactful thing that happened to me that weekend.

My grandmother's message to me had such healing power! I knew beyond a shadow of a doubt that she spoke to me that day, not only because I had always been her favorite grandchild, but because she knew that my mother had never (and very likely would never in this lifetime) taken responsibility for how greatly she had failed me. My mother's refusal to take responsibility for having wronged me had always been more painful than any of the endless ways she had actually wronged me.

I was in my thirtieth year when I got my first tattoo. As a redhead, I have a pretty high pain tolerance, but I still wanted reassurance that it wasn't going to hurt too badly, so I asked the tattoo artist to describe the pain to me before he began. He said, "It's not bad; it's kinda like a bee sting." Then he began to drill; after a few minutes, I said, "You were right; it's kinda like a bee sting . . . from a whole swarm of bees . . . all at once . . . continuously . . . and for however long it takes you to finish the tattoo!" The thing was that once the tattooing had begun, there was no turning back because the very first prick of the needle had made an indelible mark; if I had chickened out, I would still have had a tattoo, but it would have been an unfinished one.

Writing this book was a similar experience. From the very first paragraph, I began to feel the sting from what I was writing; I also knew, from the very first paragraph, that there was no turning back, because it had already made an indelible mark on me. Recalling in detail so many painful experiences from my life, reaching back to before my first breath, and replaying them in HD on the movie screen of my mind took me through them all again in a way that I hadn't experienced in many years; needless to say, I was caught off-guard by the impact.

I had never before pulled all of my life experiences together in one place. Throughout my life, as each experience came at me, one after another, I had just dealt with it the best I could at the time; along the way, I had made some connections, taken mental notes, and become aware of recurring themes, but not with the clarity that came to me through the writing of this book. As you can imagine, by the time I had finished writing the first draft, I was feeling a whole new level of hurt and outrage over how I had been treated by my family and my ex-husband, and I had fresh pain to deal with.

Had I known the full effect that writing this book would have on me before I started it, I might not have gone through with it, but I would say that about most of my life experiences, as, I'm sure, would you. I'm going to take a wild guess here and say that writing this book and the impact that it had on me is yet another one of my life experiences where "I knew what I was doing; I knew exactly what was going to happen, and I was up for it." I have learned to trust the process and follow Felix, so when I was blind-sided by what came up in me, I just went with it as gracefully as I could; by gracefully, I mean with a lot of angry tears and obscenities screamed out into the empty air.

The realizations from what I had written came to me slowly at first, like a "hey . . . wait a minute . . ." moment, and then gathered speed until they were coming to me at a rapid-fire pace, like the blinding finale of a fireworks show on the Fourth of July. When everything that was coming up in me got too big for my brain to hold, I went to the page and spent about a month just free-writing it all out of myself. I never intended to share any of what I wrote further than in conversations with my adoptive mom and dad and a few close friends, but as these thing go, it became apparent that much of what was emerging would do well as an epilogue. Furthermore, I felt I owed it to you, because I was keenly aware of the fact that I had left something out of my story; I left it out because I hadn't resolved it, and I was chicken about admitting that I still struggled with it.

If you are an astute reader, and more to the point, if you are a reader who struggles with your weight, you will have noticed that I conspicuously failed to address my struggle with my weight and if or how I had resolved that struggle; throughout the course of this book, I discuss how I overcame the other major issues that I struggled with, but neglected to discuss my struggle with weight. I actually had included it in an earlier draft, because I had lost the weight during my post-divorce-put-myself-back-together phase, but unfortunately, because I lost the weight through yet another extreme weight loss program (HCG), I didn't keep it off. By the time I began writing this book, I had gained it all back. I originally included my post-divorce weight loss story in chapter five, but later removed it because I felt it would be misleading since I had gained again. I also removed mention of it from chapter three; although the hypnotherapy gave me priceless insight into my life as a whole, unfortunately, it had no impact on my struggle with my weight.

We who struggle with our weight *always* want to hear others' success stories, and *always* want to know the secret of that success in the desperate hopes that it will help us, once and for all, to have success in our struggle with our weight! If you are one of those bizarre humans who has never struggled with your weight (bizarre only to those of us who do struggle), you might not have noticed my omission, and bless you, can no more relate to this whole experience of struggle with weight than a man can understand what pregnancy and childbirth are like. If you do struggle with your weight, I imagine you may have uttered an emphatic, "Thank you!" when I acknowledged that I failed to address my struggle with mine, and you will be eager to read the rest of this epilogue. If you have never struggled with your weight, you might finish reading this epilogue out of curiosity, and perhaps you can draw a parallel from my insights to help you with a different struggle. Either way, with this epilogue, I hope to offer you the latest color I have added to my pile of crayons, with which I am coloring my exquisite purple life; if it can help you in the coloring of your own exquisite purple life, it's yours for the taking!

In the several years following my divorce, I had been able to overcome all of my self-defeating habits, except my struggle with food and my weight. I was truly puzzled that this struggle remained, because I felt happier and more empowered than I had ever felt in my life. Why wouldn't this struggle become a thing of the past like all my other struggles had? Food continued to get the better of me, my weight continued to yo-yo, and I became very discouraged; I was in danger of giving up and accepting several fatalistic limiting beliefs about myself, like, "maybe I was just born this way" or, "maybe I am not meant to overcome this struggle" and, "I guess my body really is just prone to being overweight." Thankfully, as hard as I tried, I could not resign myself to these limiting beliefs, nor could I make my peace with having a weight struggle for the rest of my life. The nagging desire to resolve this final issue would not let me go, but I still had no idea how to resolve it; what I did know was that I needed the war with food to be over and I needed to win the war, but I had no idea how to make that happen.

Through chronicling my history with food and weight issues in chapter three, it became clear to me that the perspective I had always held about my body and my life-long struggle with my weight were both completely invented and created by my mother; *none of it was ever true and it was never actually how I was born to be.* The sentence that I wrote which switched the light on for me was, "From as far back as I can remember, my mother had told me that I needed to be careful about what I ate because I was 'prone to being overweight'; *a declaration for which she had no supporting evidence or proof, but a declaration which has haunted me for much of my life."*

The reason why I wrote that my mother had no evidence or proof for her declaration that I was prone to being overweight was because, when I thought back over my childhood, I realized that *there was not a single day when I was actually overweight, not even on the day that I was born*; in fact, I was *always* at or under a healthy weight! Yet, she had me thoroughly convinced that I was fat or about to become fat any minute, so much so that I can't remember a time in my life, even reaching back to my early childhood, when I wasn't worried about my weight and obsessed about what I was eating or not eating. In my adulthood, like a self-fulfilling prophecy, I did actually become prone to being overweight, and I was often fat or about to become fat any minute; it just goes to show that what you think and what you believe *really do* create your reality even if they completely lack any factual foundation!

Another insight I gained from writing chapter three was the realization that my habit of overeating in response to food cravings had never satiated those cravings. Throughout my adult life, I had explained my inclination to overeat and the times that I would indulge in overeating by telling myself that I was making up for being starved at birth, but no amount of overeating ever seemed to actually make up for the starvation I had experienced at birth. By this point in my life, it had become clear to me that no amount of overeating would ever satisfy me or actually make up for my experience of starvation, so I had to dig deeper to find what the root problem was.

The more I thought about it, the more I came to realize that in my first month of life, I might have gotten the overwhelming craving for food confused with being alive. I theorized that in my first weeks of life when I was being starved to death, I had learned to associate overwhelming craving for food with being alive. Every time I woke up and came back to consciousness, it meant that I was still alive (phew!); overwhelming craving for food was what woke me up and brought me back to consciousness, ergo, overwhelming craving for food meant that I was alive. This may have made perfect sense to my tiny baby brain, but it was a line of logic that no longer held up and no longer served me as an adult.

In a fortuitous culmination of all that I had been processing during the month following the completion of this book, I ended up at a Healing the Heart retreat at the Chopra Center in Carlsbad, California. Through another random, seemingly unrelated sequence of events along the lines of The A-Man, I had actually registered for the Healing the Heart retreat a year prior to attending, and before I had even started writing this book. I was originally registered to attend a session which would have coincided with the start of my writing, but scheduling conflicts caused me to postpone and transfer my registration to a session later in the year, which as it turned out, fell one month after I finished writing the first draft.

In preparation for the retreat, I read the recommended book, *Free to Love, Free to Heal*, by David Simon, MD. In one of the exercises in the book, Simon asks his readers to identify what they had needed that they didn't get from the person who hurt them. As I sat thinking about my mother, all that she had done to hurt me, and what I had needed that I didn't get from her, I caught myself by surprise when I blurted out loud, "I needed to live! I needed for it to be okay that I was alive! I was entitled to live!"

The stories in this book are all true and all mine, but a lot of the phrasing and the analogies I use to convey my thoughts and illustrate my stories just came out of me (thanks in great part, I'm sure, to my muse on the other side, May). For example, in chapter three, the sentence, "I began my life dying, literally," just came out of me. The phrasing of this opening sentence stuck with me over the many months of writing this whole book, and I came to feel a new level of outrage over my mother's negligence. It dawned on me that she had almost passively killed me; she didn't try to actively kill me, by, for example, smothering me with a pillow or shaking me, but by way of her appalling neglect, she nearly killed me all the same. The way she neglected me called into question whether or not she was okay with me being alive. In so many ways, time and time again, my mother passively tried to kill me, my body and my spirit, and repeatedly gave me the message that she did not support or celebrate me being alive.

I know I was a planned pregnancy, but whether my mother actually wanted me or not, I'll never know; what I do know is that reaching back to before she even gave birth to me, she did not treat me the way that a wanted baby is treated. Through yet another story which she so callously and recklessly shared with me when I was a preteen, I learned that she had been devaluating me even before I was born.

Although my parents lived a very austere and minimalist life when I was growing up, they both came from very wealthy families. When my mother was pregnant with me, she was thrown a lavish baby shower by her wealthy family and their friends, and was given very generous and expensive gifts (along the lines of Barneys, Tiffany, Bergdorf Goodman, etc.). She told me that her family and their friends did this for her because, as she recounted it, they had said amongst themselves, "That poor baby isn't going to have much!" I remember responding to her story by saying, "Well, at least I started my life with some nice things!" With an incredulous laugh, she retorted, "Oh, no, I didn't keep the gifts! I returned everything to the store and got the money!" Somehow, even as a preteen, I was self-possessed enough to be outraged, and I angrily chided her, saying, "How dare you! Those weren't your gifts; they were for me! They were mine; you had no right to take them back!"

As I continued with the exercises in *Free to Love, Free to Heal*, I made a connection between how my mother had almost passively killed me and how my husband had been so callous and unmoved when I told him that I planned to kill myself. In an eerily similar way, by starving me of physical and emotional intimacy and ignoring the result, he also almost passively killed me. Never did he support or celebrate me being alive; he constantly treated me like a repulsive annoyance which he wished would just go away (a continuation of my mother's attitude toward me in my childhood).

As my mind continued to ruminate on this idea of having been almost passively killed by my mother and my ex-husband, I was bowled over by a third, final, and most shocking connection: *I had also spent many years of my adult life almost passively killing my own self!* Although I never ended up actively killing myself, I had daily, for decades, engaged in habits, including overeating and poor diet in combination with little or no exercise, that were known to cause death. Although the predisposition toward these self-destructive habits wasn't my fault, I was still responsible for living a lifestyle that was passively killing me. Up to this point, I had understood my self-destructive habits individually, within the context of my depression, as a result of the abuse and neglect I had suffered. I had understood them to be self-soothing mechanisms to ease my pain, which they were, but now I saw a much bigger and more all-pervasive pattern of self-destruction. Stunned, I wondered, "*Why would I do that?* After having been almost passively killed when I was helpless to do anything about it, why wouldn't I do everything in my power to help myself live the best life possible when I was no longer helpless to do something about it? *Why would I do that to myself?*"

The answer that came to me was just as illuminating as the realization I had just had…

In the same way that I had acquired the habit of communicating using the English language, because that is what was modeled for me during my formative years by the people who raised me, I had also acquired the habit of passively killing myself, because that is what was modeled for me during my formative years by the people who raised me!

It has been so mystifying to me when I have repeatedly engaged in a dysfunctional behavior that has caused me or those I love pain, because it just seems so very illogical, and yet, it has often also felt nearly impossible to defeat. Like a dizzy person trying to reach a specific spot on the other side of the room after spinning around too many times with their forehead pressed to the end of a baseball bat, I kept aiming for where I wanted to be, but have ended up left of center time and time again. The dizzy person thinks that what they need is to reach the other side of the room, and this is where they apply their efforts; what they don't realize is that what they really need is for the room to stop spinning, so they can get where they want to go.

This had been my experience with my weight struggle; I knew my eating habits were dysfunctional and that they were causing me pain—emotional, psychological, and physical pain—and I knew where I desperately wanted to be with my weight, yet no matter how many times I took careful aim at my goal, I continued to end up left of center time and time again. I thought that what I needed, as I had been told my whole life, was to be thin, and that is where I had applied my efforts. What I didn't realize was that what I really needed was to be alive, and to know that it was okay that I was alive. I needed my incarnation to be supported and celebrated, most of all by me!

When I brought together these three epiphanies about my life (1. that I had accepted my mother's lies about my body in relation to food and weight, 2. that I was most likely perceiving overwhelming craving for food as being an indicator of being alive, and 3. that I had acquired and maintained the habit of passively killing myself because I wasn't sure if it was okay for me to be alive), I felt I had *finally* unlocked the mystery of why and how I had struggled with food and weight my whole life.

At this point, I understood why it had always been so much easier for me to gain weight than it had been for me to lose weight; I had been unwittingly manifesting the lie that I was actually prone to being overweight because I had believed it, without question, when my mother repeatedly told it to me. I understood that I continued to experience overwhelming cravings for copious amounts of food because I was still confusing overwhelming craving for food with being alive. I understood that I was still choosing unhealthy food because I was still unwittingly maintaining the habit of passively killing myself, and I hadn't fully committed to being alive. For the first time in my life, I felt a glimmer of real hope that I might finally be able to make a lasting change, and put my struggle with food and my weight behind me for good.

The first epiphany was a no-brainer. As soon as I realized that the declaration that I was prone to being overweight was a lie, I flatly and unilaterally rejected it . . . in theory. Rejecting it in practice was a different animal. Being the owner and operator of my own brain, as, by this point, I knew myself to be, I had full confidence in my ability to root out the lie that had been growing and thriving unfettered in the garden of my mind. I knew it would take time and constant vigilance over my thought patterns, but I had no doubt that I could do it; old thought patterns die hard, but they will die with enough discipline and determination.

The challenge was that my current reality, which was that I was overweight, didn't provide any evidence or proof for the reality that I now understood and believed to be the truth, which was me prone to being at a healthy weight; on the contrary, my current reality appeared to be providing evidence and proof for the lie that I had innocently believed my whole life. It seemed very logical to me that if I could manifest an actual reality based on a lie with zero supporting evidence, then I could also manifest (theoretically, even more easily) an actual reality based on the truth which I now believed to have real supporting evidence; it was just a matter of time.

As I pondered the second epiphany, this theory that I might be confusing overwhelming craving for food with being alive, an answer emerged which provided me with profound clarity. It came to me that overwhelming craving for food is not an indicator of being alive; it is an indicator of being out of balance (my infant body was definitely out of balance when it was being starved). Breathing is the indicator of being alive; conveniently, breathing also restores balance. Therefore, when I experience overwhelming craving for food, I should not try to satisfy it with overindulgence; this will not restore balance, because overindulgence, by nature, is unbalanced. I should go to my breath to restore balance, and the overwhelming craving for food will subside. Breathing also manifests; therefore, when I go to my breath, I am manifesting my life as I envision it.

The third epiphany, that I was still in the habit of passively killing myself because I wasn't sure if it was okay for me to be alive, gave me much greater pause; I found this new insight that I wasn't sure if it was okay for me to be alive, and the adjunct insight that I hadn't fully committed to my own incarnation, to be curious, and I puzzled over this for much longer. How could I be here if I hadn't fully committed to my own incarnation? Wasn't the existence of my physical body in time and space evidence of my commitment to my incarnation? After much thought, I concluded that although I had obviously committed to being incarnated initially, which is why I was born, I had clearly been second-guessing my choice to incarnate ever since I got here. It was logical that my second-guessing of my incarnation was in response to the not-so-subtle messages I received from the people through whom I had chosen to incarnate, which did not support or celebrate my incarnation.

With this new realization that I had chosen to incarnate to a mother who almost passively killed me and a father who did very little to help me (not to mention the rest of the challenging life circumstances that I had also chosen), it slowly dawned on me what a spectacular badass I must have been! I could picture my not-yet-incarnated, non-local self floating around the earth looking for people to incarnate through; when I came across all the nice mommies and daddies, I must have thought, "Nah, too easy! Oooh, look at these two; now this is a challenge that will hold my attention!"

I also understand how and why I came to second-guess my incarnation choice once I was within time and space; I don't know many who wouldn't second-guess what I chose because, within the context of time and space, my choice is questionable at best, and disastrous at worst. I felt a new and even more empowering level of ownership for my own incarnation when I saw myself as an incarnating badass. It became very easy and effortless to embrace and celebrate my own incarnation, and I became so proud of myself, once again, for the life adventure I had chosen and survived!

In a follow-up webinar a week after I attended Healing the Heart, one of the facilitators of the retreat said something that jumped out at me; she said, "Ritual plus meaning equals transformation." In the weeks following the retreat, I decided to create more ritual for myself, designed to support my emerging transformation. In a conversation with my best friend about everything I had been puzzling out, I jokingly said that I had decided to join Team Aidy Lives and quit Team Passively Killing Aidy. I laughed and told her, "They have more fun, and besides, they have better uniforms." The idea of being on Team Aidy Lives stuck with me and I ran with it; I found a website for designing T-shirts, and I designed a Team Aidy Lives shirt that I now wear every morning while doing my yoga.

When I thought about all of my beautiful baby gifts, which no longer existed because my mother returned them all, I decided that I would buy myself a baby gift to celebrate my own birth. I thought about getting a silver baby spoon or rattle, but I didn't want it to be something that would just get stored away; I wanted it to be something that could be a part of my daily life to be a constant reminder that I am committed to and celebrate my own incarnation. I settled on a little gold baby's ring which was just the right size to squeeze over the first knuckle of my right pinky finger, and it stays there to this day.

Now, as I write this epilogue, I am consistently eating healthy food in appropriate amounts, and I am losing weight without struggle or superhuman willpower (which I never could sustain)—but that is truly not my focus and not where I am actually applying my efforts. My focus and where I am applying my efforts now is being fully alive, living in a way that supports me being alive, and daily celebrating my incarnation in time and space. This time, it's not about a number on the scale or a size in my closet; whether I stay a size fourteen or end up a size four is no longer important to me (ok, yes, I'd love to be a size four!). It's not even about being healthy; it goes deeper than being healthy to the underlying reason for being healthy, which is to be fully alive. It's about being a passionately committed member of Team Aidy Lives. Not only am I on the team, I am the team captain, and I have also become the most fanatical fan of Team Aidy Lives. I root for Team Aidy Lives at every event; no one wants to see Team Aidy Lives win more than I do! I now know, beyond a shadow of a doubt, that it is more than okay for me to be alive. I am now fully committed to my own incarnation and celebrate it daily . . . a mere forty-eight years after the fact . . .

 . . . better late than never!

I can think of no other situation in my life where
this cliché has been truer or more fitting.

Work With Me

Do you dream of having your own Exquisite Purple Life?

Don't you just know that you're capable of more? Don't you just know that it's possible to have more, do more, be more, and experience more? More joy, more love, more hope, more success, more freedom, more healing, more peace, more safety . . . just *more?* Don't you just know that where you're at is not all that there is? Don't you just *know* that there's *more?*

On a good day, you believe that there is more, that you can make more happen for yourself, and that more is possible. On a bad day, the more that you dream of makes you cry, causes you actual physical pain, and breaks your heart because it seems so completely impossible.

You don't have to settle! There is more, so very much more for you!

In addition to being a published author, I am a Martha Beck-trained life coach, a public speaker, and a creator of workshops and seminars to help people create their own Exquisite Purple Lives. I have made it my life's work to help others to find a safe place inside themselves where they can rest, rebuild, rebirth, rise up, and create all the more that they've always dreamed of!

If you strongly resonate with one or more of the themes in this book and would like to work with me to create your own Exquisite Purple Life, I am here for you! I have three specific coaching programs that address the three major themes of my experience as shared here in this book. In my experience, everyone's struggle is exactly the same, only different. If your struggle is different from the themes of these coaching programs and yet somehow exactly the same, and you would like to work with me to create your own Exquisite Purple Life, I am here for you!

Leaving Your Religion: This coaching program is for you if you are a survivor of religious abuse. Religious abuse is just as damaging as any other abuse; it violates your authentic self, your soul, your spirit (or whatever your word is for it). I know firsthand how painful religious abuse is, and I'm here to tell you that your wounds are legit! In this coaching program, you will get guidance and support as you heal your wounds, rediscover your state of original perfection, reconnect to your authentic self, and recreate a sacred practice that is safe for you.

Straight Up!: This coaching program is for you if you have discovered that you are or have been in a mixed orientation relationship. This is a uniquely painful experience, and it is common to feel very alone because most people around you just can't understand. I lived in a mixed orientation marriage for twenty years, and I facilitated a Straight Spouse Network support group for two and a half years; *I understand!* In this coaching program, you will have a safe place to share your experience honestly (without censoring yourself) and be heard—straight up! You will get guidance and support to find the strength inside yourself to recover and rise—straight up! *Because it really does get better!*

Do It Differently: This coaching program is for you if you are a parent who wants to do it differently with your children. The most common thing I hear from my clients who have had less-than-satisfactory childhoods, is, "I want to do it differently with my children!" I understand, because I desperately wanted to do it differently with my children in absolutely every way possible! In this coaching program, you will be able to identify exactly how, why, and what you want to do differently with your children. You will get a giant bucket full of very practical and effective parenting tools, tailored specifically to you and your children, so that you truly can do it differently.

Please visit my website at aideentfinnola.com for more information about all of my offerings. Reach out to me at aideen@aideentfinnola.com. I look forward to connecting with you!

Namaste, shalom, God bless, Goddess bless, blessed be, and so on 'til we meet again . . .

CPSIA information can be obtained
at www.ICGtesting.com
Printed in the USA
FFHW022353110419
51634729-57077FF

9 781504 396554